# CIVILIZING VOICES

# COMMUNICATIONS

George Gerbner and Marsha Siefert, Editors
*The Annenberg School of Communications*
*University of Pennsylvania, Philadelphia*

# CIVILIZING VOICES
## American Press Criticism
## 1880–1950

## Marion Tuttle Marzolf
### *University of Michigan*

**Longman**
New York & London

**Civilizing Voices: American Press Criticism, 1880–1950**

Longman, 95 Church Street, White Plains, N.Y. 10601

Associated companies:
Longman Group Ltd., London
Longman Cheshire Pty., Melbourne
Longman Paul Pty., Auckland
Copp Clark Pitman, Toronto

Executive editor: Gordon T. R. Anderson
Production editor: Camilla Palmer
Cover design: Betty L. Sokol
Production supervisor: Kathleen Ryan

Library of Congress Cataloging in Publication Data
Marzolf, Marion.
    Civilizing voices: American press criticism, 1880–1950 / by Marion Tuttle Marzolf.
    p.    cm.
    Includes bibliographical references.
    ISBN 0-8013-0286-2
    1. Press—United States—History.  2. Journalism—United States—Objectivity.
3. Journalism—Social aspects—United States.
4. Reporters and reporting—United States—Public opinion.
5. Public opinion—United States.  I. Title.
PN4864.M37    1990
071'.3—dc20
                                                              90-5498
                                                              CIP

ABCDEFGHIJ–AL–99 98 97 96 95 94 93 92 91 90

# Contents

## Chapter 3

### The Quest for an Ideal Newspaper: 1900–1910    34

## Chapter 4

### On the Road to Professionalism: 1900–1911    50

## Chapter 5

### First Steps toward Responsibility: 1912–1919    62

## Chapter 6

### Playing for the Crowds: 1920–1939    76

## Chapter 7

### Reach for the High Ground: 1923–1929    90

## Chapter 8

### Propaganda, Publicity, and Public Opinion: 1911–1928    106

## Chapter 9

### The Objectivity Standard: 1920–1948    119

## Chapter 10

### A Waning Influence: 1930–1939    133

## Chapter 11

### Press Freedom and the War: 1940–1946    149

## Chapter 12

### Press Responsibility Confronted: 1942–1950    163

## Chapter 13

### Toward a Professional Criticism: 1947 and Later    177

## Chapter 14

### The Nature of Criticism    191

## Epilogue    207

# Preface

I defined critical articles as those which evaluated the press against a set of expressed or implied agreed-upon standards or contested standards (legal, ethical, professional). Critical articles contained opinions pro or con, proposed solutions or suggestions for improvement or change, gave specific instances of negative or positive behavior of the press, or contributed to the critical dialogue over the general role of the press and its responsibilities in American society.

I have studied the popular, professional, and scholarly literature where the critical debate took place. I did not examine runs of newspapers because only the *New York Times* is indexed for all of this period, and most of the journalists and editors who gave speeches or wrote on this topic were published in popular or professional magazines and were often summarized in the professional journals. I have examined a few archives on specific critical issues, but I have not examined individual journalists' or critics' archives. I have limited the study to what was readily available to the public.

To locate the articles I examined: *Reader's Guide to Periodical Literature* from 1905–1950; *Poole's Index of Periodical Literature* for the 1800s; Carl Cannon's *Journalism: A Bibliography*; Warren Price's *The Literature of Journalism*; Susan Kingsbury's bibliography in *Newspapers and the News*; Roland W. Wolseley's *The Journalist's Bookshelf*; Emery and Emery, *The Press and America*; Linda Weiner Hausman's *Criticism of the Press in U.S. Periodicals 1900–1939: An Annotated Bibliography*; The *Journalist* from 1881–1950; Proceedings of the American Society of Newspaper Editors,

*Problems in Journalism* 1923–1949; plus *Journalism Quarterly* and the *Social Sciences Index* and *Humanities Index* for scholarly articles.

*Press Criticism* was not a subject heading in any of these bibliographies. Journals and proceedings were not indexed and had to be paged through. In order to locate critical articles, I looked under the headings: *reporters, reporting, newspapers U.S., journalism, journalists*. I looked up all the titles that suggested or implied critical views.

For the most part my text sticks to the critical debate in the context of the time period, but occasionally I have consulted and mentioned later interpretations. Criticism of individual journalists, editors, or publishers is not included, except where that forms the basis for a larger social or ethical criticism of the press.

I selected a chronological approach for organizing this material from over a thousand articles and about a hundred books. Reading by the decade has its limitations, of course, but themes did emerge to prominence roughly in two-decade spans, and I let the dominant themes determine the chapter topics. It should be pointed out that many of the basic criticisms of the press are present in all eras, but different times present different challenges, or old challenges in new modes. The examples quoted were selected for the prominence of their authors, aptness, and representativeness. In the end this sifting and winnowing of items is a matter of judgment. I tried to present what the critics said and which issues were salient in their times, not what today's perspectives would say about them.

By the time this book is published, I will have worked on it over five years. A large debt of gratitude accumulates as a result of the help, advice, and encouragement from faculty, staff, friends, and family, and I am especially indebted to my husband and to my mother. Their attention and support have sustained me on a very long road.

Testing ideas and draft portions of the manuscript was valuable at various stages along the way. Jean Ward, Karin Siune, and Niels Thomsen, along with my editor at Longman, listened to my early ideas and encouraged me. Colleagues who were willing to discuss specific topics included Jerilyn McIntyre, James Baughman, and Richard A. Swarzlose, and this was most helpful. Ed Lambeth, now at Missouri, invited me to participate in ethics seminars and share my developing ideas on criticism. Two of my current doctoral students, who are researching in allied fields, have been important in offering new perspectives and debating ideas with me. They are Peggy Kusnerz in American Culture and Barbara Petersen in Communication. Barbara also did the demanding task of copyreading the entire final draft of the manuscript. Four undergraduate student assistants helped me for a semester each, and they were cheerful diggers in the libraries. They were Mary Scheele, Dennis Clagett, Blair Williams, and Marion Davis. My classes in journalistic performance, ethics, and criticism were most valuable as a testing ground for ideas with bright, thoughtful students. And the University of Michigan Library with its vast collection continually pleased me by having most of what I needed. The cheerful help of the librarians was much appreciated.

I was given a gracious reception at the University of Chicago and Columbia University library manuscript collections, and was given permission to cite from the Commission on Freedom of the Press papers in the Joseph Regenstein Library of the University of Chicago and from the *New York World* papers at Columbia's Butler Library.

My research took me to several libraries, including the Library of Congress, and university libraries at Northwestern, Minnesota, Missouri, Washington, Michigan State, and Wisconsin. In a way, the research done on an earlier sabbatical at the media archives in Dortmund and Münster, West Germany, and at the British Museum and Bibliothèque National, and the university and Royal libraries in Copenhagen, Oslo, Gothenberg, and Stockholm was useful in providing the foreign perspective on sensational journalism. That research trip was funded by the Horace H. Rackham School for Graduate Studies of the University of Michigan.

As ever there are a few colleagues that one turns to again and again during the long process of researching and writing a book. They help discuss ideas, read drafts, test and contest my interpretations. For me, those people have been Howard Good, John Stevens, Frank Beaver, and Jonathan Friendly. They all read the manuscript and provided tough and helpful criticism. The publisher's reviewer offered several important pointers. The book is better for all this. The vision that Cathy Covert had for journalism history continues to inspire me. The mistakes as well as the interpretations are my own, but, of course, a book like this is heavily indebted to all the ideas and critics quoted and paraphrased. They created the themes, and I hope I have been faithful to their words.

# CIVILIZING VOICES

# Introduction

In this work I have tried to lay the groundwork for an understanding of the history of criticism of the modern American press in its formative years, 1880–1950, before the growth of television journalism and the maturation of the discipline of communication research with its varied methods of media analysis. I have asked the questions: what was press criticism in this era, and who were the critics? I have investigated popular and professional literature to see if there was a continuing tradition of press criticism and if there were any enduring or changing themes.

I have not analyzed the critical works and styles of specific critics, because my purpose was to compile the history of modern press criticism. I have not been able to test the critics' advice against the performance of specific newspapers to see what impact the advice had or what reception it was given. It will take many case studies of that kind to flesh out the details in order to determine specific responses to the criticism. But general trends in the criticism and in changes in press performance are discussed.

Does press criticism account for or help to account for the yellow press toning down its sensationalism after the public clamor to clean up the press? Would tabloid journalism have pursued sleaze to even greater depths if not for the public outcry over press treatment of the Lindbergh baby kidnapping? Would press agentry have filled the news columns undetected without journalists raising the alarm against mixing of self-interested information with objective news? Would privacy laws and journalistic codes of ethics have developed without public outrage against the excesses of modern reporting? These were salient issues in the period of my study, and the vigor of the discussion in public and professional circles suggests that the press was paying attention to the criticism. There were changes. How much can be credited to the reaction to criticism is still an open question.

Clearly, press criticism raises issues and establishes an agenda for what does get discussed. The perception by the leaders of the press that the public is displeased and may withdraw support is discussed by editors and publishers at their professional meetings and in their journals. When the criticism seems to represent public opinion, the press performance generally is modified over time to satisfy the audience. The best examples of that in this study are the public objections to sensationalism and violence in the 1890s and 1920s.[1] When the criticism is clearly self-interested and deviates widely from mainstream values, such as the ideological attacks from the political left or right, it rolls off the press with little impact, unless the critics represent significant size and power. The New Deal and the Nixon/Reagan eras are good examples of the latter.[2]

Press criticism certainly played an important role in the evolution of the modern press. Since the bulk of that criticism has been of a democratic, liberal character, the ideals of free speech and press, citizen involvement in self-government, and press responsibility to society have been kept alive in the face of powerful technological and economic forces. Technology, mass marketing, and an enormous and literate modern middle class created a vast potential market and the delivery capability to reach that market. Without the critics—inside and outside the press—the impersonal market forces would have had complete control. I am not convinced that the rising educational level, growth of professionalism, improved technology, and marketing strategies would have been enough to create an independent and fair-minded press, although they certainly played a role. Values guide decision making; the dynamic dialogue forced by the critics certainly had a positive influence on the creation of a responsible and democratic press in the modern era.

Although the criticism may come from all corners of society, in the main it arises from certain most interested circles: culture critics and preservers; political and social advocates; journalists and scholars. Thus, it generally tends to reinforce both the elitist value of a press ideal and the popular value of a democratic, open society. Often these two values are in opposition, but the modern general-interest newspaper of the twentieth century has usually been successful in finding the shifting balance point.

Historians point out that the turn-of-the-century era brought a clash of values in the United States. The Victorian society of small towns and countryside was being displaced by the modern, bureaucratic urban-industrial society—moving from stability to instability.[3] The modern daily newspaper was a key player in that drama, both shaped by the new culture and helping to shape it. In its role as megaphone and monitor, the modern press amplifies and shapes a multitude of messages and images for the entire society and provides a central forum for discussion and feedback to the shaping institutions. The press itself often is a subject of some of the debate, but until now there has been no attempt to capture this tradition. The more flamboyant press critics are mentioned in standard press histories, but there is little sense of any ongoing debate over press quality and performance.

I began this research on modern press criticism because I could not find an existing historical account to use in my new class on journalistic performance. I might have returned to our colonial heritage and taken the journey forward from there. But I believed that today's standards and values were mainly shaped around the turn of the century when a "new journalism" challenged and replaced an old journalism that was rooted in the partisan political tradition. That change created the need for new ways of thinking about the press. A new audience existed in an urban culture that was forging a new social style in America.

Everyone read the "new journalism," from the recently educated common laborers and maids to the clerks, salespeople, bankers, lawyers, and society leaders. In modified form, the new journalism is still today's journalism. The challenge this new style presented to society and to a budding profession offered an excellent opportunity for an examination of modern journalistic values and ideals. There was intense criticism of the press from outside and from inside. As the old and new values clashed, press critics kept raising the issues of moral purpose and democratic idealism to counter the strong forces of commercialization and impersonality. In this way, press criticism served as a civilizing force, a balancing agent, sometimes restraining and sometimes encouraging social change while protecting essential values.

American journalism is bound by ideals framed in the Bill of Rights of the American Constitution. Publishers, editors, and the public generally believed in the press as an important molder of public opinion. In addition, the values and ideals held by the leaders of political parties that supported the early partisan press also helped shape the old journalism. When a popular form of news-oriented journalism, called the penny press, was introduced in the American cities in the 1830s, the publisher began to be freed from intimate political and economic ties with the political party. The penny press, with its emphasis on news and entertainment, was free to follow any event or issue where it led. Because there were thousands of newly literate, potential readers of these newspapers congregated in the cities and with pennies to spare, the potential for success was great. Publishers could produce large quantities of newspapers on the new, faster presses and get them on the street quickly and at low prices. An industry was born.

The Civil War whetted an appetite for constantly changing and updated news. This news-hunger was nourished after the war by energetic reporting of domestic tragedies, crimes, political battles, revealing personal interviews, and tales of city life from the upper crust to the guttersnipes. Lengthy editorials, advertisements, and legal documents that had formally covered newspaper front pages were tucked inside, modernized, or dropped.

## NEWS A COMMODITY

The penny newspapers led the way in the presentation of news as the central commodity the press had to sell. To survive, traditional newspapers had to modify their stodgy style of writing and design. Advertising followed circulation. Ample ads and mass readership made the politically independent press economically free of the entrenched powers. Was this popular press still to be a molder of public opinion? If so, what values and morals would guide its editors?

This became a key issue in the press criticism of the late nineteenth century in America. When Joseph Pulitzer showed New York City the power of the "new journalism," it enlivened the discussion. Pulitzer's journalism had first flourished in the newer industrial cities of the Midwest and West Coast. Transplanted to New York City, the new journalism became an instant success in the 1880s. Pulitzer's newspaper supported Democrats on the editorial pages, but the rest of the newspaper was intended for all kinds of readers. The division of news and editorial opinion became standard for the modern American press.

The new journalism efficiently supplied entertainment and information that readers could use. In the penny press tradition, these papers were also marketed on the street like pretzels and apples, with something for all tastes. What readers thought about the news was their own business. They could take or leave the editorials. Many fretted that these new papers speaking to thousands were a frightening political power. Not even the President of the United States had such a megaphone. Would the new journalism serve and connect with its local community, or would it be just another piece of merchandise bought and sold without regard for the larger social welfare?

The critics were alarmed. Free speech and free press guard all other freedoms in the American democracy. Freedom of expression, religion, press, and assembly are bedrock rights. What role would they play in the new high-speed journalism that was rolling off the presses into the waiting hands of the masses? Would popular journalism drive out the ideas and serious discussion? How could the pillars of society be certain that the public interest was maintained without resorting to censorship and control? A spirited debate arose. Those inside and outside the press were involved. Civic and moral issues were intertwined with free speech and politics. If the new journalism became the only American journalism, what responsibilities would it, could it, assume for informing, enlightening, and educating the public, and for maintaining the public forum and marketplace of ideas?

## THE CRITIC AS CIVILIZING AGENT

In a sense, all the criticism of the modern American press during its first seventy years revolved around two issues—the role of the free press in safeguarding other freedoms in a democracy and the socio-cultural role the press was to play. The critics act as a conscience, nagging the press to live up to higher standards, ideals, moral behavior. Alarmed by the vulgarity of the masses, the critics sought to be a civilizing influence, guarding the old high culture and seeking to manage the new machine with its primitive appetite.

By the early twentieth century, the new journalism had become the standard journalism and a powerful institution in society. The journalist was on the way to becoming a professional who accepted a standardized body of values and practices that balanced societal and commercial interests. The older journalism had been personified by vigorous and visible owner-editors who were respected members of their communities; the new journalism was built on large staffs of reporters and editors who fed the hungry printing presses like so many faceless coalhandlers. The newspaper assumed its own special flavor and character, and the scrambling reporters became the visible embodiment of the institution. Owners and publishers, with some notable exceptions, slipped into the comfortable business set and shared those values.

The early exuberance of the new journalism was moderated gradually by a growing concern over respectability and stability. The marketplace needs of a huge and variegated populace and hungry advertisers desiring the greatest possible reach for their messages helped to develop a journalism that tried to appeal to all and to offend few. Reporters and editors yearned for respect and status. Objective reporting with the partisan bias shorn away served the professionalism of the staffs, the business needs of a mass-market, journalism, and the democratic ideals of an educated citizenry that could think for itself.

This study traces the public criticism about the performance and responsibility of modern journalism from 1881 to 1950. The period is formative in the development of contemporary standards for journalistic practice. The closing date of the study is about two years after the 1947 release of a national critical study of the press by the so-called Hutchins Commission. Some of the reaction to that document, "A Free and Responsible Press," is included. The study does not cover the introduction of radio news and the postwar ascendance of television news.

Seen in the context of decades of criticism, the Hutchins Commission's recommendations seem less controversial and more a culmination of decades of debate than they were regarded in 1947. The intense negative reception from newspaper editors and publishers suggests an opportunity missed. The tendency in journalism at the time had been to move toward greater responsibility and professionalism, but old political and cultural animosities erupted to bury this proposed agenda for change. It would be at least two decades before some of the Commission's suggestions were actually tried by the press, and then with only limited success, although their arguments favoring diversity were particularly apt in the 1970s and 1980s.

At the end of the 1980s, the earlier journalistic values forged for the modern press were still in place and journalistic ethics had reemerged in another era of intense press criticism. Now, however, there are more sources of formal, regular criticism—national journals of press criticism, reader representatives, and media critics at individual newspapers, national conventions, seminars, and workshops where issues are regularly debated, and increased research in the social science and the humanities traditions. The criticism continues informally to monitor the moral, social, and political performance of the press. Corporate mergers, computers, and video and satellite technology are rephrasing the questions of press power and responsibility. This study offers a look at the early development of these values and attitudes in the hope that knowing where we have been may be helpful in determining where we are going.

## NOTES

1. W. Phillips Davison, "The Third Person Effect," *Public Opinion Quarterly* 47 (Spring 1983): 1–15.
2. This may be an example of the third person effect—or the action taken by someone in response to a perceived effect on a third party. Professors James Baughman and Rick Perloff are studying this phenomenon as applied to journalism history.
3. Robert H. Wiebe, *The Search for Order 1877–1920* (New York: Hill & Wang, 1967), vii, and Henry Steel Commager, *The American Mind* (New York: Yale University Press, 1950), 50.

# CHAPTER 1

# Old Values and New Realities: 1880–1900

A new kind of journalism was introduced to New York City and the East in 1883, when Joseph Pulitzer transformed the stodgy *New York World* into a newspaper for the working class. This "new journalism" was identified with the American Middle West, where it had made significant progress in cities like Chicago, Cleveland, Detroit, and St. Louis. Joseph Pulitzer's *St. Louis Post-Dispatch* was a leading example of the two-cent people's papers that offered lively coverage of the day's news, aggressive crusading for civic improvements, and entertaining reading about the drama and pathos of city life. These newspapers posed an immediate challenge to the older, established newspapers and threatened the genteel Victorian culture with a brassy, modern urban blast.

The decades between 1880 and 1900 brought dramatic changes in the United States. The population increased 50 percent, and national wealth more than doubled. The urban population had quadrupled between 1860 and 1900. Streetcars and elevated railways, street lighting and high-rise buildings, as well as motley crowds of new urbanites from rural and small town America and from overseas gave vigor and style to the booming cities. City dwellers put pressure on the city services, swelled school enrollments, and quickly emerged as a new audience for the mass media of newspapers, magazines, and books. The super rich and the abject poor, working men and women, and white-collar professionals passed each other in the city but lived in their own enclaves. The city provided ample news of crime, violence, despair, elegance, and decadance. The old stable society, its Victorian moral code, and its cultural leaders were threatened and gradually replaced by the new, professional/managerial middle-class urbanites.[1]

It was also a time of unparalleled growth for the daily newspaper.[2] The change to mass production of goods in the new industrial-commercial cities created a need for national distribution and advertising of products. Newspapers and department stores were ideal vehicles. To attract and serve ever larger populations in the cities, the newspapers required better and faster machinery, larger staffs, and greater capital. The newspaper became not just a modern business, but a big business, introducing new business management and chains or groups of newspapers under common ownership.

Although the newspaper remained a community enterprise, emphasizing local news and goods and circulating mainly in the city and nearby region, it also provided access to national events and trends through national news association dispatches, syndicated columns, and features. The modern city made the new journalism possible by concentrating the mass of newly literate readers. The average American had only had five years of schooling by 1900, but this created a vast new market for newspapers, magazines, and books written in spritely and straightforward language.[3]

The traditional daily newspapers still sold for five cents a copy and were bound by political party alliances. In contrast with the new journalism, their style was dull and ponderous. Political discussion and literary essays filled many columns as editors carried out their traditional role as molders of public opinion. The new journalism followed the penny newspaper tradition of the 1830s in emphasizing news. Political opinion and support were included, but the editor was free to choose sides. The Civil War encouraged the news-reading tradition, and the new journalism adapted action reporting to the urban locality. News was the business of newspapers, and the city with its teeming population and explosive growth provided the stories. To attract reader interest the on-the-scene dramatic incident, the exclusive interview, and the human interest story dominated the new journalism.

Editors of the old style journalism acted more like magazine editors, sitting in their offices, clipping exchange newspapers and writing long editorials. The new journalism sent scoop-minded reporters about the city, poking their noses into everybody's business, gathering up gossip and tidbits, ignoring social conventions and cultural taboos. Each new edition of the newspaper offered new revelations and excitement throughout the day as newsboys and newsgirls shouted the latest headlines to curious throngs.

In 1885, five New York City dailies had circulations of 100,000 to 190,000 and a few approached half a million by the late 1890s.[4] The vast circulations attracted ample advertising, which produced financial independence from political party support. This made the newspaper a new power in the culture and in politics, one with direct access to the urban masses and their votes. Much of the criticism of the new journalism was in response to the recognition and fear of this new power.

People who had no previous tradition of reading were quickly attracted to the breezy style, lively headlines, and ample illustrations. The defenders of the old culture saw their grasp on the public mind slipping, replaced by the vulgar new journalism. The ideal of the press as a pillar of culture and molder of public opinion was endangered because a public raised on trivia might lose its ability to concentrate or to take an interest in serious debate and uplifting culture. The ideal of the rational, informed citizen was being undermined by the irrational mob, and the upholders of the traditional, civilizing values lost no time in crying the alarm.

## PULITZER'S NEW JOURNALISM

Joseph Pulitzer saw New York City as a prime market for his aggressive newspaper for the working man and woman. There were one and a half million inhabitants in the metropolitan area and nearly a million in the city itself. Although there were many competing daily and Sunday newspapers, only the *New York Herald* and the *New York Sun* attracted massive audiences; most were in the 10,000 to 20,000 range like the *World* that Pulitzer purchased. Visitors to New York City noted its "almost unalloyed materialism" and lack of taste and refinement, the intense speed, pressure, restless energy, and ambition.[5] Pulitzer caught this mood and pace and readers flocked to his *New York World* in 1883. In a little over a year, circulation rose from 15,000 to 100,000. By 1887 it had reached a quarter million, passing the *New York Herald* and the *New York Sun*, the old penny press pioneers in New York City.

Pulitzer declared that he intended to create a truly democratic paper that served not only the masses, but humanitarian causes. To capture the interest of millions, he said, he would attract them with bright news and entertainment and address them about matters of importance on the editorial page. "I want to talk to a nation, not a select committee," he declared, underscoring the contrast with the traditional *New York Post* and the *Nation*.[6] The *World* quickly engaged in exposures of bribery and corruption in city government, campaigned to help the poor, hungry, and needy, and persuaded the common people of America to show their appreciation to France by donating their pennies, nickels, and dimes to pay for a base for the Statue of Liberty. The readers were engaged and inspired; they were also entertained. Pulitzer gave them comic strips, short stories, travel and adventure stories, puzzles, and ample illustrations.

Critics were offended by this vulgar new journalism, and they were quick to mount an attack in defense of the old. The new journalism ignored important social and political issues, they charged, while wallowing in trivia. Editors and writers in the literary and cultural journals led the attack against vulgarization.[7] New magazines in the 1880s like *Arena*, *Forum*, and *North American Review* featured debates on cultural matters and considered the role of journalism an interesting and timely subject.

They were joined by the quality genteel magazines, such as *Harper's Monthly*, *Atlantic Monthly*, *Scribner's*, and *Century*. The members of this group of editors had attended the best universities, socialized in the good clubs, and pictured themselves as "missionaries in the cause of culture," says John Tomsich in his study of the Gilded Age.[8] They were part of America's literary establishment, fighting hard to develop and retain a respectable literary tradition in America in the face of the rapid decline in public taste.

The cultural split in journalism between quality and popular newspapers mirrors the schism in literature, the arts, and society in general. As Santayana explained, America was a country with "two mentalities, one a survival of the beliefs and standards of the fathers, the other an expression of the instincts, practice, and discoveries of the younger generations." Religion, literature, and moral emotions still kept the hereditary spirit, he said, which "floated gently in the backwater, while, alongside in invention and industry and social organization the other half of the mind was leaping down a sort of Niagara Rapids."[9]

An accommodation would be reached after a few decades of struggle. The essential values attached to free speech and press in a democratic society would remain, but the style and daily standards of journalism would change dramatically. The most energetic critics of new journalism upheld the old genteel values and urged that the growing middle class strive to reach them. The critics' concern centered on the nature of the new audience and how to attract it.

"The newspaper is a product of its age," observed Charles Dudley Warner in a speech in 1881. As coauthor with Mark Twain of the *The Gilded Age* and a former daily newspaper editor, he was a close observer of the contemporary press. Although the newspaper was a business enterprise that had to make money, Warner thought that it need not be superficial. Its chief function "was to print news," then to elucidate, comment, and show its relations, and "finally to furnish general reading matter." But the modern daily was "lacking in providing background necessary to increase the public's understanding of events and issues, even though its news enterprise was admirable."[10] A daily diet of reading the hodgepodge of contents of the popular press, Warner speculated, could lead to "superficial knowledge and an appetite for the unnatural." It would make it hard to sit down and read a book, study history, or "acquire the intellectual development and strength which comes from thorough reading and reflection."[11]

Although European visitors appreciated the enterprise and democratizing tendencies of the American papers, they were shocked by their vulgar character. Visitors were amazed to see everyone from wagon drivers and scrubwomen to matrons and bankers reading these newspapers, which Europeans took as evidence that the American experiment in democracy was working. European newspapers were still directed at the affluent and well educated, since Western European populations lagged a couple of decades or more behind the United States in providing common school education.[12] In London, for example, Alfred Harmsworth (later Lord Northcliff) would discover a similar "new audience" for popular journalism and build a powerful media empire on it in the twentieth century.[13]

The English press belonged to the editorial writers, and the American to the reporters, observed Arnot Reid, an editor from Scotland. The Americans want "a condensed record of the day's news and short, pithy editorials." The Englishman seeks a "literary finish." American reporters turn in "bright, racy, trivial, contemptible stuff which should interest no one of any intellectual capacity," he pointed out, "but which does interest 99 out of 100 people."[14] That fact was rapidly dawning on traditional American publishers.

## NEW CONTENT AND NEW READERS

The most highly regarded voice among the American critics was that of E. L. Godkin, editor of the *Nation*, the prestigious, conservative weekly offshoot of the *New York Post*. Godkin had a long and distinguished career on both publications, where he took a sharp, adversarial tone in his critiques of the new journalism. He called it childish—juvenile intelligence for boys and girls.[15]

Throughout the 1890s, Godkin showed a "mounting distaste for popular government," according to his biographer, and his attacks on popular journalism were as vehement as those he had leveled earlier at the penny press, especially the *New York Sun*.[16] When the masses share power, there are problems with democracy, Godkin believed. His fears were confirmed as he watched the *New York Journal* and *New York World* push sensationalism to its extremes during the Spanish-American War in a gigantic battle for mass circulation. Godkin was also distressed over their attention to sensational crimes and immorality, and he worried that the modern newspaper already had a greater influence on the popular mind and morals than either the pulpit or the book. Newspapers would be "shaping the social and political world of the twentieth century," he predicted, because the new generation was pouring out of the public schools in the tens of millions and was "getting its tastes, opinions, and standards" from the newspapers.[17]

People who formed the habit of reading short bits of newspaper information, he warned, would lose the ability to give "continuous attention" to books or other documents that "require attention of the eye as well as the mind." Neglect of this habit of reading that had to be acquired in youth, Godkin believed, would make it "all but impossible" to take up again.[18] The newspaper was easy to understand; it did not require the mind to be "fixed on any topic more than three or four minutes." Each topic "furnishes a complete change of scene," said Godkin in explaining its popularity. This development was creating a gulf between the cultivated circles who read books and the common men and women. The only remedy was to improve the newspaper and make it a "better channel of communication to the masses of the best thought and most accurate knowledge of the time."[19]

He called this one of the most serious problems facing the country in the coming century:

> The solemn truth is, that the printed matter of some of our metropolitan dailies has now for a dozen years been making it impossible for the people of this city to read anything, long or short, on any serious subject. The young people who leave the public schools with reading and little else, make the newspaper their only literature.[20]

A fellow critic echoed Godkin's sentiments in a pithy style. The newspaper has become "the common sewer for public and private immorality." It tells the "sins, the crimes, the misfortunes, and the weaknesses of our poor humanity; sensationalism is its dominating principle." He warned that "this tide of filth" was degrading the public morals and that no one was safe from its "unfeeling" and "impersonal prying."[21]

One New York newspaperman made an early attempt to substantiate the contemporary press criticism by examining the contents of several Sunday newspapers for April 17, 1893, and the same date in 1881. J. J. Gilmer Speed found that the New York dailies had increased the amount of space devoted to gossip, scandal, and crime and had decreased news of science, religion, literature, and other significant matters.[22] A newspaper is not "the history of the world for a day," as is often believed, said Speed. "Nothing could be falser. Instead, everything is so covered with sensationalism that few can get the truth." He expected decent people to demand news of good taste and moderation as civilization improved.[23]

Richard Watson Gilder, editor of the conservative *Century* from 1880 to 1909 and leader of a fashionable literary salon, also realized that the readers had become fickle. Readers used to stick with one paper of their own political persuasion, he pointed out, but "now take this or that paper because it happens to be convenient or cheap." Editorial opinion, consequently, had less weight and the paper had less power as readers were urged to draw their own conclusions.[24]

Gilder had worked as a newspaper reporter, and he deplored the Western-style sensationalism that had taken over the press. He thought the lack of responsibility, the faking and contriving of news, led to the reporter's "degeneration in character under pressure to produce what is demanded by cynical employers." In spite of his feelings, he believed that since the sensational papers reflected "with more or less accuracy" what the people were thinking, they were important to politicians. Editors also monitored their readers' letters in order to market their newspapers better. So, he observed, "a newspaper both creates public opinion and is largely regulated by it."[25]

With all its faults, "the press, even the sensational press, has certain generous qualities that make it ready to facilitate any disinterested work taken up by public-spirited members of the community. The greatest service the press does for civilization is in the searchlight it throws on dark places," Gilder said. The cleaning up of the city tenements happened largely because of the threat that newspaper publicity would reveal the names of the landlords, Guilder pointed out.[26]

Still, for Gilder, the really discouraging thing was to see that so many "members of the more intelligent portion of the community will buy the very papers they abuse and despise...." He thought it was understandable that people without culture would be attracted to the vulgar "swash" served in these newspapers. But Gilder told *his* readers it was their public duty to shun the sensational press.[27]

Sunday newspapers provoked special criticism, especially in religious circles. Critics believed the popular reading and advertising matter was distracting families from better Sunday activities, and some seemed to think that the newspaper staffs violated the Sabbath by preparing Monday's paper on Sunday. The Sunday newspaper first appeared during the Civil War and was accepted on the Sabbath only because of the urgency of the war news. After the war there were separately produced Sunday newspapers in many cities—100 in 1883 and 250 (mostly Sunday editions of the dailies) in 1890. Since Sunday feature sections were prepared early in the week, they were filled with an array of material from the expanding feature syndicates. Artists' drawings accompanied the long articles and decorated the department store ads.[28]

The Sunday newspapers offered entertainment for the entire family, including comics for the children. They were similar to the weekly magazines and competed with them for writers, artists, readers, and advertisers. The Sunday staffs were the real sensationalists at the *World* and *Journal*, and as they pioneered tactics that increased circulation, the daily staffs were pressured to do the same. The Sunday newspaper had become so important by 1886 that Julius Ward said in the *Forum* that it rivaled the pulpit in directing life, reaching people, and forming public opinion.[29]

## ALREADY A PROFESSION

Occasionally a critic saw something positive in the new journalism and urged its further improvement by developing its professionalism and ethics. One critic pointed out that press critics should discriminate between the good and bad newspapers, because many did refrain from publishing all the brutal details of crime and from lying, spying, and fabricating. The press does good and mischief—"liberty can run into license, but to restrict it is an even greater evil."[30]

Professionalism should be encouraged, Eugene Camp of the editorial staff of the *Philadelphia Times* told the Alumni Association of the Wharton School at the University of Pennsylvania. Journalism "ought to be a profession," as was being contemplated at Cornell University, with its own place for study as a distinct subject. Camp recommended a strong liberal arts program plus instruction in writing, editing, and news judgment. This would broaden the journalist by knowledge and develop him by research. Camp urged that the best brains of the nation be attracted to journalism, so that it "could be raised from a trade . . . to the dignity of the learned profession that it ought to be."[31]

A sign of journalism's nascent professionalism was the arrival of its first weekly trade publication, the *Journalist*. It was founded in 1883 and devoted to the improvement of journalism. Editor Alan Forman took heart in the growing number of college graduates entering the newsrooms in the late 1880s. He advocated the use of bylines to encourage reporters' responsibility for their own work. Editors feared creating high-priced stars once readers learned the reporters' names. Publishers were not required to run lists of responsible editors, and many publications carried no masthead.[32]

Professionalism of the journalist continued to be a theme of press criticism, and one issue of the *Forum* brought together three top journalists in 1893 to discuss their field. One of them was J. W. Keller, New York City reporter for thirteen years, who called journalism in its "essential qualifications a learned profession" but in actuality a trade with low pay, job insecurity, and wage-earner obedience to the boss. Further, the impersonality of the work and lack of public recognition "whittled away at the creative individual's self-esteem." It was a young man's job, he said, and if he did not leave to write for politics or theater, he would be "pitched out on the dust heap as useless when his legs wear out."[33] Keller charged that publishers hired the best brains and then turned them into hacks serving the publishers' personal needs. The picture was one that would become familiar in literature and biography—the modern journalist as victim, talented, underpaid, degraded by assignments, scorned by polite society, and torn between idealism and cynicism. Keller had no illusions about the prospects for a journalists' union because journalism was a "trade in brains," not brawn, and success required business and editorial competence. Some who left the newsroom did write damning portraits of journalism's voracious appetite for youthful idealism.

"Anxiety about the status of journalism runs like a fault line through newspaper fiction," said Professor Howard Good in his recent study of the journalist in American fiction. "The newsroom was a schoolroom or a cemetery," he said, "while the country journal still held out hope as a refuge."[34] Similar views are found in the autobiographies and contemporary writings of journalists of this era.

Some critics thought that journalists, like other professionals, should adopt a code of ethics. "The liberty of the press, like all liberty, means action within the great principles of ethics, not emancipation from them," said W. S. Lilly. He called newspapers guides, philosophers, and friends of the masses, teaching them what they think on most subjects, making the press extremely important in a free society. Thus it was the correspondent's duty to state facts, base arguments on them and to denounce abuses and advocate reforms in order to enlighten others based on what his reason and conscience say is truth.[35]

*Dial* magazine set forth its idea of the proper ethical standard for newspapers: (1) to collect news, pure and simple, in the scientific spirit, with accuracy of statement placed above all other considerations; (2) to select and arrange news for news, not sensational, values, and for the benefit of the public; and (3) to make honest comment that stood for well-defined principles and expressed sincere convictions of the newspaper's intellectual head.[36]

It was too easy to apply the counting room argument as a test of successful journalism, editorialized *Dial*. "If journalism is to be considered a form of business and nothing more, then the only proper tests of success are the daily circulation, the number of advertisements and the annual balance-sheet." The *Dial* editorial recommended using an ethical standard for tests of journalistic service to society.[37]

Two leading newspaper publishers who had grown up in the old tradition of the partisan and penny press, Charles A. Dana of the *New York Sun* and Whitelaw Reid of the *New York Tribune*, shared the genteel critics' values in many respects and worked for higher standards within the profession. The press is a "pretty powerful agent," said Dana. "It takes men when their information is incomplete" and "suggests, intimates, insinuates an opinion and a judgment." That power inspired Dana with a solemn sense of his responsibility over the minds of people who might know nothing of the subject reported. He did not expect much change until "the individual becomes more intelligent and able to form and guide his own judgment," freed from suggestive influence and control.[38] Dana believed the newspaper should be an informal check on the executive branch of government and a force against despotic rule.

Dana had made the human interest story and bright style the trademark of the *Sun*—a fine training ground for reporters and writers. Dana sought college graduates with liberal education and trained them to be reporters. The *Sun* remained a "newspaperman's newspaper" long after Dana's death.

## THE IDEALS OF MODERN JOURNALISM

Whitelaw Reid was well aware of the flaws and excesses that accompanied journalism's commercial growth at the end of the nineteenth century. In 1879, when he spoke to the Ohio Press Association, he predicted that the next great change in newspapers would be "better newspapers, the story better told;

better brains employed in the telling," papers dealing with the more important of current matters "in such style and fascination that they will command
the widest interest."[39]

He deplored the fashion of berating journalism, even though he agreed
that the press often was "crude, shallow, coarse, unjust, impertinent, distorted," reckless with the truth, and craved sensations "to turn a few extra,
dirty pennies." But he pointed out that if the newspapers taught disjointed
thinking and encouraged shallowness, the same could be said of pamphlets,
cheap books, and quarterly reviews. He wondered if the critics ought not also
include the "twin brothers" of the popular press, the common schools. "I
only insist that whether you consider the common school or the free press,
faulty as each may be, it is a necessary concomitant of our civilization and our
government; that it has been steadily growing better, and that the best way to
remedy the evils it works is to make it better still."[40]

Reid charged his audience of editors to look beyond the business considerations. "Make your newspaper so good, so full of news, so truthful, so
able, that people must take it; make its circulation so great that advertisers will
plead for the privilege of getting into it—those seem to me the two great business commandments of our better journalism." Good newspapers grounded
in these commandments "would no longer be able to afford to suppress or
soften the truth in any business interest," Reid said.[41] The good newspaper
would keep the rights of readers paramount, he believed, and journalism
would become master, not the tool of party and would tell the truth and
"command the general confidence."[42]

When he was asked to talk about the press two decades later in 1901,
Reid still believed the press could improve. He insisted that a bad paper was
"the fault of the community that supports it. But if the bad paper tends to
make the community worse, that is the fault of the men who issue it." He
wisely pointed out that a newspaper can't uphold a standard that a community
does not want and will not maintain, unless it is subsidized in some way.
"Free your minds about their shortcomings if you like, but do not forget that,
whatever their faults, your community chooses to sustain them (newspapers),
and that most of them are surely printing what they think they have reason to
believe the largest numbers desire."[43]

The modern newspaper was like an encyclopedia that people dip into, he
explained. It was no longer the expression of one man's personal whims or
partisanship. Reid simply wanted newspapers to "tell the truth and be fair."
In return, the community should support a good paper and not the other
kind, and let the courts uphold fairness and truth in libel cases. He concluded
that the newspapers are better than their audiences, so "when people criticize
the newspapers, they are criticizing themselves."[44]

By the end of the 1890s the lines of debate over the modern daily newspaper had been set. The newspaper was still seen as the people's educator and
as such had a moral responsibility to serve the public. Its independence from

advertising and political parties was, therefore, considered essential. But dominance by the commercial side was tipping the press toward the immoral, degrading vulgarity that threatened impressionable minds and put it on a runaway course toward irresponsibility and ever higher profits.

Beginning in the 1890s magazines published more articles criticizing the new journalism. By 1911 there were thirty or more a year, compared to about ten a year in 1880.[45] Most were written by editors or regular writers for the monthly magazines. A few were by newspaper editors, ministers, or professors. It was essentially an insiders' discussion among the elite reading public of the cultural magazines and the editors, publishers, and reporters and their trade publications like *Newspaperdom* (1882–1925), the *Journalist* (1884–1907), the *Fourth Estate* (1894–1927).[46]

As the battle for bigger circulations escalated at the end of the century, predictions became gloomier. William Randolph Hearst had purchased the *New York Journal* in 1895, and by the last years of the decade Pulitzer's and Hearst's New York City papers each reached half a million daily. Critics chastized the public for buying the sensational newspapers, and even more the publishers who were responsible for offering this trash.

Charles Dudley Warner in 1890 repeated his belief that the American people "have the newspapers they deserve." He put some of the blame on the public, but said the actions of the editors "make it worse." Warner admitted that the American newspaper was a "marvel of "intelligence and enterprise." It exposed misconduct of public officials and made the whole people "inspectors of all that concerns them...." He said its great service was to inform public opinion and regretted that not all papers had a conscience or sense of responsibility.[47] Warner pointed out that the public had legal remedies for the invasion of privacy or injury to reputation by the press. He still hoped that the public might see sensationalism as "windy, unprofitable daily food—that wit and gayety [sic] and a lively presentation of news are not inconsistent with decency and with respect for individual rights and sensibilities...." If readers would discriminate in their reading, the quality of the newspaper would rise. The literacy of the multitudes explained the large-circulation journals. "This is the penalty of cultivating the ability to read in advance of the taste to discriminate," he observed.[48]

## THE SEARCH FOR SOLUTIONS

Critics sought remedies. The idea of an endowed newspaper was mentioned as early as 1890 in an article in the *Arena* by W. H. H. Murray. This idea would gain force in the following decades and never entirely disappear from the public debate. Murray thought an endowment would free the paper from vulgar personalism and slanderous attack and let it follow the ideals of "honorable and right thinking journalism."[49] The endowed newspaper would explore all political viewpoints because it had no political or commercial aim to serve. Lies and fabrication in the American press were bad, Murray said, but the system permitted it. The editor is an employee and "writes what he is told." The reporters are "bright and manly but act under orders." The power that commands them is money, he said. "Money has no conscience, no honor, no patriotism, no sympathy with truth, right, and decency, and never has had. It loves and seeks but one thing—profits." This leads to the publication of sensations in order to sell more. An endowed press, he thought, would bring fairness, accuracy, and moral conviction that would raise journalism to the level of the professions and elevate the status of the editorial page.[50]

An endowed press, said an editorial in the *Dial* of January 1893, would have a "civilizing influence" over city and country. *Dial* observed that journalism was the public teacher and could not be just another business enterprise. It must "exercise a trust no less than the legal, medical, or teaching profession." But *Dial's* editors feared this was being lost sight of in the "modern scramble for wealth."[51]

The growing enthusiasm for an ideal newspaper brought a group of gentlemen together in New York City in 1896. Professor Harry Thurston Peck of Columbia University, an editor of the *Bookman*, reported that they all believed that "in spite of the excellence and ability and enterprise of our existing newspapers," not one of them was truly representative of the "soundest and sanest public opinion."[52]

Inaccuracy, faked stories, concocted interviews, sensationalism, and "a morbid craving for personalities" were some of the main criticisms from this group. They said that the same prominence was given a barroom brawl and a great diplomatic negotiation. There was too much about political candidates' looks and clothes and personalities and too little about arguments and issues, he said. "Partisanship that tinctures all political news and opinion, including the language used to describe political leaders," resulted in a lack of fairness.[53] Due to lack of time, reporters often sacrificed accuracy. Peck thought America had a "large and very influential class of trained and thoroughly intelligent men, who are not to be influenced by cheap jokes and tawdry rhetoric and big, black scare-heads." This audience would appreciate a serious newspaper that would set forth news and arguments "rationally, crisply, convincingly."[54]

That audience was small. The *New York Times* under Adolph S. Ochs after 1896 would establish its bright reputation by appealing to that very audience with "all the news that's fit to print." Ochs came to New York City from Chattanooga, Tennessee, where he had built the *Chattanooga Times* into a strong local newspaper. The *New York Times* had been staggering under the impact of the "new journalism," but Ochs liked the challenge of creating a quality, nonsensational newspaper in that yellow market.[55] He took the 9,000 circulation daily to 75,000 by 1899, bragging that this was a reliable newspaper that "did not soil the breakfast cloth." By 1901, The *Times* sold for three cents with 100,000 circulation while the *World* and *Journal* were at two cents for substantially larger circulations.[56] It was the *Times* that critics singled out for praise and emulation.

At the turn of the century, newspapers in New York City and nationwide continued to pursue the lucrative sensationalism that critics decried. This line of 1890s criticism would not change very much as "yellow journalism" exaggerated sensationsalism at the end of the decade, and it would increase in volume until some publishers finally paid attention.

# NOTES

1. Arthur M. Schlesinger, *The Rise of the City 1878–1898*, vol. X of *A History of American Life* (New York: Macmillan, 1933): Sean Dennis Cashman, *America in the Gilded Age* (New York: New York University Press, 1984/1988); Robert H. Wiebe, *The Search for Order: 1877–1920* (New York: Hill & Wang, 1967), vii, 129; Henry F. May, *The End of American Innocence* (New York: Knopf, 1959), vii.
2. Edwin Emery and Michael Emery, *The Press and America*, 5th ed. (Englewood Cliffs, N.J.: Prentice-Hall, 1984) 253–280.
3. Edwin Emery, *The History of the American Newspaper Publishers Association (ANPA)* (Minneapolis: University of Minnesota Press, 1950), 11.
4. Emery, *Press*, 288: Theodore Child, "The American Newspaper Press," *Fortnightly Review* 44 (December 1, 1885): 827–37.
5. Bayrd Still, *Mirror for Gotham* (New York: New York University Press, 1956), 205–08.
6. James Creelman, "Joseph Pulitzer—Master Journalist," *Pearson's* 21 (March 1909): 246.
7. The author examined articles listed under *journalism* and *newspapers* in *Poole's Index* and the *Reader's Guide to Periodical Literature* for the period studied and has identified as many of the authors as can be located in standard biographical sources.
8. John Tomsich, *A Genteel Endeavor, American Culture and Politics in the Gilded Age* (Stanford, Calif.: Stanford University Press, 1971), 6.
9. Tomsich, *Genteel*, 1–2.
10. Charles Dudley Warner, *The American Newspaper* (Boston: I. R. Osgood, 1881), 19, 42.
11. Warner, *American*, 61.
12. Marion T. Marzolf, "The American 'New Journalism' Takes Root in Europe," *Journalism Quarterly* 61 (Autumn 1984): 530–31.
13. Marzolf, "American," 691.
14. Arnot Reid, "The English and the American Press," *Nineteenth Century* 22 (August 1887): 529–536, 691.
15. Allan Nevins, *The Evening Post: A Century of Journalism* (New York: Boni & Liveright, 1922), 549.
16. William M. Armstrong, *E. L. Godkin: A Biography* (Albany: State University of New York Press, 1978).

17. E. L. Godkin, "Newspapers Here and Abroad," *North American Review* 150 (February 1890): 197–204.
18. Godkin, "Newspapers," 202.
19. Godkin, "Newspapers," 204.
20. E. L. Godkin, editorial, *Nation* 68 (27 April 1899): 295.
21. Condé Benoist Pallen, "Newspaperism," *Lippincott's Monthly Magazine* 38 (November 1886): 470–77.
22. J. J. Gilmer Speed, "Do Newspapers Now Give the News?" *Forum* 15 (August 1893): 710.
23. Speed, "News," 710–11.
24. Richard Watson Gilder, "The Newspaper, the Magazine, and the Public," *Outlook* 61 (4 February 1899): 319.
25. Gilder, "Newspaper," 319.
26. Gilder, "Newspaper," 320.
27. Gilder, "Newspaper," 321.
28. Emery, *Press*, 256–59.
29. Julius Ward, "The Future of Sunday Journalism," *Lippincott's Monthly Magazine* 37 (June 1886): 389.
30. Junius Henri Browne, "'Newspaperism' Reviewed," *Lippincott's Monthly Magazine* 38 (November 1886) 721–28.
31. Eugene M. Camp, "Journalists: Born or Made?" A paper read before the Alumni Association of Wharton School, First Annual Reunion, University of Pennsylvania, March 27, 1888 (Philadelphia: Philadelphia Social Science Association, 1888), 3, 15.
32. *Journalist*, 19 December 1885. See also: "*Editor and Publisher* Marks Its Sixtieth Anniversary," *Editor and Publisher* (25 March 1944): 11.
33. J. W. Keller, "Journalism as a Career," *Forum* 15 (August 1893): 691–704.
34. Howard Good, *Acquainted with the Night: The Image of Journalists in American Fiction, 1890–1930* (Metuchen, N.J.: Scarecrow, 1986), 89.
35. W. S. Lilly, "Ethics of Journalism," *Forum* 7 (July 1889): 503–07.
36. Editorial, *Dial* 15 (16 August 1893): 79.
37. Editorial, *Dial* 80.
38. Charles Anderson Dana, "The Modern American Newspaper," in *The Art of Newspaper Making* (New York: Appleton, 1895), 20.
39. Whitelaw Reid, "The Future of the Newspaper," *Nation* 95 (26 June 1879): 432–33.
40. Whitelaw Reid, "Journalism as a Career," in *American and English Studies* II (London: Smith, Elder, 1914), 199.
41. Reid, "Career," 221.
42. Reid, "Career," 226.
43. Whitelaw Reid, "Journalistic Duties and Opportunities," in *American*, 317.
44. Whitelaw Reid, "The Practical Issues in a Newspaper Office," in *American*, 269.
45. See note 4.
46. "*Editor and Publisher* Marks Its Sixtieth Anniversary," *Editor and Publisher* (25 March 1944): 7.
47. Charles Dudley Warner, "Newspapers and the Public," *Forum* 9 (April 1890): 198–207.
48. Warner, "Public," 201.

49. W. H. H. Murray, "An Endowed Press," *Arena* 2 (October 1890): 553–59.
50. Murray, "Endowed," 556.
51. Editorial, *Dial* (16 January 1893): 36.
52. Harry Thurston Peck, "A Great National Newspaper," *Cosmopolitan* 24 (December 1897): 209–20.
53. Peck, "Great," 217.
54. Peck, "Great," 220.
55. Emery, *Press*, 327.
56. Emery, *Press*, 328–29.

# CHAPTER 2

# The Deluge of Yellow: 1895–1900

The race between William Randolph Hearst and Joseph Pulitzer for the biggest circulation and control of the market in New York City gave rise to the term "yellow journalism." It was used by critics as shorthand for the blatant degeneration of a modern journalism gone wild in pursuit of profit. Hearst tried to turn the nickname to advantage by saying it was the journalism that got things done by fighting the establishment in the name of the little people. But the negative "yellow" label stuck and today is still associated with faking, deception, prying, insensitivity, and arrogance by powerful mass media.

Hearst had entered the New York City market in 1895 with the purchase of the *New York Journal*, a lackluster newspaper started by Joseph Pulitzer's brother Albert. Hearst had studied Joseph's success with the *World* and had remade the *San Francisco Examiner* in that image. He brought some of his top staff to New York where he also snared several of the *World's* star reporters, editors, and artists by offering them better pay. As Pulitzer had done before him, Hearst set a penny price for the *Journal*, forcing Pulitzer and others to lower prices to compete. Pulitzer later admitted that this penny cut was a telling blow to the *World's* financial stability, but he had wanted to keep his lead.[1]

Hearst drove up circulation at the *Journal* to 150,000 the first year and passed the *World* in the second year of competition using the new journalism tactics of interesting and exciting news, extensive use of stunts, crusading editorial page, regular self-promotion of the newspaper's scoops, low price, innovative use of illustrations and cartoons, and readership campaigns.[2]

By 1897 both papers had Sunday editions of about 600,000 and somewhat smaller morning and afternoon editions.[3] The Sunday editions became the battleground for readers and advertisers, where hyped content and garish displays of type, art, and words were made possible by the improvements in color printing, engraving, and high-speed presses. The Sunday *World* had introduced an eight-page comic section, with four pages in color. The *Journal* came out with its own competing eight-page color comic supplement in the fall of 1896, advertised as "eight pages of iridescent polychromous effulgence that makes the rainbow look like a lead pipe."[4]

The *World* ran a popular comic panel that covered about half a page called "Hogan's Alley" drawn by R. F. Outcault. It featured a brash, streetwise bald-headed urchin in a nightshirt who dropped irreverent and timely remarks on life in the contemporary slum—the original "Yellow Kid." Don Seitz, the *World's* business manager, tells the story of his yellow origin. The printers were experimenting with color, which they hoped would drive up circulation. The pressman complained that he "got no results from the wishy-washy tints turned out by the art department." The art department responded with pure yellow for the nightshirt.[5]

It was right, Seitz recalled. "The solid color stood out above all the colors in the comic." The comic became so successful that Hearst hired away the artist and his feature; Pulitzer had to retaliate with a new artist, George B. Luks, who drew his own version of the yellow kid.[6] The yellow journalism label is credited first to Ervin Wardman, editor of the *New York Press* who used it to describe both the *World* and the *Journal*, and then to C. A. Dana, publisher and editor of the *New York Sun*, who made frequent use of the term in referring to the extremes of decadence on both newspapers.[7]

Yellow journalism is really only differentiated from sensationalism by the matter of degrees of tactics used to promote the stories to attract readers. It built on those familiar subjects—crime news, scandal and gossip, divorce and sex, disaster and sports—and added scare-headlines in large black or red ink, "lavish use of pictures," (sometimes stolen or faked); fraudulent and misleading stories, faked interviews, and thrilling pseudo-science stories; Sunday color comics and human interest stories; and "ostentatious sympathy with the underdog."[8]

## THE COLOR OF DECADENCE

Yellow was the color associated with the end-of-the-century decadence and with renaissance, explains Holbrook Jackson. Critics saw the yellow-clad urchin as an apt symbol of urban social decay.[9] Yellow was also associated with provocative new departures in the fine arts, like Aubrey Beardsley's little magazine, *Yellow Book*, and with poetry and paintings that typified the "fine de siècle" mood. In the popular arts, the yellow press was also rejecting the old ways and was "alive to the desires of the crowd."[10]

Yellow journalism was democratic in its capture of a vast new audience for newspapers and often helped to improve the lot of the working man and woman while entertaining them. A few critics were willing to credit these positive features. Criticism that began with the introduction of the "new journalism" and sensationalism accelerated along with the spread of yellow journalism beyond the borders of New York City. A moral war, similar to that waged against the first penny press of the 1830s, ensued, led by the high-brow magazines. They were joined by new scholars of the social sciences who were examining the city and its institutions. European visitors saw the press as an example of the rawness and uncivilized level of the new nation. The American newspaper is a "conglomeration of news—political, literary, artistic, scientific and fashionable, of reports of trials, of amusing anecdotes, gossip of all kinds, interviews, jokes, scandals—the whole written in a style which sometimes shocks the man of taste, but which often interests and always amuses," said French correspondent Paul Blouët. Blouët was a fan of American democracy, and he predicted that American style journalism would accompany democracy as it made progress in Europe.[11]

American critics at the turn of the century, when yellow journalism was at its most flamboyant and powerful, emphasized its bad taste and moral decay that made the world worse, its encouragement of lawlessness and class hatreds, its childishness and lack of ethics, and its hypocrisy in maintaining that it was only giving people what they wanted.

Elizabeth Banks, who had been a yellow journalist, could see no virtue in the work. Women could be trapped in the career of yellow journalism, she warned, and it would eat away at their wholesomeness and purity. They were driven to work to earn money to support themselves and their families, and their assignments exposed them to risk of life and honor. To do the job they had to lay aside their feminine squeamishness and scruples, but Banks acknowledged that women were doing some of the most difficult, enterprising, and sensational journalism. To flee that fate, Banks had gone to London to become a freelance writer for the respectable magazines.

She was merciless in unmasking the pretenses of American editors who asked reporters to engage in immoral tactics to produce moral lesson stories for the yellow press. They champion the weak and defenseless and send women reporters out to encounter the evils in society, she said, but "if nothing happens, there is no story." Banks told of one woman who had traveled steerage with immigrants to America to get an inside story. The woman had written about the deplorable conditions on the ship, but she had not been molested on the trip, so the editors refused her story. Another, sent to interview a mayor, learned he had just left town, but was told to fake the story anyway and have it ready in two hours, according to Banks.[12] Autobiographies and fiction depicting yellow journalism are filled with similar incidents.

"There can be no denying the fact that yellow journalism has become a power in the United States—a power for evil in the main," Banks said.[13] Intelligent American readers had been "warned about the yellow press" but looked on it as a "vulgar fad among vulgar people."[14] Now those same people, Banks charged, had become alarmed over yellow journalism's influence among the lower classes. "Any institution having at its command almost untold millions of money, must, of necessity, become a power—whether for evil or for good rests with those who have it in charge."[15]

Banks said that if the legitimate newspapers wanted to compete, they should lavish equally large sums of money on the brightest literary talent. The yellow journals had attracted hundreds of former men and women workers from the more dignified newspapers. Among them, Banks said, were former editors-in-chief of a number of leading newspapers:

> It would be funny if it were not so pathetic—the sight of a man well advanced in years, who, for the better part of his life, has presided over the destinies of a dignified Republican newspaper of the old school, sitting at a yellow journalistic desk and turning off "jingo" editorials, denouncing the Republican President for whom he voted, and passing his opinion upon the issue of "scare-heads" for the next day![16]

## THE PROBLEM OF AUDIENCE

Sensationalism was to be found more in the appearance than in the facts of the stories, Professor Harry T. Peck of Columbia University pointed out. American life was "so much more open and lived in public than European" and the excess of personal gossip was a carry over from village life. The American casualness was a part of journalism, but Peck thought a line should be drawn in coverage of personal lives of public figures. Even after defending the popular press, Peck had to admit that what he wanted was a newspaper for the growing class of educated and intelligent people, a newspaper that would treat serious matters fairly and in proportion to their importance, one that was fair in political discussions without being dull or vulgar.[17] This would become an increasingly popular theme in the decade to follow.

One reader praised an unnamed, good Chicago newspaper that was free from sensations and scare-heads and still presented all the news. It had the largest circulation. "If the people really want blanket-sheet sensationalism, why do they buy this paper?" he asked. He believed that people would buy a good paper when it was offered and predicted that the "herculean effort" of the yellow press to advertise itself was a sign of weakness. Dogma and money would not forever sustain the newspapers, he said, and finally the public would get the newspaper it really wants.[18]

Charles Dudley Warner, still concerned about the state of American journalism, pointed out that the audience was at least partly to blame. The newspapers that pander to the lowest taste do have the largest circulation, he observed, and they make money, so rivalry is tremendous. The newspaper is sold too cheap, he said: "so long as it is cheap it tends to be nasty." Because the cost of news gathering and editing had increased tremendously, the paper depends on advertising for its financial support. "The sole effort of the paper, then, is to gain circulation. No matter *what* sort of circulation. . . ."[19] Warner's solution—to reform people so they will become "moral enough, clean enough, intelligent enough or refined enough to prefer a real 'news' paper and a decent paper to the 'fake' paper and the unclean." Newspapers could easily charge three times the price and still be the cheapest thing in the market, he said, and if they concentrated on news, they would be less costly to produce.[20]

Many of the criticisms were reprinted or summarized in the weekly trade publication, the *Journalist*, where editor Allan Forman often defended the successful new sensational press. The *World* and the *Journal* were "continually doing things in which the public is interested . . . sending thousands of sick children to the seashore every summer, exposing fraud, fighting corruption." He suggested the "sober, clean, self-respecting journals" take an interest in this kind of work and get closer to the people. Forman said that it was the ablest writers, the brightest writing, and its "warm, generous heart alive to the troubles and miseries of humanity and anxious to alleviate them" that brought the readers to the yellow press, not the fakes and intrusions of privacy.[21]

The enormous funds spent and efforts made by the *Journal* and the *World* to promote the news coverage of the Spanish-American War and to boost their own circulations to over a million a day during the six-month war have been thoroughly covered in journalism histories. "How do you like the *Journal's* war?" boasted the Hearst newspaper. Godkin at the *Nation* certainly didn't and frequently said so: "The power of making war in a democracy must always, in the last resort, no matter what the constitutional arrangements may be, reside in the mass of the people," he declared.[22] But he saw that power passing into the hands of the worst elements of the press that were using it to forment war, to increase their circulation at the expense of sorrow and loss for the rest of the community.

What made the matter deadly serious, said Godkin, was that "for the first time in American history, an irresponsible force" had assumed this power without any restraint. "From every such discipline or restraint, except libel suits, the yellow journalist is absolutely free. His one object is to circulate widely and make money." People were clamoring for war, so Congressmen feared loss of their seats if they did not press for war. "This is an absolutely new state of things," warned Godkin. The multitude "now sets fleets and armies in motion . . . a blackguard boy with several millions of dollars at his disposal has more influence on the use a great nation may make of its credit, of its army and navy, of its name and traditions than all the statesmen and philosophers and professors in the country. If this does not supply food for reflection about the future of the nation to thoughtful men, it must be because the practice of reflection has ceased."[23]

Godkin exemplified the culture custodians who saw the newspapers allied with the most vulgar and crass elements in modern American life. He blasted away at the publishers who created the "yellow press," and at the advertisers and readers who supported it; but he steadfastly supported freedom of expression for all and robust discussion, even when hotter heads were advising some censorship after the McKinley assassination in 1901:

> The real offense of yellow journalism is . . . that its pervading spirit is one of vulgarity, indecency, and reckless sensationalism; that it steadily violates the canons alike of good taste and sound morals; that it cultivates false standards of life, and demoralizes its readers; that it recklessly uses language which may incite the crack-brained to lawlessness; that its net influence makes the world worse.[24]

## A CALL FOR PUBLIC ACTION

Godkin was not alone in calling for public action against the vulgar press. A group of Baltimore Quaker women in 1897 in *Dial* magazine called for the purification of the press. They wanted newspapers to show "reticence in the detail of crime and scandal, that the purely sensational shall be excluded, that pictures and advertisements both personal and medical, which so insidiously lead the innocent and unspecting from the path of virtue, shall find no place in your columns. . . ." But *Dial*'s editor mused that the yellow editors were not likely to pay much attention to these "gentle pleadings." The average American journalist had long since lost any conscience and had substituted a "hypocritical accent and leering mien," said *Dial*. The "modern substitute for a conscience in journalism . . . (was) preaching virtue in such a manner that it in nowise interferes with the practise of vice," editorializing on the "brutal tendencies of the age" while filling columns of the same issue with highly-colored accounts of brutalities.[25]

According to *Dial*, the Governor of Illinois had asked for legislation "to protect men from wanton assaults upon their character" by such "foul sheets." Public libraries and clubs in Eastern cities were "excluding from their reading-rooms the two most conspicuously objectionable newspapers that are published anywhere in the country." These actions suggested that "some such crystallization of sentiment on the subject of American journalism, its duties and its responsibilities, may soon take place."[26] People have the government they deserve; cities are equally responsible for the newspapers they support, said *Dial*, asking all good citizens to treat these newspapers like the "moral outcasts" they were and shaming them "out of existence or into amended lives."[27]

The real mission of the American press was to be "a potent agency of enlightenment and a pillar for the support of republican institutions." The yellow press had used its power to excite and fascinate the masses so that its opinions were no longer taken seriously because they were not reached by a process of serious reasoning. "Most of the newspapers published in our large cities are so devoid of principle that they constitute a perpetual menace to every genuine interest of our civilization," *Dial* declared.[28] Retention of that old, secure way of life was precisely what these high-brow critics wished to preserve. The press was a visible and apt symbol of the nation's shifting cultural standards.

The sensational journals had attained the power to "manufacture public prejudice" and have become tyrants in the use of that power," said Judge John Henderson Garnsey in the *Arena*. "They indulge in the open boast that they can make or unmake any man or women, any set of men or any institution, any line of thought or any reform; and they are pretty nearly right," he said. The people have no protection against this influence, he complained, because the current libel laws were nearly powerless and no other force checked the press.[29]

The press, unlike other individuals and institutions, answered to no one, Garnsey argued. He did not advocate press censorship because that would violate the constitutional principles of the country, but emphasized the need for "some protection from the flood of journalistic filth issuing from the great cities." That the reader "wants this sort of thing" was specious reasoning, he believed, because the reader is taught to think this is what he wants by the press; he reads "to see to what depths his neighbors have descended." Give the people a real choice and they would support it, he said.[30]

## SOCIAL RESPONSIBILITY PROPOSED

Leadership was an issue in a content analysis study of newspaper sensationalism in 1900 that was frequently quoted in its day. Dr. Delos F. Wilcox, a social psychologist, examined 147 major city newspapers in 21 metropolitan areas. He measured the space devoted to categories of news and sensations, and found 47 newspapers that were yellow, 45 conservative, with the rest in the middle. He classified 23 characteristics of press content and found a few that fit 15 papers generally agreed upon as representing the two extremes. Crime, vice, illustrations, want ads, medical ads, and self-advertising belonged to the yellow press, while conservative papers had more political news, business news, letters, exchanges, and miscellaneous advertisements. All 23 categories were measured for all the papers in the survey, and Wilcox found that those that fit the yellow end also had the largest circulations and cheapest prices, and thus, according to Wilcox the "greatest potential influence."[31] Wilcox admitted that it was difficult to define "yellow journalism," but to him it meant the use of extreme sensationalism and playing on passion and follies of people in the quest of wealth or power, which made it a social vice.

The newspaper business was becoming more and more institutional, Wilcox warned, requiring large capital outlay, but it had public responsibilities to distribute information. It ought not be controlled by "irresponsible individuality," he said. The ideal newspaper, he asserted, would be free of either private or factional interests.[32] "Newspapers should be responsible to society just as teachers must be," Wilcox declared in an early discussion of the notion of social responsibility for the press. Newspapers should provide a review of the day's events, factually and briefly, without distortion, passion or prejudice, he said.[33]

If we believed in ideal democratic government, "we could have the newspapers under government control." But we think "government is a necessary evil, and so we will not trust government with control of the newspapers." Wilcox had little faith in the idea of an endowed newspaper; instead, he called for the "development of the sense of social responsibility for the use of brains and money." As society improved, social intelligence would improve and better newspapers would be demanded, he observed, and the good that was "mixed with the evil of even the yellowest journals" would be retained in the evolutionary process.[34] Wilcox was one of the first to develop the theme of social responsibility, which a national commission would propose nearly half a century later as the new philosophy suited to modern American journalism.[35]

Yellow journalism won't last, predicted a critic in the *Catholic World*. The writer, Charles B. Connolly, said that yellow journalism was only ten years old and had flourished because of the technological developments, absolute freedom from restraint in press utterances, and Americans' love for anything new. Connolly surmised that there could be no code of ethics for a profession that "let you ruin a man's reputation without incurring blame, that encouraged you to lie and cheat and deceive both the sources of your information and your competitors in order to get a beat on the story, and that encourages faking in order to fill an editor's demands to do the impossible."[36]

He believed idealistic youth would either be corrupted by journalism, or would turn away from it. Connolly detected a "tide of reversion" already setting in which would "slowly but none the less surely compel the abandonment of many of the methods at present in vogue," and would allow the reporter "to become a professional man, a scholar and a gentleman, and not a professional meddler, amateur detective, and inventor of plausible impossibilities all in one."[37]

## TRIAL BY NEWSPAPER

The allegations that the yellow press was eroding the judicial system, undermining stable institutions and setting class against class emerged at the turn of the century along with stepped-up interest in some form of control. The yellow journals make "venomous attacks upon the rich, respectable and influential members of society, thus arousing feelings of envy and animosity on the part of the poor and humble," argued the *Inland Printer*. "This raising of ill-feeling between classes is one of the most dangerous tendencies of our sensational times, for discontent is easier aroused than allayed." The allegation that these journals were setting class against class and creating distrust in the social institutions was a common one.[38] Historians note that a war between the rich and the poor seemed plausible to some in the 1890s in the context of Populism and labor strife.[39]

Attorney George W. Alger argued in the *Atlantic Monthly* in 1903 that the yellow press was a "pernicious influence" on the courts of justice in criminal trials. Advance publicity with incriminating evidence leaked to the press was causing people to be "tried by newspaper" before a case ever came to trial, and making it difficult to obtain an unprejudiced jury.[40]

Through constant repetition the yellow press "made the ignorant and poor think that justice is not blind but bought; that the great corporations own the judges . . . that American institutions are rotten to the core, and that legislative halls and courts of justice exist as instruments of oppression and to preserve the rights of property by denying or destroying the rights of man. No greater injury can be done to the working people than to create in their minds this false and groundless suspicion concerning the integrity of the judiciary," he said. He did not defend specific allegations of prejudice or wrongdoing, but opposed the yellow press charges of wholesale corruption in the judiciary.[41]

## THE PUBLISHERS REACT

The predicted crystallization of opinion against the yellow press was at hand. Although it was not known until later when Don Seitz's papers were available for study, Pulitzer sought a truce with Hearst. The two publishers held a series of negotiations for the purpose of agreeing on a way to share the market.[42] Yellow press circulations had dropped following the war. For example, Hearst's morning *Journal* was losing 10,000 to 15,000 subscribers a week, but he could still go on pouring family money into his newspaper ventures. In 1897 he was willing to deal with Pulitzer because he was anxious to extend his chain of newspapers across the country. He proposed raising the morning paper from a penny to two cents; each would secure a share of the market without raiding the other. Pulitzer objected that the evening and Sunday papers were not part of the arrangement, so they discussed it again in 1902–03. Although a similar arrangement had been worked out in 1898 among Chicago newspapers, Pulitzer and Hearst never came to terms. Instead, their editorial decisions began to lead the papers toward different publics. Hearst continued the yellow tactics in Chicago and nationwide in his chain and built a famous media empire.[43]

Pulitzer regretted some of the yellow tactics he had allowed on his newspaper in the battle with Hearst, and piously ordered his editors to go after a better class of readers. "We cannot do—must not do what the *Journal* does in recklessness and disregard of good taste and public opinion." A staff memo in 1903 told editors: "There will be no faking. Tone down the worst of divorce, murder, salacious stories. Keep the tone higher on the first page showcase." The memo allowed the Sunday paper to be lighter in tone, since it was to entertain the entire family.[44]

His new target market was the type of reader who liked the *Herald* or *Times*, Pulitzer said. He wanted to change the *World*'s tone to attract them without losing the masses. The idea was to walk a line between the sensational and the vulgar, but his editors sometimes found it hard to see the distinction.[45] Pulitzer worked to reestablish himself as a serious and responsible publisher, and he spoke out on the issues facing journalism:

> A newspaper can never be influential if it seeks no more than to please the unthinking or echo the cries of ignorance and passion. Indeed, to become truly commanding, a newspaper must have convictions, must sometimes fearlessly oppose the will of the very public on which its existence depends.[46]

According to some of his biographers, this was the real Joseph Pulitzer speaking, and they describe his newspapers as toned down after this. Meanwhile, Pulitzer began plans to enhance his professional legacy, announcing an endowment to fund a school of journalism in New York City at Columbia University. This tension in the modern newspaper institution between the publisher's profession of a public-spirited ideology and mean-spirited, profit-centered institutional practices continues to plague the print mass journalism and its electronic counterparts. It forms a central motif in a century of press criticism. Efforts to curb these institutional practices face an uphill fight today, as they did at the start of the century.

# NOTES

1. Frank Luther Mott, *American Journalism* (New York: Macmillan, 1962), 521.
2. Emery, *Press*, 247; Mott, *Journalism*, 437–39.
3. Emery, *Press*, 249.
4. Mott, *American*, 525.
5. Don Seitz, *Training for the Newspaper Trade* (Philadelphia: Lippincott 1916), 90–91.
6. Seitz, *Training*, 90–91.
7. Mott, *American*, 526.
8. Mott, *American*, 539.

9. Frank Luther Mott, *A History of American Magazines*, Vol. 4, 1885–1905 (Cambridge, Mass: Harvard University Press, 1957), 196–97.
10. Holbrook Jackson, *The Eighteen Nineties* (New York: Knopf, 1922), 23.
11. Marzolf, "New Journalism," 532.
12. Elizabeth Banks, "American 'Yellow Journalism,'" *Nineteenth Century* 44 (August 1898): 328–40.
13. Banks, "Yellow," 320.
14. Banks, "Yellow," 332.
15. Banks, "Yellow," 330.
16. Banks, "Yellow," 333.
17. Peck, "Great," 220.
18. John Henderson Garnsey, LLB, "The Demand for Sensational Journals," *Arena* 18 (November 1897): 686.
19. Charles Dudley Warner, "Better Newspapers," *Journalist* (1 May 1897): 14. Exerpted from *Harper's Monthly* (April 1897).
20. Warner, "Better," 14.
21. Editorial, *Journalist* (1 May 1897): 12.
22. E. L. Godkin, Editorial, *Nation* 66 (5 May 1898): 336.
23. Godkin, "Editorial," 336.
24. Godkin, "Editorial," *Nation* 26 (September 1901): 238.
25. Editorial, "The Decay of American Journalism," *Dial* 22 (16 April 1897): 238.
26. "Decay," *Dial*, 238.
27. "Decay," *Dial*, 239.
28. "Decay," *Dial*, 238–39.
29. Garnsey, "Demand," 682.
30. Garnsey, "Demand," 684–85.
31. Delos F. Wilcox, "The American Newspaper: A Study in Social Psychology," *The Annals of the American Academy of Political and Social Science* 16 (July 1900): 76–77, 86.
32. Wilcox, "Study," 86–87.
33. Wilcox, "Study," 88.
34. Wilcox, "Study," 90–92.
35. The study by Wilcox was usually only cited for its statistics on sensationalism, and the social message was ignored, which is probably why Dr. Wilcox has not received credit for this early formulation of what would become the social responsibility theory.
36. Charles B. Connolly, "The Ethics of Modern Journalism," *Catholic World* 75 (July 1902): 456.
37. Connolly, "Ethics," 462.
38. "Yellow Journalism," *Inland Printer* (October 1901): 89.
39. James MacGregor Burns, *The Workshop of Democracy* (New York: Knopf, 1985), 224.
40. George W. Alger, "Sensational Journalism and the Law," *Atlantic Monthly* 91 (February 1903): 148.
41. Alger, "Law," 150.
42. "Hearst-Pulitzer Feud Cost Millions, Ended in Draw," *Editor and Publisher* (27 June 1957): 182, 184.

43. William Robinson Reynolds, *Joseph Pulitzer* unpublished doctoral dissertation (Columbia University, Political Science, 1950), 300–308.
44. Reynolds, *Pulitzer*, Chap. 19.
45. Reynolds, *Pulitzer*, 462.
46. Piers Brendon, *The Life and Death of the Press Barons* (London: Secker & Warburg, 1982), 451.

# CHAPTER 3

# The Quest for an Ideal
# Newspaper: 1900–1910

Out of the clamor over the evils and dangers of the yellow press, a vision of
the ideal newspaper began to emerge in the first decade of the new century.
The culture critics and religious leaders were joined by the social scientists,
who offered supporting evidence that the sensational press would undermine
the moral fiber of society. The growing commercialism of the press became a
favorite target of the press reformers in the Progressive Era, and the endowed
press and a financially independent press were suggested as popular alternatives. The yellow press did have a few defenders; even its critics acknowledged the democratic virtues of this popular press—it expanded the audience
for news and helped educate the common people.

The struggle between the old and the new journalism mirrored a larger
social dynamism in a nation that was gradually loosening the bonds of the
nineteenth century and adapting to a modern society and scientific spirit.[1]
The new journalism, even in its detested "yellow" form, was imbued with the
go-ahead spirit of the contemporary American city; it was lively, modern, and
interesting. If its infantile, vulgar, and immoral features could be curbed, the
yellow press might be redeemable. The task would be to make a popular press
that conformed to the standards of respectable society without having to
resort to legal sanctions, such as the despised suggestion of censorship.

Yellow journalism, according to its supporters, went out and got results
for the poor and powerless people. It brought the newly or barely literate,
urban public together and gave it a sense of itself and of the city life. "The
daily newspaper is an urban institution," said sociologist Robert Park. It had
become a necessity in the modern American city with its rich mix of national,
rural, and urban peoples, and it let them know what was going on. It

encouraged a reading habit, even though most of that reading was sensationalized and trivialized. The independent press "was driving the old time newspapers to the wall," Park explained. It was clear that circulation could be "greatly increased" by making literature out of the news." Dana had done it with the *Sun*, Park observed, and the yellow press "grew up in an attempt to capture for the newspaper a public whose only literature was the family story paper or the cheap novel." It wrote the news to formula—"love and romance for the women; sport and politics for the men."[2] The form culminated in the Hearst and Pulitzer Sunday newspapers, Park pointed out. In so doing it "enlarged the circle of a single public of a larger number of people and wider range of interests and intelligence than any other type of newspaper has ever done before." Park noted that total circulation of newspapers between 1880 and 1921 increased from 3,566,395 to 33,741,742. Whatever else it was, said Park, the yellow press "was at least democratic."[3] He saw no remedy for the existing condition of newspapers. They were "about as good as they could be." The newspaper's improvement would come about only with better education of the people and better organization of political information and intelligence, Park said, advising journalists to think more objectively and not wholly in moral terms.[4]

Yellow journalism was an American cultural phenomenon, growing out of the particular blend of newly literate urban inhabitants, booming economy, technological innovations, and entrepreneurs who sized up the new market. The yellow press was an entertainer that competed with other forms of urban entertainment, offered a release from the monotony, drabness, and strain of urban life, and built on an old tradition of sensational stories that abound in folk tales, broadsides, almanacs, and ballads. Some sensationalism could be accounted for because "we know so little about life," Park commented, and are shocked by what we read.[5]

Modern city people, explained Professor Carroll D. Clark, had the same appetites and desires as their village ancestors. The yellow press provided "news as surrogate for primary contacts," a substitute for the village corner, and it gave emotional color to urban life and taught moralistic lessons. The breakdown of old ways of life and the challenges of the urban experience produced problems and a search for solutions and understanding among these new city people. The yellow press filled a need, Clark said, even as it shocked the established society. "Yellow journalism disappeared," according to Clark, as its techniques became standardized and modified by the modern journalism and then were "no longer regarded as yellow by the masses."[6] The new front page, the big stories, illustrations, and Sunday newspapers became a part of the mainstream press tradition.

Arthur Brisbane, one of Hearst's highest paid editors, defended yellow journalism as the "journalism of action and responsibility," attracting attention by detecting crime, sending relief trains to help flood victims, fighting the encroachments of class or capital on popular rights. When yellow journalism criticizes Wall Street or brings suits against the trusts, it frightens the big public plunderers, he claimed. But the people "know their side is being heard."[7]

Such arguments were not accepted by the *Journalist*, which retorted that Brisbane used socially acceptable behavior to defend his newspaper's yellowness. The saving of a young women from Spanish tyranny and contributing funds to the starving and the suffering were good deeds of public welfare, but they were also excellent examples of self-promotion that helped sell the newspaper, a motive the *Journalist* called suspect.[8]

Another advocate took refined society to task for objecting to yellow journalism's catering to the low tastes of its readers. To Lydia Kingsmill Commander, it was just a difference in cultivation. The refined reader thrills to Sherlock Holmes, Poe's horror tales, and Balzac's gruesome stories, she pointed out, and high literary skill makes such writing acceptable to the cultured few. "Yellow journalism is vulgar and emotional, but it is kind and generous, active, wide-awake and progressive. It guards the peoples' interests and is a strong educational force." Commander thought it taught ordinary people to read regularly, as well as to put the masses in touch with the world, its scientific progress, and great leaders.[9]

"Yellow journals are not 'nice' and 'proper.' But neither are the people they are intended to reach," she declared. "America has an enormous population on a very low level of intelligence.... Yet, if men, they can vote and help determine the destiny of the nation," she said. The yellow journal was helping educate and uplift this mass. As one editor put it, it was better "to raise a whole city one inch than to hoist a few men or women ten feet in the air."[10]

## SOFTENING THE BRAIN

What most worried many critics about the yellow press was its emphasis on crime and sensation. A *Nation* reader said it contributed to the prevailing spirit of lawlessness, encouraging readers to take the law in their own hands.[11] A steady diet of yellow journalism would "gradually wear out the power of the brain-cells to take impressions," decrease the ability to remember, and stunt growth, creating a "morbid craving for emotional excitement," warned Doctor Frederick Peterson in *Collier's* magazine in 1906.[12] A steady diet of yellow journalism would waste away the moral fiber of the nation in the same way bacteria poisons the physical body, he believed.

After a dozen years as a daily newspaper reporter, William Salisbury recalled that Hearst editors did not want just facts. "They wanted us to tell stories," he said. The whole structure of yellow journalism was built upon fabrication and distortion, he believed, not to inform or uplift readers, but to make them think that's what was being done. "We want to thrill and charm and entertain them. People are just a lot of grown-up children."[13]

The childish nature of the yellow readership was a popular explanation for yellow journalism's popularity. It was widely believed that readers of the yellow press were especially susceptible to the power of suggestion and would model their behavior on what they read. But "A Newspaper Reader" wrote *Outlook* magazine that all the press, not only the yellow press, was guilty of giving "Lessons in Crime Fifty Cents Per Month." This reader offered a list of examples clipped from one of the "so-called best newspapers" showing detailed examples of how crimes were committed. As the reader put it: "There was ten times as much educative material for would-be lawbreakers, that any one not feeble-minded or insane would interpret by the very act of understanding what was done or attempted; but in these several cases the lesson in crime was patiently and lovingly unfolded and explained, so that any one so caring to do could add it to his or her repertory."[14]

When a defender of the yellow press tried to justify crime reporting as a deterring lesson about the punishment of evil, the typical retort was that most of the interest in such criminal proceedings is due to a distinctly morbid curiosity. The *Independent* warned that a natural abhorrence toward these crimes is lessened by familiar repetition. "It is well known now that suicides, as reported in the papers, constantly furnish suggestions for further unfortunate beings to put an end to their existence." New methods and types of poisons reported in the newspapers are quickly adopted, said the editorial. A tripling increases in the number of suicides among young people during the previous twenty-five years, it was believed, could be attributed to the great increase in numbers of young people between ages fifteen and twenty who read newspapers over those of a generation ago.[15]

## A SUGGESTIVE INFLUENCE

Young people were more susceptible to suggestive influence, the editorial pointed out. The average age of the suicides was becoming lower, indicating that the power of suggestion over those "who have less mental resistance to the hardships and the trials of life" was great. "There is no doubt at all that suggestion plays a large role in bringing about the commission of unusual crimes of this kind.... Familiarity with them only enhances the morbid curiosity that tempts to abnormal experiences...." This pattern had been recognized by common sense before, said the editorial, and "is confirmed by the advances in modern psychiatry."[16]

Modern sociology was in its early stages of development, and the city and its institutions were important research subjects for the sociologists at the influential University of Chicago. The press, a major urban institution, quickly came under scrutiny. Professor W. I. Thomas, of the University of Chicago's Department of Sociology, explored the nature of mankind's attraction to the morbid in an article in *American Magazine*. The appeal of the yellow journal is to "something lying very deep down in us, something of the nature of impulse or appetite, and almost as blindly elemental as hunger itself," he explained in an early analysis of the yellow press. People don't like to admit the presence or power of this force, Thomas pointed out, but man is a social animal only in a secondary sense, with "a disposition deeply imprinted with the traits of anger, hate, fear, and exultation in disaster to others."[17]

The two influences that temper and socialize man, according to Thomas, were "the affections growing up with marriage and children and the comradeship which arises among men prosecuting vital interests in common." He thought that the yellow journal existed because of the primitive emotions, which are essentially antisocial but pleasurable.[18]

The methods of the yellow press went beyond singling out shocking events, and distorted and perverted facts, and manufactured stories that would produce far greater shock than the exact truth, Thomas explained. The artist and caricaturist add their talents and further isolate and overemphasize certain features. It was successful, Thomas asserted, because "the popular mind is essentially childish." The conditions of contemporary America—free schools and mass immigration—created a "great population that has really just learned to read, and which, though lettered, is childish, or, that which amounts to the same thing from the psychological standpoint—savage; and to these the yellow journal gives endless stories, both real and make-believe."[19]

The modern publisher is able to produce great numbers of issues at a price far below the real cost because of the advertising subsidy. The result was a subversion of the social role of the newspaper, Thomas believed. Speech and printing were the main agents for the dissemination of knowledge, he pointed out, and the daily press has been one of the premier agents for this in the modern democracy. "We have been slow to perceive and credit the essential viciousness of the operations of the yellow press," said Thomas.[20] "Language is a powerful instrument of control because through it, knowledge, tradition, standpoint, ideals, stimulations, copies are transmitted and increased." In this way government, religion, and other elements of the culture exert a control over knowledge and memory to benefit a stable society.[21]

## AGENT OF CRIME

But the public faith in the press was departing, according to Thomas, who observed that many people no longer believed what they saw in the press, and were starting to coalesce around the need to reform the press. The real immorality of the yellow press, according to Thomas, was its serving as an active agent of vice and crime, instead of exerting positive influence through language by promoting a better, more civilized and responsible way of life. Thomas thought it was time for an "eleventh commandment": "Thou shalt not have the perversion of truth for a gainful occupation."[22]

One of his students, Frances Fenton, took up the study in her doctoral dissertation, summarized in the *Journal of Sociology* in 1910–11, just as the public began to organize national meetings and campaigns for a clean press. Fenton noted the public's growing belief that the yellow newspaper contributed to crime. Most of the articles in the magazines, she pointed out, were based on the conjecture and conviction of the authors. Even those that analyzed newspaper content were not comparable because they used differing criteria, Fenton said, when she provided her scientific evidence applying the psychologists' theory of suggestion.

Fenton's study examined newspaper presentation of crime and other antisocial activities to see how this influenced the growth of crime and antisocial behavior. She measured and categorized newspaper content from 103 sample issues using three comparative dates. She also looked at court records and talked to judges and case workers to detail examples of known copying of criminal or antisocial behavior. Her findings showed that crime and antisocial news occupied from 5.01 to 20.02 percent of the news and editorial content of the papers in her study, with the higher percentages belonging to the largest circulation newspapers. She found enough cases of direct newspaper suggestion leading to crime and antisocial activity that her belief in a strong correlation between the two was strengthened.[23] But she did not claim that there was a direct, causal relationship, and since she read only newspaper copies that the librarians were willing to part with, her sample lacks the kind of rigor later developed for content analysis.

The newspaper presents detailed descriptions of crimes and immoral acts, illustrations and writing that glorifies these activities, and "influences people directly, both unconsciously and consciously, to commit antisocial acts," Fenton said. There was a more indirect antisocial influence on public opinion during criminal trials through accounts of these trials and partisan selection of evidence. She concluded that the newspaper aided in "building up antisocial standards, and thus in preparing the way for antisocial acts."[24]

Because the newspaper was such a tremendous influence in the community, Fenton recommended that in the future suggestive antisocial matter be excluded. The newspaper should be an educative and dependable medium, she believed. "Large type, vivid and picturesque writing, illustrations, colored type, diagrams, etc., are just as easily the media of social as of antisocial suggestion and when the content conveyed by them is of a social character they are indispensable for readers who are fatigued, or who read in poor light," she said, outlining a prosocial role for the newspaper.[25]

Fenton recommended new and adequately enforced laws that would restrain newspapers from detailing certain crimes and types of antisocial facts. She dismissed the idea of an endowed newspaper as impractical. Law was the only solution, in her opinion, while hope for the general improvement of society was misguided optimism.[26]

## DECLINING INFLUENCE

Legal solutions raised the spectre of tampering with freedom of speech and press. Although there were efforts to strengthen libel law and introduce privacy law, such legal reforms could not remedy the even more fundamental problem that occupied press critics in these years. That was the problem of the declining influence of the press in its editorial role as a leader and educator of public opinion. The elitist critics yearned for the old opinion-leading days when newspapers and cultural leaders cooperated in preserving the status quo and stifling the unruly masses. The *Journalist* contended that the loss of influence on the editorial page was the result of a better educated public doing its own thinking.[27] The influence of the modern press came through the news columns, it pointed out. The modern political reporter, police reporter, sports reporter, and others exercised a power "none the less potent because it was unobtrusive," said the journal. The reporter shapes the story by the manner in which he tells the news, and this "unconsciously molds in a certain degree the minds of his readers." Reporters were recognized by the circles they reported as wielding power behind the "editorial throne."

The old days of the personal, powerful editor was gone, a casualty of the Civil War, according to Virginia journalist R. Gray Williams in *Editor and Publisher*. But the war had also vitalized modern, impersonal journalism and would give us "better and more satisfactory newspapers than we have ever had before, as soon as the people resent extreme methods of make-up and disreputable presentation of content." The new journalism had gone too far and was already "slowly tempering some of its methods," he said. It would become responsive to decency and respectability if the public demanded it. The growth of press associations, which could provide an ample news service to newspapers of any size across the country, and the growth of specialized reporting made the new newspaper an aggregation of many specialists, no longer bound by the personal ideals of one all-powerful editor and publisher.[28]

These views were echoed by General Charles H. Taylor as he celebrated thirty years' leadership of the *Boston Globe*. His first change had been to "alter the spirit of a party newspaper." Taylor believed that "the news columns . . . should be entirely independent and give impartially the news of all parties." He was not out to reform the world, he said, but he intended to make an accurate and truthful newspaper that did good in the community.[29]

By the end of the decade, a long-time journalist was charging in the

*Atlantic Monthly* that the recent New York city elections had shown that the public could and did ignore the press and would elect a mayor of their choice. It was not really astonishing in such a skeptical age, added Francis Leupp, that people had such a low valuation of the press and completely ignored its advice. What worried him was that this posed a serious problem for democracy if the "citizen of fair intelligence and education" had lost so much faith in the newspaper as an organ of opinion and was just sneering at it as "mere newspaper talk."[30]

## A COMMERCIAL INFLUENCE

Many critics in this era thought the commercial influence in modern newspapers caused its declining status. The modern formula of pricing newspapers less than they cost to produce put advertisers in the power seat and made editors dependent on the advertising to pay well over half their costs.

"Yellow journals are most in awe of the mob, while the so-called respectables fear the advertising interests," claimed Hamilton Holt, managing editor of the *Independent*. Holt leveled his charges in a series of lectures at the University of California, which were published in book form in 1909 and widely discussed in the contemporary journals.[31]

Democracy is ruled by public opinion, and editors had become the "moulders of public opinion" by common consent, Holt said. But the editors were not as free as people believed to say what they thought, because journalism had grown into a business in recent years, he charged. The printing industry had increased thirtyfold since 1850, while other industries had increased fifteenfold. There were 21,394 dailies, weeklies, and monthlies with an average 47 percent income coming from advertising. There were enough daily newspapers to supply one paper to every four people, enough weeklies to supply one for every two people and enough monthlies to supply one to every person for nine months of the year, he pointed out.[32]

Advertising grew rapidly after the Civil War, and enabled the "press to outdistance its old rivals, the pulpit and platform, and thus become the chief ally of public opinion," said Holt. "It has economized business by bringing the producer and consumer into more direct contact . . . abolished the middle man in many cases."[33] He saw advertising as "the greatest menace to the disinterested practice of a profession upon which the diffusion of intelligence largely depends." And he warned: "If journalism is no longer a profession but a commercial enterprise," it was "due to the growth of advertising and nothing else."[34]

Journalism had been on the verge of developing a system of professional ethics, Holt thought. But the great editors had been replaced by impersonal and invisible owners and editors who were in turn subject to pressure from press agents seeking free publicity masquerading as news and by advertisers who wanted to "twist editorials" to their own ends.[35]

## THE ENDOWED PRESS

The yellow press had brought about a "general deterioration of reporting," Holt said. It served up sensations and fakes, and hurt reputations, but was not going away. So he believed that the sophisticated reader must turn to the *Atlantic Monthly* or the *Nation*. Thoughtful, moral leadership of opinion had shifted to the weekly and monthly journals, he pointed out, which filled the public opinion vacuum left by the weakened dailies.[36]

Although Holt himself was a leading editor of a respected journal of opinion, he was not cheered by the loss of editorial leadership in the press. To him, newspapers played a leading role in the formulation of public opinion and were better able to discuss and influence local community problems than the national journals. Holt hoped that yellow journalism would lose its influence, and he thought people were already awakening to the need to overthrow the bad influences of commercialism that infected the daily press. He offered four remedies, including their flaws:

1. Newspapers could attain such large circulations that they could ignore advertisers, but still would have to "truckle" to popularity.
2. Newspapers could be endowed in the manner of theaters and universities, so that they could say what "ought to be said irrespective of anybody and everybody and can serve as examples to the not so fortunate," but the industry is too big for it all to be endowed.
3. Newspapers could be combined into a trust, a publishers' trade union, that would work to investigate fraudulent advertising, but this was not democratic.
4. An old remedy—"personal integrity and character if sincerely applied —would solve most of the ills of society. Integrity in the newspaper profession as in life was the only thing that really counts."[37]

An article in the *Atlantic Monthly* by Richard A. Haste carried a similar warning. New journalism had weakened the Fourth Estate and caused people to have little confidence in newspapers. Magazine muckraking had helped open the public's eyes to corruption in business and government, said Haste, but he feared magazines had grown weary of the reform fight and had already started to tone down their reporting:

Whenever a newspaper, posing as a member of the Fourth Estate, is run purely as a business proposition or as a special advocate, and in the chase after dollars or in its efforts to accomplish other ends, suppresses or garbles the news and devotes its editorial influence to selfish ends alone, it becomes a public menace, worse than a venal public servant—worse than a pirate on the high seas.[38]

The foremost proponent of the endowed newspaper was sociologist Edward Alsworth Ross at the University of Wisconsin. His *Atlantic Monthly* article in 1910 summed up his views. "The modern newspaper did not give the news, the budding spirit of professionalism and ethics has wilted and left nine out of ten newspapermen of 15 years' experience cynics," Ross said. Newspapers had been subordinated to the commercial role of "paying property" needing to attract the crowd, protect the owner's "sacred cows," and suppress important news. He thought muckraking had been helpful in waking up the public, but it was declining.[39] He called for endowment of newspapers with private funds from public-spirited men of wealth who would place control of the paper in the hands of a high-minded foundation that would govern to benefit the community. The endowed newspaper would print the interesting news of the day—society, accidents, sports, politics, business and crime—but would "not dramatize crime or gossip of private affairs . . . not fake, 'doctor' or sensationalize the news. . . ." It would be a *corrective newspaper* and would keep the big papers from smothering or "cooking" the news. As Ross envisioned it, such a newspaper, even if it only printed a fraction of the news, would exert a great deal of influence.[40]

## THE DANGER OF IMPERSONAL JOURNALISM

Building on the current debate and the mounting evidence, James Edward Rogers explored these issues in a modern book-length study of the urban newspaper in 1909. He warned that the impersonality of modern journalism brought with it a decadence of power and a decline of journalism's educative and moral force in the community. He expected it to "degenerate into a mere bargain-counter sale of ad space and irresponsible narratives of daily events." Rogers warned that the newspapers were still "allied to political party interests," still colored the news and twisted the facts in the news columns to sway readers. They flouted the law and "thought they were immune."[41]

Rogers reminded readers that the press wielded the "power to suggest to a whole community what it should think and do." This was power "for good or evil," he explained, because Americans were such inveterate newspaper readers and got most of their education there.[42] For millions of immigrants who did not go to the American common school, the newspaper became the school. Since people's reading habits gave rise to habits of thought and action, the daily reading of the newspaper can influence and improve the daily life and the morality of readers or build distrust and cynicism, Rogers believed. "If you can influence habits of thought and habits of action, you have power," so the continued reading of ugly, vulgar, low material would form bad habits.[43]

Since the newspaper, which once had been reading for the privileged few, was now read by everybody, it had become "crucially important." The messages carried in the press about the government, the law, politicians, and the courts would impact on the views of the public. Europe has "the censor," Rogers said, but America has a free press that "can do or say anything" and has "bred a loose conception of the responsibility of the press that seems to exempt newspapermen from the laws that bind other individuals."[44]

Rogers believed newspapers mirrored public opinion more than shaped it. When the newspaper plays to the passions of the crowds, it is in turn influenced by them. Rogers called for leadership from the press and a rise in standards of the newspapers, which would raise public morality and vice versa. "Degrading each lowers the other."[45]

Rogers blamed yellow journalism squarely on the American love of change, curiosity, independence, and competition—a youthful nation rushing to become a modern urban society. "The American paper is sensational because the American is sensational," Rogers declared, but he expected both newspapers and public would and could change.[46]

## WANTED—HONEST JOURNALISM

Critics frequently asked if honest journalism was possible, and replied with their own solutions to the problem. President Arthur Twining Hadley of Yale University, for example, said editors will make newspapers that people want, and a few would make them better in an attempt "to educate people up to a higher level." Yellow editors were only responsible to a degree for the low quality of journalism, whereas "to a larger degree the responsibility lies with the public that will buy and read their news." During the Spanish War newspapers wrote of battles that never occurred, only to sell more newspapers, he recalled. And people kept buying the extras, not even caring enough to ask for evidence. "If a man fools me once, shame on him; if he fools me twice, shame on me," said Hadley. The editor "was responsible for the first offence; the public is responsible for encouraging him to repeat it."[47]

It was the duty of every member of society to take an intelligent interest in the news, to examine the facts and the evidence and live up to the responsibility of citizenship. Hadley pointed out:

> If the public cares more for sensations than it does for facts, more for excitement than it does for evidence, it is obvious that its opinion will be based on wrong data and often on dangerous ones, and that its conclusions will be unwise and irresponsible, and as long as public opinion is unwise or irresponsible, the government of the country will be bad.[48]

## THE IDEAL NEWSPAPER

Only a few critical voices offered a viable alternative for the problem, one that would have to come from inside the newspaper institution itself. In 1901, Alfred Harmsworth, editor of the London *Daily Mail*, a popular newspaper modeled on American new journalism, told American editors: "The best brains are not going into American journalism." He urged editors to find ways to attract them, because he believed there was "great potential for positive influence and leadership in the national tendency toward business concentration" in America. He did not advocate a newspaper trust, because news writing, editing, and salaries would improve if newspapers were more financially independent.[49]

National newspapers could be published simultaneously in many locations in England and France, "minimize political differences and bring about unity of thought and action," Harmsworth said. Such newspapers would "be free to advocate the best interests of the country and could do so with an influence far wider in scope than has hitherto been possible." They would not have to have a party slant, and they would require "thoroughly capable journalists" who were in touch with the public.[50] The simultaneous newspaper existed in a simple form in the weeklies with their use of patent insides, and widespread adoption of wire and syndicated copy.[51] But what Harmsworth envisioned was more on the order of contemporary satellite printing operations.

Harmsworth foresaw the domination by great, monopoly newspapers in the new century, and acknowledged that they could abuse their power, but he thought public opinion would not tolerate it.[52] "People are not obligated to buy newspapers, like food, so the press had to live on public approval." Harmsworth believed in the "sound sense and practical power of the people." Public sentiment has often "forced the hand of the politician and monopolist," he pointed out, and would "equally stay the hand of a corrupt and mischievous press."[53]

Freedom of press does not mean "a license to say what we please, or do whatever we like, but a freedom from outside interference or censorship," he said. Harmsworth was not advocating monopolies, he said, but he saw that they were practicable and thought America's twentieth century newspapers would have greater power, responsibility, and freedom than party journals of the past. He believed the American press was "in step with the progressive age" in casting off the party domination and restraining traditions, and had its face set "steadfastly toward the light."[54]

Whether a financially stable and independent press or an endowed press was to be the ideal replacement for the yellow press, it was clear that the critical view was crystallizing around a set of values that people thought ought to be incorporated in modern American journalism. The ideal journalism would be ethical, fair, factual, authoritative, responsible, and respectable, and the independent press would make journalism a force for good in the society.

After surveying 3,000 newspaper readers, Professor W. D. Scott of Northwestern University announced that readers wanted "facts, local news, politics, sports, and finance—in that order." The ideal paper "would have to do only with facts." News would be "well written, but the interest would be mainly in the news itself and not in the reporter's or publisher's views concerning it."[55]

A contemporary New York editor wrote that the model newspaper would possess "a soul of its own," something more than the aggregate of all the work of all the men who work on its staff. The paper's tradition will modify the product of any man who writes for it, save only one whose personality is so dominant as to give the paper something of his own character, like Greeley with the *Tribune* or Bowles with the *Springfield Republican*.[56]

What this editor wanted was a return of the "note of authority." The contemporary newspaper seemed unable to translate European ideas into American terms or to present well-argued editorials or thorough information, he complained. What was needed was a newspaper with honesty of purpose, high ideals, seriousness, and ethical standards of performance. "News in the yellow journals becomes one continuous shriek," appealing to class hatreds and group conflict in society, but the ideal newspaper would be "popular and of real technical merit."[57]

"The public wants an independent newspaper . . . critical rather than constructive," he said. The public was changing; more and more attended college and had learned to think for themselves. Party regularity was declining because of these independent thinking voters, he pointed out. To serve this new public, the newspaper would have to be independent and examine many points of view on issues, serving as a healthy critic of all branches and functions of government. The public wants "a newspaper which treats its reader not as a child or a sage, neither as a hero nor as a fool, but as a person of natural good instincts and average intelligence, amenable to reason, and one to be taught tactfully to stand upon his own feet, rather than to take his principles ready-made from his teacher. What an ideal!" Such a newspaper would serve the shopgirl and the Senator equally, he declared.[58]

## A CIVILIZING AGENT

"The press is the highest agent in modern civilization," said Dr. Albert Shaw, because it "sweeps the whole world and every day keeps alive in us a sense of the common interest in the affairs of our country. It lifts us out of the local rut and gives us the broader spirit and intelligence of common citizens of a great country." He saw the press as a key agent of change in getting society to live up to progressive ideals.[59]

A Chicago journalist recommended that "trust the public" should become the motto for the newspaper, replacing "give the public what it wants." The public should be credited with sanity and fairness, and seen as rational and reputable men and women. This journalist believed that if editors saw the audience this way they would edit their papers very differently.[60]

Democracy "becomes an exquisite absurdity if it be taken to mean that in these matters there is to be no guidance, no attempt to uplift the general taste, no function higher than that of supplying an untrained demand," *Dial* said in response. The public had been acquiescent too long in allowing yellow journalism to rationalize its existence on the specious plea of giving the public what it wants. "Taste grows by what it feeds on. When that is garbage . . . it loses its appetite for better food." *Dial* urged the public to press for newspaper reform.[61]

One of the most respected editors of the day, Henry Watterson of the *Louisville Courier-Journal*, summed up the problem in a talk comparing English and American newspapers. Daily journalism's function was telling "the history of yesterday," he said. But most newspaper editors also want to teach, influence, and mold public opinion, but too often private interest "colors its narrative and shapes its oracles," said Watterson. He called for a paper with a "proper sense of responsibility which was the very soul of honest journalism."[62] The pressure for responsibility would continue to mount, he predicted, as more people inside and outside journalism engaged in the debate. The ideal newspaper, in his opinion, would have a duty to truth and decency, upright purpose, and "a proper sense of professional respect."[63]

Responsibility would come as an internal reform in response to public pressure, Professor Wilcox had predicted at the turn of the century. The newspaper was a public institution, he said, "the principal organ of society for distributing . . . (its) working information." He saw complete independence and subordination of the editorial page to the news column "coming to be widely recognized as the ideal of journalism." "The newspaper should render easily accessible to the individual all widely interesting news as promptly as is consistent with accurate reporting, and should furthermore give concise reviews of public events just passed."[64]

An endowment scheme was not practical, Wilcox argued, since the public had already "endowed" the press through advertisements. The solution was to make news and advertising pay for itself, he said. Newspapers might be made legally responsible to publish reliable news, which would develop a sense of "social responsibility for the use of brains and money" and raise the level of society's involvement and education.[65]

Wilcox offered no concrete solution. It was one thing to say the press should be responsible to society and to idealize its potential, but quite another to figure out how this might be enforced beyond moral public pressure. Accountability would become a key concept in modern press criticism, posing a conundrum for democratic society with its guarantee of free speech. Accountability raises the issue of control, and it would become the essential tension between the American press and society.

## NOTES

1. Wiebe, *Search*.
2. Robert E. Park, "The Yellow Press," *Sociology and Social Research* 12 (1924): 3, 9; and "The Natural History of the Newspaper," in *The City* by Robert E. Park and Ernest W. Burgess (Chicago: University of Chicago Press, 1925/1968), 95.
3. Park, "Yellow," 11.
4. Park, "Natural," 97–98.
5. Park, "Natural," 96.
6. Carroll D. Clark, "Yellow Journalism as a Mode of Urban Behavior," *The Southwestern Social Science Quarterly* 14 (1933): 241, 245. See also: W. I. Thomas, "The Psychology of Yellow Journalism," *American Magazine* 65 (March 1908), 492.
7. Arthur Brisbane, "The American Newspaper: Yellow Journalism," part 4, *Bookman* 24 (June 1909): 403.
8. Editorial, *Journalist* (9 July 1904): 190. See also: Michael Schudson, *Discovering the News: A Social History of American Newspapers* (New York: Basic Books, 1978), 9.
9. Lydia Kingsmill Commander, "The Significance of Yellow Journalism," *Arena* 34 (August 1905): 151.
10. Commander, "Significance," 155.
11. Letter to editor, "Newspaper Responsibility for Lawlessness," *Nation* 77 (20 August 1903): 151.
12. Frederick Peterson, M. D., "The Newspaper Peril, a Diagnosis of a Malady of the Modern Mind," *Editor and Publisher* (1 September 1906): 7 (abridged).
13. William Salisbury, *The Career of a Journalist* (New York: B. W. Dodge, 1908), 204.
14. A Newspaper Reader, "Lessons in Crime Fifty Cents Per Month," *Outlook* 84 (2 February 1907): 276.
15. Editorial, "Newspapers' Sensations and Suggestions," *Independent* 62 (21 February 1907): 450–51.
16. "Suggestions," *Independent*, 451.
17. Thomas, "Yellow," 491.
18. Thomas, "Yellow," 491.
19. Thomas, "Yellow," 493.
20. Thomas, "Yellow," 495.
21. Thomas, "Yellow," 496.
22. Thomas, "Yellow," 496.
23. Frances Fenton, "The Influence of Newspaper Presentation Upon the Growth of Crime and Other Anti-Social Activity," *The Journal of Sociology* 16 (January 1911): part 2, 559.
24. Fenton, "Influence," part 2, 560.
25. Fenton, "Influence," part 2, 564.
26. Fenton, "Influence," part 2, 564.
27. Editorial, *Journalist* (10 October 1903): 388.
28. R. Gray Williams, *Editor and Publisher* (20 December 1902): 13.
29. "General Taylor's Review," *Editor and Publisher* (21 November 1903): 4.

30. Francis Leupp, "The Waning Power of the Press," *Atlantic Monthly* 105 (February 1910): 155.
31. Hamilton Holt, *Commercialism and Journalism* (Boston & New York: Houghton Mifflin, 1909), 38.
32. Holt, "Commercialism," 2, 5.
33. Holt, "Commercialism," 21–22.
34. Holt, "Commercialism," 34.
35. Holt, "Commercialism," 58.
36. Holt, "Commercialism," 93–94.
37. Holt, "Commercialism," 99–105.
38. Richard A. Haste, "The Evolution of the Fourth Estate," *Arena* 41 (March 1909): 352.
39. Edward Alsworth Ross, "The Suppression of Important News," *Atlantic Monthly* 105 (March 1910): 303–05.
40. Ross, "Suppression," 311.
41. James Edward Rogers, *The American Newspaper* (Chicago: University of Chicago Press, 1909), 94.
42. Rogers, "American," 101.
43. Rogers, "American," 111–12.
44. Rogers, "American," 125.
45. Rogers, "American," 164.
46. Rogers, "American," 185.
47. Arthur Twining Hadley, "Is Honest Journalism Possible?" *Current Literature* (June 1909): 47.
48. Hadley, "Honest," 47.
49. Alfred Harmsworth, "The Simultaneous Newspapers of the 20th Century," *North American Review* 172 (January 1901): 76.
50. Harmsworth, "Simultaneous," 88.
51. Harmsworth, "Simultaneous," 84.
52. Harmsworth, "Simultaneous," 90.
53. Harmsworth, "Simultaneous," 89.
54. Harmsworth, "Simultaneous," 90.
55. Review of W. D. Scott's *Psychology of Advertising, Editor and Publisher* (26 September 1908): 1.
56. A New York editor, "Is an Honest Newspaper Possible?" *Atlantic Monthly* 102 (October 1908): 442.
57. Editor, "Honest," 443–44.
58. Editor, "Honest," 446–47.
59. "Press as Civilizer," *Editor and Publisher* (19 June 1909): 4.
60. An Independent Journalist, "Is an Honest and Sane Newspaper Press Possible?" *American Journal of Sociology* 1t (November 1909): 334.
61. Editorial, "What the Public Wants," *Dial* 47 (16 December 1909): 500.
62. Henry Watterson, "English and American Journalism," *Munsey's* 34 (January 1906): 423.
63. Watterson, "English," 424.
64. Wilcox, "American," 86–88.
65. Wilcox, "American," 91.

# CHAPTER 4

# On the Road to Professionalism: 1900–1911

Efforts to reform journalism in the pre–World War I era were strengthened by the formation of the first journalism departments and schools and by the start of professional organizations to promote common ideals and values. Many of the founders of these institutions saw journalism reaching the status of law and medicine. This led to an emphasis on ethical codes of conduct, standardization of academic requirements, and licensing for professionally educated journalists. These critical voices from inside the profession turned the debate toward remedies and inculcated standards of performance through classroom lectures, textbooks, and sponsorship of regional and national professional meetings that linked universities and professional journalists. The new academic field produced research on journalistic history, ethics, practices, and social effects. These early educators believed they could improve journalism by infusing the new generation with high standards and by service to the working professionals through workshops and other programs.

Professionalism was a less threatening and more credible means of press accountability for journalistic insiders than either the endowed press or legal restraints. Professionalism encouraged high ideals and personal accountability to the voluntary codes, which it was anticipated would elevate the national standard of performance. Further, it offered a way for the reporter and the editor to regain some of the lost prestige suffered during the era of yellow journalism. What the old personal, partisan owner-editors had lost in their presumed power to shape public opinion would be regained by modern professionals whose fair and responsible work would be done on behalf of the enlightenment of the general society.

The early schools of journalism were grounded in this progressive philosophy, and their curricula embraced the liberal arts plus specialized, technical, and applied journalistic skills. The journalist would be a caring, discerning, watchful but detached observer, more a modern social scientist than partisan essayist or creative writer. Modeled on the other professional schools, these journalism schools demanded seriousness of purpose and ethical behavior, quality writing and solid scholarship. They were imbued with the public-service philosophy that saw journalism as a central pillar in the democracy and the role of journalist/editor as one of a high public trust. Accuracy, honesty, fairness, and decency were fundamental values.

The schools worked to rally the professionals of their states and regions to raise the standing of the whole field. But the low pay and low esteem that clung to reporting remained a constant problem and mocked the self-sacrifice and dedication being asked of the novices. Personal satisfaction from the reporting and writing experience would draw many, but the split between the proponents of reporting as a craft to be learned on the job and journalism as a serious study surfaced in the early debates over education and remained for decades a drain on the professional movement for journalism.

One of the earliest statements about modern journalistic professionalism appeared in 1903 in the *New York World*'s announcement of Joseph Pulitzer's intended gift of a two million dollar endowment to Columbia University for a Department of Journalism. President Nicholas Butler quickly accepted. Said the *World*:

> In every other pursuit, where men are under an equal moral responsibility to the public for the proper discharge of their duties, they are prepared for those duties by years of careful and conscientious study; but the newspaper men, who are in many directions the informers and teachers of the people, the exponents and to a degree the makers of that public opinion which rules communities and governs States and the nation, have hitherto received no special preparation for their delicate and important duties.[1]

A university was the proper place for journalism to take its place among the learned professions, Pulitzer believed. If they were established on the same ratio of faculty to practitioners as the law schools, journalism would need 26 colleges and 291 faculty members to serve a field that currently had 30,098 practitioners, according to the *World*.[2]

## TWO APPROACHES

When the idea of journalism education began to be discussed seriously, Harvard University President Charles W. Eliot was asked for his views. His proposed course of study for journalism was: literature, history, government, political science, geography, newspaper ethics, press history, and law, plus newspaper administration and production. He emphasized the liberal arts, saying that the teachers of journalism would have the task of developing the students as writers and interpreters of those varied subjects for the general audience. He also proposed that a student newspaper was the way to develop practical experience while in college.[3]

President Butler told Columbia University's Board of Trustees that a "new academic field is entered upon" with the establishment of journalism at the university. He acknowledged its experimental status, but felt it had support of a large and influential portion of the press. Natural aptitude and experience were necessary, Butler said, but the university could provide "the study of principles and practices, the acquirement of the subsidiary information which must be drawn upon, and the practice under criticism which gives the beginner the benefit of the experience of others.... It can and will train students to become good newspapermen, if they have the root of the matter in them."[4]

Reaction to Butler's announcement was swift. Most opponents emphasized the need for practical experience for journalists. Horace White, an old colleague of Godkin's, said practical experience had served him well since 1854, and the classical education was still his ideal. "Harvard and Yale, without a School of Journalism, might conceivably be better equipped to train men for editorial work than Columbia with one," he asserted. No techniques in the profession needed to be taught in college, in his opinion, and the necessary gentlemanliness and character began in the family. What needed to change was internal to the newspapers, he believed. Editors and publishers should demand men of the highest merit and reward them for dignified work.[5]

Lincoln Steffens, a noted muckraking journalist, remarked that he was not sure anyone really knew what journalism was, so the first task would be to assemble the experience and knowledge of the field. The teachers would have to create reporters with broad knowledge of life and people, with human sympathy, ethics, and imagination who could write about complex and difficult subjects for anyone to understand.[6]

Both trade publications, *Editor and Publisher* and the *Journalist*, supported the Columbia plan, and praised Pulitzer for not giving up his plan twelve years earlier in the face of criticism.[7] Critics called the scheme "visionary" and "unnecessary." Pulitzer responded with a long article in the *North American Review*, in which he predicted that before the century closed the schools of journalism would be generally accepted in higher education just like schools of law and medicine.[8]

## THE PULITZER PLAN

"They object, the critics and cavillers, that a 'newspaper man' must depend solely upon natural aptitude, or, in the common phrase, that he must be 'born, not made,'" Pulitzer said. He was unable to name a born editor. "The only position that occurs to me which a man in our Republic can successfully fill by the simple fact of birth is that of an idiot." Pulitzer suggested that the "born editor" really was a man with unusual ability and aptitude for his chosen profession and one who had especially applied himself to his work with whole heart and mind.[9] He agreed that the "news instinct must be born," but it had to be tempered with "sound judgment bred by considerable experience and training," or it would just provide more work for the lawyers. One of the chief difficulties for journalism was to keep "news instinct from running rampant over the restraints of accuracy and conscience."[10]

The educational program that he proposed excluded the business side of journalism. In this he disagreed with President Eliot of Harvard, he said, because a College of Journalism is to train journalists not business managers and publishers. "A journalist is the lookout on the bridge of the ship of state. . . . He is there to watch over the safety and welfare of the people who trust him."[11] The business office, Pulitzer believed, must remain separate from the editorial rooms where it is a "degradation and a danger. Once let the public come to regard the press as exclusively a commercial business and there is an end of its moral power."[12]

Pulitzer proposed courses in style, law, ethics, literature, truth and accuracy, history, sociology, economics arbitration, statistics, modern language, physical sciences, principles of journalism, and news. High ethical ideals were to pervade all the courses. He saw the press as a great moral force "upholding the standard of civic righteousness."[13] Some critics had charged that his college would "establish class distinctions in journalism," and Pulitzer hoped that it would—"between the fit and the unfit"—not on money but on morals, education, and character.[14] "A cynical, mercenary, demagogic press will produce in time a people as base as itself," warned Pulitzer. "The power to mold the future of the Republic will be in the hands of the journalists of future generations."[15]

Pulitzer's proposal generated so much controversy especially over his role on the advisory committee, that the plan was shelved until his death, even though the groundbreaking ceremony had been held in 1904 and the architects hired. The school was officially founded in 1912. Meantime, the University of Missouri established the first College of Journalism in 1908.[16] In 1910 there were at least a dozen colleges or universities offering journalism courses with over 400 students enrolled in all, and by 1912 there were three professional schools, Columbia, Marquette, and Missouri. According to Professor Frank W. Scott in a 1910 survey, "it was inevitable that professional journalism education would take its place in the college curriculum along with the contemporary subjects of business administration, public affairs, political science and sociology."[17]

The propriety of professional study in liberal arts colleges would remain a matter for debate for decades, and the two competing approaches also remained in journalism education. Eliot's plan emphasized practical education and laboratory newspapers and was immediately popular and lasted many years. As Professor Albert A. Sutton of Northwestern University explained in his study of journalism education in the United States, the Harvard president was the leading educator of his day and his view was accepted by other educators. Early journalism educators also liked the laboratory emphasis for its close approximation of the practical work of newspapermen, who in turn might be more likely to support the schools.[18]

Journalism can be taught, insisted George Harvey, editor of *Harper's Weekly*, when he gave the prestigious Bromley lectures at Yale University in 1908.[19] The journalist must have "conscience, character, conviction: his aim must be to uplift humanity, not to profit by its degradation." He must be independent of politics and of provincialism, his responsibility is "to the whole people." Harvey described the master journalist as "the guardian of all, the vigilant watchman on the tower ever ready to sound the alarm of danger, from whatever source, to the liberties and the laws of this great union of free individuals."[20] The university life "produces nobleness of mind," said Harvey, and so it is an ideal place for the development of character—"the first and indispensable requisite of true journalism."[21]

Harvey emphasized the importance of a liberal education because the journalist was one person in an "age of specialism" who was charged with "the need of breadth of knowledge to conduct the daily teaching of our millions."[22] The university would also improve the journalist's "clarity in thought and lucidity of expression" by exercising the practice of criticism and writing.

## THE LAB NEWSPAPER

To supplement his lectures, Harvey produced his own version of the "ideal newspaper" for the future. It was a four-page sheet, with condensed service listings for entertainment and cultural activities in the city, financial news, professional sports, art news, and an editorial page, along with brief, key national daily news items on the front page.[23]

His ideal caused some derisive criticism, but his proposal that student journalists should be encouraged to produce such newspapers in university laboratories the way scientists and engineers applied their learning to the practical demands of the laboratory raised much more controversy. Harvey wanted an endowment that would set up a newspaper laboratory with an outstanding editor at its head, assisted by professional working journalists who would have the time in the lab to train the young.[24] Harvey argued that a novice got little training in the newsroom. It was the university's duty, he challenged Yale, to improve both journalism and journalists.[25]

The *New York Times* gave grudging approval to the idea of an endowed laboratory newspaper.[26] Others called for sticking to the liberal arts. But the student laboratory was made an important feature at Missouri and many of the land grant colleges that introduced journalism education. Missouri's first dean, Walter Williams, was a former newspaper editor and he was in the Eliot/Harvey tradition, creating a program that would produce "well-equipped men for leadership in journalism with high ideals and special training."[27]

The first courses at Missouri included: history and principles of journalism, newspaper making, newspaper administration, magazine and class journalism, newspaper publishing, newspaper jurisprudence, news gathering, correspondence, and office equipment.[28] The first class attracted ninety-seven students, including thirteen women. Six, including one of the women, formed the first graduating class of 1910.[29]

By 1918 the growing importance of the social sciences strengthened the second approach, the one identified with Joseph Pulitzer. Gradually an emphasis on a broad study of journalism and its relationship to society was advocated, and social science began to dominate many journalism programs and their research. By the 1930s the journalism schools offered their own social science–based courses linking journalism and public opinion, psychology, sociology, political science, and economics. Along with a shifting emphasis from technical competence to grounding students in the social sciences came a system of national classification of schools and accreditation.[30]

Journalism courses also developed within liberal arts colleges and grew into programs or departments. At the University of Michigan, for example, an early course in "Rapid Writing" offered in 1890–91 led to a journalism program in 1916 and a department in 1929. Michigan's approach, explained by Professor John L. Brumm, first department chairman, was to emphasize the broad, liberal education of the journalist who would be responsible for reporting, editing, and commenting on the news. Practical professional courses were designed to adapt to that goal. Brumm focused on developing a "critical appreciation of modern civilization and the institutions through which this civilization expresses itself." He said that "since the highest responsibility of the journalist is to deal competently with the news, he must understand the structure of society, the process by which public opinion is molded and the nature and tests of the sources of the news." He called for mastery of a scientific technique of recording objectively, reporting impartially and authoritatively, and developing the ability to penetrate and discern significance. Internships and extracurricular work on school publications provided most of the laboratory experience beyond the one course in producing the experimental *Michigan Journalist*.[31]

## THE IMPORTANCE OF ETHICS

The growing professionalism in journalism encouraged journalism teachers to form their own group. In 1910 they began meeting informally. They formed the American Conference of Teachers of Journalism in 1912 in order to discuss academic interests and gather statistics. Professor Willard G. Bleyer of the University of Wisconsin was elected the first president by the twenty-five members in attendance. In 1916, the group advocated a study of teaching, public service, and research in journalism, standardization of their teaching programs and of journalistic writing, more stress on research, and a code of ethics. They reaffirmed efforts to place journalism on the plane of other professions, and location of several journalism units in key Land Grant colleges, which encouraged giving academic recognition to new professional disciplines, was an asset.[32]

The importance of journalistic ethics was underscored by Dean Walter Williams of the University of Missouri School of Journalism in a speech to the Wisconsin Press Association in 1910. He opposed fakes, falsehoods, scandal mongering, acting as private detective, and coloring of the news to give a false interpretation. Williams said editorial opinions should never be for sale. As an all-purpose motto, he said you should never write anything you would *not* be ashamed to own or like your mother or sister to read.[33]

By 1914 one of its graduates insisted the Pulitzer School of Journalism was "no longer an experiment." It had graduated thirteen men and two women in 1914, and the current second class was equally successful.[34] Journalism as a profession was making immeasurable progress in 1916, according to Chester S. Lord, the much-admired former *New York Sun* managing editor, who had trained a generation of editors. He recalled that fifty years earlier journalism reflected "the supreme importance of a few editors, but that importance has been transformed into the supreme import-ance of the newspaper." Lord pointed out that journalism did take intellectual effort, but differed from the other professions in that it involved study "in almost every realm of human knowledge." It was not considered a profession by some because it required no specific study. Anyone, it was thought, "ignorant or careless or immoral, may start a newspaper." But he believed that college journalism would "enlarge and strengthen and uplift the standard of the profession as well as revolutionize the business."[35]

## MUCKRAKING THE PRESS

The concern over the corruption and moral decay of newspapers was given greater public attention in 1911 in *Collier's* in a long series of articles on the newspaper by Will Irwin.[36] Irwin, formerly a *New York Sun* reporter and a *McClure's Magazine* editor, had joined *Collier's* as a special writer. Publisher Robert Collier asked him to do an investigation of the American newspaper.[37] Collier believed that as the magazine muckrakers revealed corruption in the American cities, it had become clear that the newspapers in those cities had done nothing to expose the wrongdoing. It was time for the press itself to become the subject of muckraking.

After a year of researching and interviewing reporters and editors around the country, Irwin learned that there was scandal, that some newspapers were indebted to advertisers and protected them, but that other newspapers were strong, successful, and courageous. His vivid and documented series made such a splash that Irwin in turn was scorned by some of his colleagues as one who had "fouled his own nest."[38] But Irwin's was much more than just another a muckraking exposé; he wrote American journalism's first social history. In it he announced that the power of the press had clearly shifted from the editorial to the news pages.[39] The publishers and editors he interviewed had alerted him to this development.

"Journalism was still finding itself," he wrote in his autobiography. "It had no formal code of ethics. The moral outlook of its practitioners varied from those of Oswald Garrison Villard's *New York Evening Post*, bowed down with responsibility for making this a better world, through Adolph Ochs's *New York Times*, which professed merely to be manufacturing a sound and honest commodity, to a Western newspaper which was admittedly the organ of a pair of showmen out for money and power...."[40]

The ability to select and display news gave editors great power in furnishing the raw material for public opinion, Irwin observed. The newspapers, which put views into the news columns and related news from a bias of opinion, could educate the public and could implant a number of ideas. Editors were able to develop interest in certain subjects by playing them heavily, Irwin said, offering several examples. "The influence peddlers," he said, had already realized this and were trying to bribe and influence public opinion.[41]

Irwin charted the progress of the American press from its partisan beginnings through the rise of the penny press to the importance of the reporter and the "scoop" mentality of the late nineteenth century. "During a half-century in which the press grew from a humble professional enterprise to a great business, turning out its millions in profits every year, there was nothing to restrain the baser members of the craft except public disgust as expressed by the withdrawal of public patronage, or the opposition and exposure of better contemporaries. This force surprised civilization; it was born without the law; its power kept it above the law."[42] The *New York Sun* under Charles Dana had introduced witty and bright writing, and the yellows brought monstrous growth, cheapened the product, raked in profits, and taught press and public how to use the newspaper to fight entrenched power, according to Irwin.[43]

Yellow journalism had influenced the rest of the press, Irwin said, improving the writing and attracting more college graduates to its ranks, creating more newspaper readers and making journalism into a big business. But yellow journalism was on the decline, Irwin thought, perhaps partly because of Hearst's attempt to use it to get into politics. Some of the decline, he thought, had to do with the nature of the readers, who were believed to "read out" of the yellow press regularly, so that it was estimated that the entire readership turned over every six years. Immigrants, women, and other new readers of the press moved on to other publications, Irwin said.[44]

His research suggested that publishers and editors set the moral character of the press. News is a "departure from the established order," and editors in selecting what goes into the paper were guided by what the public likes and what it will tolerate, he said. The business-minded editor paid attention to what the public wanted, and the professional-minded editor cared about what the public needed.[45] The publisher-owner sets the tone for the newspaper and infuses it with a point of view or morality, Irwin explained, but the reporter "wields the real power" within boundaries set by the publisher. Reporting was part craft and part art, and "gives the public its perception of events." Good reporters, according to Irwin, had qualities of mind and heart that permitted them to see, record, and observe.[46] But Irwin also warned that the colorless uniformity of press bureau and wire service reporting was eroding the artistry and personal style that had given life and vitality to American journalism. "The sense of romance, thrill of life, and power of expression" that makes journalists in the first place should not be lost or turned into mere mechanics.[47]

## A GROWING PROFESSIONALISM

Irwin detected a kind of professional spirit or code of ethics that had been evolving across the nation. Good reporters never published information learned at a friend's home or at the club, never published information without full permission of informants (except criminals), never sailed under false colors, and respected the privacy of others. The newspaper, Irwin said, should be a gentlemen and a watchdog for the public—"an electric light in a dark alley."[48]

His era, Irwin explained, was a time of transition for the country and for journalism. The better trained and educated writers had improved the press, so there was less dishonesty and corruption, but the financial structure still presented a problem. He decried the growing influence of advertisers and business interests in directing the newspapers, and was opposed to the publishers' close association with other business and social leaders. Although few newspapers were actually "edited" from the business office, Irwin said, some "sold out to special interests." He warned that several newspapers had died following such activities.[49]

"In the profession itself lies out greatest hope," Irwin concluded. He doubted that endowed newspapers would work. But journalists were beginning to see the need for improvement and the potential usefulness and status of their profession.[50] They would elevate the standards so that the press would live up to the "franchise it had from the American people, which made it the freest press in the world. The American people expected in return that the press would be the guardian of our liberties."[51]

The deans and heads of the first schools and departments of journalism played key roles in shaping the standards, ideals, and ethics of modern journalism for thousands of students who came flooding into the field as opportunities expanded along with the modernizing nation. Their early stress on journalism as a liberal education, bolstered by specific studies and professional training, and on adherence to ethics and responsibility, gave journalism a tradition of professionalism that would help counterbalance outsider efforts to impose accountability on the press. Professionalism has not received much credit for that. "Old school" practitioners prefer the roughneck image of the "newspaper game," while some scholars warn that professionalism without autonomy allows reporters and editors to disengage from personal moral responsibility for their work, leaving newspaper owners and unscrupulous promoters free to manipulate the institution for their own ends.

## NOTES

1. "The Pulitzer School," *Editor and Publisher* (22 August 1903): 1–2.
2. "Pulitzer," *Editor and Publisher* 1.
3. "Pulitzer," *Editor and Publisher* 1. Neither Harvard nor Yale offered journalism curricula, and their official academic resistance to the new field is still used in some circles to invalidate journalism and communication as a scholarly discipline. Harvard was not interested in Pulitzer's proposal for a college of journalism, and astonished many with its establishment of the Nieman journalism fellowship center in 1937.
4. "Reports on School," *Editor and Publisher* (10 October 1903): 1.
5. Horace White, "The School of Journalism," *Journalist* (16 January 1904): 220.
6. Lincoln Steffens, "The New School of Journalism," *Bookman* 18 (September 1903): 175.
7. Editorial, "The College of Journalism," *Editor and Publisher* (7 May 1904): 4. See also: "A Real School of Journalism," *Editor and Publisher* (22 August 1903): 274–75, and "That School of Journalism," *Journalist* (29 August 1903): 292.
8. Joseph Pulitzer, "The College of Journalism," *North American Review* 178 (May 1904): 642.
9. Pulitzer, "College," 642.
10. Pulitzer, "College," 644.
11. Pulitzer, "College," 656.
12. Pulitzer, "College," 659.
13. Pulitzer, "College," 679.
14. Pulitzer, "College," 649.
15. Pulitzer, "College," 680.
16. Edwin Emery and Joseph P. McKerns, eds., "AEJMC: 75 Years in the Making," *Journalism Monographs* 104 (November 1987): 2–3.

17. Frank W. Scott, "College Training for Journalism," *Independent* 69 (13 October 1910): 814.
18. Albert Alton Sutton, *Education for Journalism in the United States from its Beginning to 1940* (Evanston, Ill.: Northwestern University, 1945), 14.
19. The Isaac H. Bromley Chair at Yale was founded by his widow in 1901. Bromley was a journalist and the Bromley lectures were devoted to journalism, literature, and public affairs.
20. George Harvey, *Journalism, Politics and the University*, Bromley Lecture at Yale University, March 12, 16, 1908 (New Haven: Yale University Press, 1908), 1.
21. Harvey, "Journalism," 4.
22. Harvey, "Journalism," 3.
23. Harvey, "Journalism," 5–6.
24. Harvey, "Journalism," 7. Pulitzer and Camp had made similar suggestions for working laboratories.
25. Harvey, "Journalism," 8.
26. Harvey, "Journalism," March 16 lecture, 8–18.
27. The continued use of "men" and "newspaper man" indicates the status of women in journalism in this era. Although there were women reporters and even a few editors, they were still rare. See: Marion T. Marzolf, *Up from the Footnote: A History of Women Journalists* (New York: Hastings House, 1977).
28. "A New College of Journalism in the West," *Harper's Weekly* (27 June 1908): 22.
29. Maurine Beasley, "Women in Journalism Education: The Formative Period 1908–1930," (AEJMC Convention paper, Memphis State University, August 1985) 6.
30. Sutton, *Education*, 14–39. First efforts at accreditation were made between 1925 and 1939 by committees representing the professional associations and colleges and universities. Standards have continued to be a hot topic of debate ever since. See: Emery and McKerns, "75 Years," 22, 75.
31. John D. Stevens, "Journalism Instruction at the University of Michigan, 1929–1979," (Ann Arbor: Department of Journalism, 1979).
32. "Teachers' Conference," *Editor and Publisher* (7 December 1912): 1.
33. "Equipment for Journalism," *Editor and Publisher* (20 August 1910): 4.
34. B. O. McAnney, "Preparing Students for Strenuous Newspaper Life," *Editor and Publisher* (13 June 1914): 1082.
35. Chester S. Lord, "'Boss' Lord Praises Journalism Schools," *Editor and Publisher* (13 May 1916): 1563.
36. Will Irwin, *The American Newspaper* (Ames: Iowa State University Press, 1969): reprinted from *Collier's* (January–July 1911).
37. Robert V. Hudson, *The Writing Game: A Biography of Will Irwin* (Ames: Iowa State University Press, 1982), 68.
38. Will Irwin, *The Making of a Reporter* (New York: Putnam, 1942), 71–72.
39. Irwin, *Making*, 164–69.
40. Irwin, *Making*, 164–69.
41. Irwin, *American*, part 1, 18.
42. Irwin, *American*, part 2, 16.
43. Irwin, *American*, part 3–4.
44. Irwin, *American*, part 4, 20. Newspaper management in 1988 considered "circulation churn" (replacing lost subscribers) at metro daily newspapers a key

problem, with worst case example having to replace an entire subscriber base each year. See: "How Newspapers Can Win the Battle to Retain Subscribers," *Editor and Publisher* (3 September 1988): 52.

45. Irwin, *American*, part 6.
46. Irwin, *American*, part 7, 21.
47. Irwin, *American*, part 7, 35.
48. Irwin, *American*, part 8, 30.
49. Irwin, *American*, part 15, 15.
50. Irwin, *American*, part 14, 23.
51. Irwin, *Reporter*, 164–69.

# CHAPTER 5

# First Steps toward Responsibility: 1912–1919

The demand for the ideal newspaper raised the issue of responsibility. The press was free, but didn't that guarantee of freedom imply some measure of public accountability in return?[1] That was the question behind the debate over forms of external versus self-regulation of the press in the years before World War I. Some believed newspaper leaders incapable of setting and maintaining their own standards, so they pressed for alternatives like the endowed newspaper or tougher laws. A few states adopted privacy laws to stop prying journalists, and a few briefly tried licensing of journalists. The Federal government imposed a postal regulation requiring the filing of financial data about all top owners and stockholders in commercial newspapers and magazines. Codes of ethics, bureaus of accuracy, and correction boxes were in-house reforms.

A campaign to create endowed newspapers received national attention when Hamilton Holt, the managing editor of a religious journal called the *Independent*, revealed his plan to a national audience of scholars, editors, and journalists in 1912. Holt was supported by one of the nation's leading sociologists, Edward A. Ross.

The three-day meeting, held at the University of Wisconsin in Madison where Ross taught, addressed the question: "Are newspaper reporters free to tell the truth?"[2] Discussions underscored the growing public feeling that many newspapers had become a menace to the social order. Two decades earlier they might have blamed the yellow press for these problems, but in 1912 the problem appeared more widespread. Even the small-town papers complained that they were being hurt along with the big-city newspapers.

During the meeting Holt argued that an endowed newspaper was desirable and opportune because the ordinary commercial press neither adequately performed the important social functions of giving reliable and complete information at the time it was needed for public opinion, nor presented a complete discussion from different points of view. The commercial press had found that it did not "pay" to be thorough or impartial, Holt said, whereas an endowed paper could speak frankly and offer all opinions. Such a newspaper would be a positive force in the formation of public opinion among its readers, and would force other newspapers to "raise their standards of accuracy and fairness."[3]

Holt called for a national weekly newspaper controlled by a "board of trustees composed of the most eminent men of different political parties and social classes." They would supervise the endowment, select the managing editor (a professional journalist), and monitor the paper's performance. The journalists and contributors would be drawn from the entire United States and foreign countries. Advertising would be open to products, services, political views, and personal editorials published at an author's own expense. The paper would be nonpartisan, "or rather polypartisan," and the motto would be "comprehensiveness, impartiality and accuracy."[4] More than one version of a controversial event would be published. Criticism of the arts and literature and of consumer commodities would be presented, Holt promised.

Other previous attempts at subsidized or endowed journals, such as those published by political parties or religious organizations, Holt said, had presented only single points of view. The municipal organs of a few cities provided colorless but useful official information. These were not what Holt had in mind. He assured potential supporters that his paper would be attractive and competitive with the "highest standard of typography, literary style and pictorial illustration." He needed a $5 million endowment and called for donors.[5]

Andrew Carnegie agreed to support the national newspaper if others would. Nothing came of that.[6] Holt and Ross were still promoting the idea two years later at another national newspaper meeting, but it was doomed. Most critics realized it was totally impractical and would create the potential for constant bickering among the various partisans involved.[7] All assumed it would cost far more than Holt anticipated. However impractical the notion, its appeal and idealism illustrate the direction criticism was taking.

## UNDERSTANDING PUBLIC OPINION

Professor Ross's books, *Social Control* and *Social Psychology*, were influential in the development of modern sociology, especially in the school at the University of Chicago. Ross believed that enlightened public opinion would prevail over the mob. He endorsed the plan for an endowed newspaper because it would correct the distortion of the commercial press, which he complained "did not present the news."[8]

Accountability was a major concern at several state and national meetings of professional journalists and editors in the pre–World War I years. Professor Merle Thorpe, Dean of the College of Journalism at the University of Kansas, reported that in 1913 alone, 20 states had considered some form of regulation, and Congress had several bills before it, most dealing with advertising.[9] In 1912 Congress passed the Bourne Act prohibiting the mailing of false advertising and requiring the registration of all editors, publishers, business managers or owners of every newspaper, magazine, periodical or other publication, plus their stockholders, bondholders or large financial investors. All ads had to be labeled. Failure to comply could result in loss of mailing privileges.[10]

Thorpe said the contemporary criticism of the press dealt with four issues: (1) carelessness that amounted to criminal negligence in handling news; (2) suppression of important news to the advantage of certain interests; (3) conspiracy with advertisers to mislead honest buyers; and (4) pandering to antisocial instincts of readers through yellow journalism.[11] The first and last of these items attracted the greatest critical attention at the turn of the century, but in the second decade there was increasing discussion and concern over the domination of business and advertisers as muckraking journalists revealed press abuses.

## LICENSING OF JOURNALISTS

At a national journalism conference held during Kansas Newspaper Week at the University of Kansas in May 1914, all of these issues of press criticism were discussed by critics from inside and outside journalism.[12] It was here that the idea of licensing of journalists and binding journalists to codes of ethics were first raised to the level of national concern, although both matters had been discussed earlier in the professional publications.[13]

As *Editor and Publisher* had said a couple of years earlier when Pennsylvania was drafting a licensing plan: "There has been a growing conviction for some time that something should be done to keep out of the newspaper profession men who for various reasons are a disgrace to this, one of the most important businesses of the commercial world." The Pennsylvania State Editorial Association advocated the license plan in 1912 and intended to establish a state board to examine and pass on the qualification of would-be practitioners. *Editor and Publisher* agreed licensing would be a "good thing" for journalism and for the public.[14]

It was pointed out at the Kansas meeting that no one could practice medicine or law without meeting licensing standards, and newspapers had become so important as the "only instrument of publicity that goes to the whole community" that it demanded the highest abilities, sense of responsibility, idealism, and public duty from journalists and editors. The time had come to discuss licensing, said the chairman of the meeting.[15] Lieutenant Governor Barratt O'Hara of Illinois was asked to defend the notion.

O'Hara had been a journalist in Chicago before starting his own newspaper, and he had attended the University of Missouri when yellow journalism was on the rise. He had prepared a bill for the licensing of journalists in Illinois and gathered support from several newspapermen as he prepared the proposal. Licensing was a way to guard against insensitivity of the press and enhance its responsibility, he said. It would "lift the responsibility for willful misrepresentation, malicious scandal and other diseases of colored and impure news from the impersonal publishing corporation and place it personally with the reporting and editing parties."[16]

Licensing would remove the publisher's and stockholders' sacred cows and pet peeves and give the reporter the right to say: "I cannot manufacture colored and impure news for your columns without losing my license, and when I lose my license I cannot work for you any longer." This placed the reporter's and the public's interest first, explained O'Hara. He believed that the reporter's ethics and personal honesty "are of the highest order," but "he is a cog in a machine . . . labors anonymously . . . is miserably paid." Until he was better compensated and regarded, the "American newspaper cannot hope completely to harmonize with the American spirit and satisfactorily embrace an ever broadening opportunity for service."[17]

O'Hara said his bill had not been introduced in the last session of the state legislature because of a clogged calendar, but news of it leaked and provided a "storm of bitter editorial opposition, reaching from coast to coast." He was astonished at the reaction, because his consultations had led him to believe other editors supported the idea. He still intended to introduce the bill and thought it would pass.[18]

The Illinois proposal was for a State Board of Journalism that would provide licenses for journalists who were of legal age, had completed high school or the equivalent, had two years at a recognized college of journalism or the same length of time as an apprentice reporter at a newspaper office, could furnish proof of good moral character, and had passed an exam in writing conducted by the Board. A license could be revoked if the holder was convicted of a felony or found guilty in a trial by jury of his fellow practitioners for "willful misrepresentation, malicious writing of scandal, acceptance of money or other prize tendered as bribe for the deliberate and unjustified coloring of news items, or other conduct unprofessional, reprehensible and dishonest."[19]

Opinions from the audience and others solicited in advance were mixed. The main criticism was that licensing conflicted with the constitutional guarantee of a free press. Many assumed that the new schools of journalism and the press associations in the states would accomplish the necessary raising of standards, and that licensing would not be needed. Advocates, however, favored the model of law and medicine and thought licensing would standardize professional development and guard against a licentious press.[20]

The discussion over licensing of journalists trickled along during the next few years without dramatic results. There was not much enthusiasm for it, but Dean Talcott Williams of the Columbia School of Journalism in New York City in 1915 still advocated an "examination for journalists." This time *Editor and Publisher* commented that there would be "unanimous objection to any such interference by the state to regulate the newspaper as contrary to the spirit of independence that has hitherto characterized the American press."[21] The schools and courses of journalism were setting standards for their students, but access to the reporting profession should be kept open to individuals without a test or license, the trade journal believed.

Licensing continued to meet strong resistance. For example, the Connecticut state legislature proposed a licensing exam for journalists with six months of experience. This brought forth a biting *Chicago Herald* column that spoofed the questions on the proposed exam:

- When is the last analysis in hand?
- How does a scion differ from a rich man's son?
- What is the middle initial of Jack Frost?
- How long after a woman is arrested for shoplifting does she become a former actress?[22]

## ACCURACY BUREAUS

Suggestions for accuracy bureaus and speedy publication of corrections, along with the development of codes of ethics, met with greater favorable reaction than licensing at the Kansas meeting. After the talk by Isaac D. White, a former top *New York World* police reporter and then director of that newspaper's year-old Bureau of Accuracy and Fairness, the conference voted to set up a committee to pursue this approach and recommend it to others.[23] White warned the conference that newspapers had to stop jumping "behind the Bulwarks of our Civilization and hoisting the Star Spangled Banner" every time someone proposed a new law that might affect newspapers.[24] People were looking at newspapers as they used to look at policemen who were too free with their nightsticks. "Journalistic clubbers" have to be stopped, he said, "and fairness, truth and accuracy have to be the standards." Otherwise, warned White, Congress and the state legislatures would find ways to regulate the press.[25]

White also urged the public to use the existing libel laws to prosecute those newspapers that abused press freedom. He pointed out that the press was protected against a libel conviction if it could prove it told the truth and was not malicious or was providing a fair and true account. The current laws protected both the free press and the citizen, White pointed out, but the press had to live up to the law and the citizen had to fight back when necessary.[26]

Accuracy had improved and the number of libel cases had declined at the *World* in the first six months of the bureau's work: 190 cases investigated, 108 complaints sustained, 73 corrections or explanations published, 11 fakes uncovered, 3 libel suits. That was "a low-water mark in the Legal Department," he reported.[27]

The Bureau was the idea of Ralph Pulitzer, Joseph's son who was then president of the *New York World*. He had begun working on the plan at about the time he lectured to the Pulitzer School of Journalism at Columbia about his father's belief in accuracy. "Accuracy in newspaper writing was, with him (Joseph Pulitzer) a religion. He had a ravenous craving for information . . . specific facts were what he wanted, and from them he preferred to draw his own conclusions. This craving for exact facts naturally carried with it an insistance on accuracy and an utter detestation of inaccuracy. He hated an inaccurate statement as another man would loathe a lie. He was inexorable in running it down, ruthless in tearing it to pieces." Ralph Pulitzer told the students that he was proud to have grown up with this legacy, and he expected that the school would pass on that tradition to them.[28]

The students should be dedicated to truth. "Truth telling is the sole reason for the existence of a press at all," said Pulitzer. The students should elevate the profession, consider newspaper work a solemn trust, and stimulate its ideals "without which no calling can remain a profession."[29]

Pulitzer told those celebrating the *World*'s twenty-fifth anniversary to keep in mind the picture of his father, who "in the throes of sightlessness and suffering . . . listened with painful attention to catch and collect any slightest suspicion of misstatement in a fact, any slightest shade of overemphasis in an adjective, any possibility of conveying an impression that was not altogether accurate and scrupulously just."[30]

When the Bureau was introduced, the *World* sent announcements not only to its New York staff but to all its correspondents and to U.S. consulates, newspaper publishers, and editors nationwide. Reaction was positive, and the Bureau published excerpts from these letters in its first report. The Bureau announcement set forth its ethics standards and punishments: deliberate faking and chronic carelessness would result in dismissal; carelessness (including misspelling of names) or unfairness would get a reprimand, suspension, or dismissal. Penalties were imposed by editors, not the bureau. Journalism schools expressed interest and support, and a few other newspapers said they were thinking of adopting the plan.[31]

In selecting White to head the Bureau, Pulitzer chose the man who had headed the paper's legal department for several years and had already developed a systematic procedure for checking on those who involved the newspaper in libel actions. Each time a libel complaint was brought, the legal staff inquired into the matter and reported findings on an index card keyed to both reporter's and copyreader's names. The department also started running corrections and retractions. The card system made it easy to track the careless and unfair employees and to encourage the bosses to take action. White's responsibility was expanded with the introduction of the new bureau. After that his office looked into all complaints of inaccuracies or unfairness and discussed these with staff people involved.

The Bureau's procedures were similar to those of post–World War II ombudsmen. First the Bureau obtained a copy of the article in question and went over it with the reporter and copyreader involved. A written report was required. After that, a correction was prepared, if warranted, and a copy of the correction clipping sent to the complainant along with a "polite note." Finally, the complaint was registered on the card index, charged to whomever was found responsible. This report went to the managing editor for consideration or action.[32]

The complaints and corrections covered a wide range of matters, from the coverage of major political news to the spelling of names, wrong causes of death, misstatements or suspected slights, and wounded dignity of sources. The Bureau was still active in 1931 when the *New York World* was sold to be merged with the *New York Telegram*. A report covering libel suits between 1910 and 1931 shows libel claims of $1.2 million had been settled for about ten percent of the damages, and White believed the Bureau got much of the credit for this record.[33]


## CODES OF ETHICS

Ethical codes had received special attention at the Kansas meeting, perhaps because in 1910 the state press association had been the first in the nation to adopt a code of ethics. The conference looked at the twenty-five-year-old example of the British Institute of Journalists as a possible model for professionalism in the United States.[34] It set forth standards and codes and regulated the performance of English journalists. Professor James Melvin Lee, director of New York University's School of Journalism, advocated a code of ethics for journalists, saying that American journalism "has learned slowly that honesty is the best policy." He warned that the public was demanding that the press be put in a "moral test tube" and then judged by the reactions it provides. Legislators were tinkering away with an ethical code for newspapers, he added, and the government is demanding accurate circulation figures. "The rumbles you hear are the approaching storm." Editors should get "out from under it before lightning strikes," he declared.[35]

Lee pointed out that fraudulent ads in general as well as immoral personal ads had mostly been eliminated from the press; and fraudulent medicine and patent medicine ads were being excluded, and circulation lies curbed and monitored. The ethics of the family newspaper should be those of a welcome guest in the household—those of a gentleman. "If he does something wrong, he will apologize quickly." Lee praised those papers that were beginning to publish corrections, but wanted a code of ethics even if "we won't always live up to it."[36]

## AN ETHICAL TRIBUNAL

The strongest plea for an ethics code came from Oswald Garrison Villard, then editor of the *New York Post*, who said that the "widespread mutterings among the people" and the fresh laws regarding our business show that "we have to a considerable degree lost the confidence of the people who no longer believe what they read in the papers." He told the conference that the newspapers were considered dupes of Wall Street.[37]

Villard listed the reasons for the public's mistrust: (1) refusal to right editorial wrongs; (2) suppression of news for profit or fear of powerful interests; (3) false emphasis on news; (4) lack of accuracy in reporting; (5) invasion of privacy of public men; and (6) deliberate falsification of news and facts.[38] Although most newspapers are more respectable and better than they were, he said, restoration of lost prestige was badly needed.

"Has not the time then come for us to codify the public opinion within our own ranks, to begin to deal in our press and editorial associations, our publishers' organizations, with other things than errors of technique or increasing our gross incomes?" he asked. Villard wanted an ethical tribunal like those for bar and medicine. "If we do not set our house in order ourselves, our glorious freedom from a hateful supervision and control will crumble away and with it many of the present day splendors, powers and opportunities of our craft."[39]

From the vantage point of a family with 96 years in American journalism, Villard declared that "no commercial returns, however great, can compare with the moral satisfaction attained by the editor whose lance is ever ready for the public enemy . . . no achievement of huge circulations can compensate for the lack or loss of public respect."[40]

Thorpe published many of the conference papers plus additional essays in his book, *The Coming Newspaper*, in 1915. At that time he noted that there were 2,074 students and 72 teachers in journalism in 39 American universities and colleges. The Kansas meeting had raised the consciousness of Kansas newspapermen, he said, and his book was intended to place these issues before the larger public and to inspire other newspaper workers.[41]

Writings by Thorpe and other pioneer journalism teachers were widely used in the new classes and certainly had an influence in the formulation of values for the new crop of academically trained journalists. By 1916 the student numbers had risen to 3,500, and there were 175 teachers in 55 schools.

Newspapers need a standard for ethics, said Norman Hapgood, editor of *Collier's* magazine, then known for its muckraking journalism. In a lecture to students at Yale University in 1909, he said that some newspapers held back on things that might hurt the business of the community, and that others suppressed the truth to protect advertisers, or gossip that might injure favored individuals. The newspaper had no right to do "everything that is popular, especially when it ends by harming others," he said.[42]

## PRIVACY LAW DEVELOPED

The newspapers would have to recognize the line between privacy and publicity, lawyers Samuel D. Warren and Louis D. Brandeis had argued in an 1890 *Harvard Law Review* article. "The press is overstepping in every direction the obvious bounds of propriety and decency," they charged. "The question whether our law will recognize and protect the right to privacy . . . must soon come before our courts for consideration."[43] Warren and Brandeis argued further:

> Gossip is no longer the resource of the idle and of the vicious, but has become a trade, which is pursued with industry as well as effrontery. . . . To occupy the indolent, column upon column is filled with idle gossip, which can only be procured by intrusion upon the domestic circle.[44]

"The social need which became crystallized in the right of privacy did not grow insistent until the age of great industrial expansion," explained Louis Nizer, in a review of half a century of privacy case law. Then the advances in transportation and communication "threatened to annihilate time and space" and the press was "going through the growing pains of 'yellow journalism,' and Business first became Big."[45]

Warren and Brandeis said:

> The intensity and complexity of life, attendant upon advancing civilization have rendered necessary some retreat from the world, and man, under the refining influence of culture, has become more sensitive to publicity, so that solitude and privacy have become more essential to the individual; but modern enterprise and invention have, through invasions upon his privacy, subjected him to mental pain and distress, far greater than could be inflicted by mere bodily injury.[46]

Warren and Brandeis contended that this gossip and sensationalism trivialized and dwarfed thoughts and aspirations of a people, and appealed to the weak side of human nature. Their essay noted support for privacy in the common law and in existing property law that could be used to invoke a protection of privacy from invasion of "the too enterprising press, the photographer, or the possessor of any other modern device for recording or reproducing scenes or sounds."[47]

But they continued that this right would not prohibit the publication of matter of public or general interest. The point was to protect the privacy of private life, not of public life, and their essay indicated that privacy law would make similar distinctions between private and public people along the lines of libel law.[48]

The roots of privacy went back to common law, Nizer explained, but the development of privacy laws in the states was a response to needs created by the complexities of modern life. "Privacy is antisocial," explained Nizer, demanding the individual's right to a life of "seclusion and anonymity, free from prying curiosity.... Opposed to this ideal is the principle that the white light of publicity safeguards the public, that free disclosure of truth is the best protection against tyranny."[49]

Modern civilization can spread information instantly around the world, so the individual needed protection from instant exposure, Nizer said in his review of the cases from 1893 forward. He found that the first state to pass a privacy law was New York in 1903, and the first case to recognize the right was in 1905.[50]

## TREATMENT OF PUBLIC FIGURES

The struggle over individual rights and the rights of society quickly distinguished in practice the treatment of ordinary private citizens and the treatment of public officials. Paul M. Brice, at a South Carolina Press Association meeting, said there had evolved a principle of journalistic ethics that the individual must be treated with "consideration and respect." But when someone becomes a public character through holding office or seeking it, "the circumstances and conditions may change." Brice added that some think a public man's official acts are "legitimate objects of criticism only," but he argued that there were exceptions. "Public office is a public trust, and the manner in which any man will fill that trust largely depends upon his private character. A corruptionist will not become incorruptible by the mere fact that he is placed in office by public favor or factional politics."[51]

Brice argued that it was appropriate to make private acts and matters of general conduct the subject of "legitimate investigation and criticism," and if the person "is found wanting, lacking in that character and those high attributes which would make him the proper custodian of the people's moral and industrial welfare, it is not unethical for a newspaper to publish proved, unquestioned facts as to his private life which will inform the people of the manner of man he is and what they may logically expect should they confer their suffrages upon him." Brice said this was not license, but the "duty of the public serving newspaper."[52]

An experienced New York City newspaper reporter, Julius Chambers, made the same point a few years later saying it was the duty of the press to inform the public of the wrongdoing of its public officials. Editors live in glass houses and the "scurviest of critics may throw stones from the cover of anonymity." But editors must be personally held responsible for the columns they direct and must act for the public good, without malice.[53]

Editors are obligated to tell the citizens when politicans are doing wrong, Chambers said. He added:

> The upright, non-tricky public official has the same legal protection as the commonest citizen. But many things are properly printable concerning the public official that are utterly unwarranted to lay before the neighbors of a civilian, even though they be true. Inaccurate as the assumption often is, the public official is expected to stand forth as a representative man.
>
> If a private citizen by a long record of uprightness has lived down a criminal act of his youth, it is venal on the part of an editor to blazon forth the facts; but if that same man be a candidate for country treasurer or for a place of distinction that will invest him with pardoning power, whereby punishment of criminals may be lightened and the chastening effect of conviction nullified, it is the duty of the press to state the record of that man, dispassionately. Voters have a right to know. The right is an inherent as that of liberty and the pursuit of happiness.... When a man asks his fellow citizens to elect him to office, he should "come with clean hands."[54]

Chambers pointed out that the press can't cease its "clamoring" and "meddling," as some critics call it. It has a lofty mission, like that of doctor, minister, or lawyer, and editors have to do their duty for the public even if the facts are unfavorable to a public official, he said. It was the duty of the press to advise and admonish the public official, Chambers said, and he saw that as a "high, not a low, ideal."[55] This debate over the private lives of public and private persons has continued with roughly the same distinctions being made in recent years. Presidential candidates, as Gary Hart learned, are scrutinized for clues to their potential leadership style and competence not only through their political programs and leadership records but also through evidence of their moral codes and behavior.[56]

The shame of the sensation-seeking press had reached such proportions that some church groups began campaigning for clean newspapers. Churchmen and journalists exchanged views in public debates. In 1908 Mary Baker Eddy turned the early Christian Science publishing efforts into the *Christian Science Monitor*, a full-scale daily newspaper that provided an alternative, clean, wholesome newspaper with no exploitation of crime and vice.[57] The charges of corruption and moral decay of the newspapers were greatly amplified with the publication of Will Irwin's series in *Collier's* early in 1911.

World War I deflected the critics' interest in the professionalism of journalism to the more pointed issues of the balance between patriotism and national defense and censorship and wartime propaganda. But, after the war, the concern that became paramount was the growing concentration of ownership of the press and the big business mentality that came with that. Profit and growth dominated the thinking of the newspaper owners, critics said, and the brief but eye-catching success of the urban tabloid after the war underscored their point.

## NOTES

1. The debate over this issue from the late 1890s into the 1940s was always cast in terms of responsibility. The critics urged self-improvement and justified it by moral and social arguments. The responsibility was implied in the granting of free speech and press in the First Amendment. In using the word accountability, I am suggesting that these pressures toward legal restraints, such as privacy law and licensing, were attempts to force responsibility on a press that was not initiating it. The first critic I found using the term accountability was Archibald MacLeish in his 1946 draft of the Hutchins Commission report, and he said that he meant "owner accountability" to the larger society. See Chapter 12 for a discussion of this report.
2. "First National Newspaper Conference, August 1912, Madison," *Outlook* 101 (17 August 1912): 847–48.
3. Hamilton Holt, "A Plan for an Endowed Journal," *Independent* 73 (1919): 301.
4. Holt, "Plan," 302.
5. Holt, "Plan," 303.
6. James M. Lee, *A History of American Journalism* (Garden City, N. Y.: Garden City, 1917/23), 410.
7. Lee, *History*, 408–9. Sources differ on the longevity of *Daybook*, an adless newspaper published in Toledo from October 1911–1917 (*New York Times*, 7 July 1917, 9).
8. Ross, "Suppression," 303–11: and Julius Weinberg, *Edward Alsworth Ross and the Sociology of Progressivism* (Madison: State Historical Society of Wisconsin, 1972), 128, 132.
9. Merle Thorpe, *The Coming Newspaper* (New York: Henry Holt, 1915), 2–3.
10. *U.S. Statutes at Large, 2d Congress 1911–13*, 37 Pt. #1 (approved 24 August 1912). The Bourne Act of 1912 was H. R. 21279 Public #336.
11. Thorpe, *Coming*, 5.
12. For a detailed discussion of the licensing issue see: Barbara K. Petersen, "Thinking the Unthinkable: Licensing of Journalists in America—An Historical Perspective," unpublished doctoral student paper, University of Michigan, Department of Communication, March 1988.
13. "Proceedings of the First National Journalism Conference held during Kansas Newspaper Week, University of Kansas, Department of Journalism May 10–14," *University of Kansas News Bulletin* 14 (1914): 14–15.
14. Editorial, "Licensing for Newspaper Men," *Editor and Publisher* (4 May 1912): 8.
15. *Kansas Bulletin*, 8.
16. Thorpe, *Coming*, 156.

17. *Kansas Bulletin*, 17–19.
18. Curtis D. Mac Dougall, *Newsroom Problems and Policies* (New York: Dover, 1963), 69 says that it did not pass.
19. *Kansas Bulletin*, 155–56.
20. *Kansas Bulletin*, 17–19.
21. Editorial, "Should Reporters Be Licensed?" *Editor and Publisher* (16 October 1915): 476.
22. "Licenses for Journalists," *Literary Digest* 54 (7 April 1917): 1021.
23. *Kansas Bulletin*, 22. The bureau lasted from 1913 to 1931 when the paper was sold.
24. *Kansas Bulletin*, 26.
25. *Kansas Bulletin*, 30.
26. *Kansas Bulletin*, 30.
27. Thorpe, *Coming*, 7.
28. Ralph Pulitzer, *The Profession of Journalism: Accuracy in the News—An Address* (New York: School of Journalism, Columbia University, 1912), 3.
29. Pulitzer, *Profession*, 16.
30. Isaac DeForest White, speech draft, the *World* (N.Y.) archives, Box 1913, folder Bureau of Accuracy and Fair Play (BAFP) (Butler Library, Columbia University). From *The World* (New York) Collection, Bureau 51 Accuracy and Fair Play Report 1910–1931. Copyright © 1910–1931 by Columbia University Library. Reprinted by permission.
31. "Notice *to* World Correspondents, the *World* (N.Y.) archives, Box 1913, folder BAFP (Butler Library, Columbia University).
32. Letter from White to David S. Taylor, *World* archives, Box 1913, folder BAFP—Initial Reaction.
33. 1931 List of Libel Suits 1910–1931, *World* archives, Box 1931, folder BAFP January–August.
34. In professional journals and meetings in the early twentieth century the British Institute of Journalists was frequently praised as a model for the Americans.
35. Thorpe, *Coming*, 172.
36. Thorpe, *Coming*, 186–87.
37. Thorpe, *Coming*, 51.
38. Thorpe, *Coming*, 58.
39. Thorpe, *Coming*, 74–75.
40. Thorpe, *Coming*, 70–77.
41. Thorpe, *Coming*, 1.
42. Norman Hapgood, *Everyday Ethics: Page Lecture* Series (New Haven, Conn.: Yale University Press, 1910), 6.
43. Samuel D. Warren and Louis D. Brandeis, "The Right to Privacy," *Harvard Law Review* 4 (15 December 1890): 196.
44. Warren, *Right*, 196.
45. Louis Nizer, "The Right of Privacy: A Half Century's Development," *Michigan Law Review* 39 (February 1941): 526.
46. Warren, *Right*, 196.
47. Warren, *Right*, 206.
48. Warren, *Right*, 215.
49. Nizer, *Privacy*, 528–29.

50. Nizer, *Privacy*, 535.
51. Paul M. Brice, "Newspaper Ethics," *Editor and Publisher* (29 July 1905): 7.
52. Brice, "Ethics," 7.
53. Julius Chambers, "The Press and the Public Official," *Forum* 44 (July 1910): 14–25.
54. Chambers, "Press," 19–20.
55. Chambers, "Press," 25.
56. See: John B. Judis, "The Hart Affair," *Columbia Journalism Review* 26 (July/August 1987): 21–25.
57. Erwin D. Canham, *Commitment to Freedom* (Boston: Houghton Mifflin, 1958), 39.

# CHAPTER 6

# Playing for the Crowds: 1920–1939

The social menace of an increasingly commercial press was a continuing theme in the 1920s, gaining strength because of the vocal critics that took up the cry—socialist muckraker Upton Sinclair, professional journalist-editors Silas Bent, Oswald Garrison Villard, Don Seitz, and H. L. Mencken. Perhaps more than any other era this one is widely associated with identifiable press critics, whom one scholar has called "first generation" critics.[1] Their criticism was considered provocative enough to be published in books, popular and serious monthly magazines, and in the trade journals. Tabloid journalism, new on the scene, intensified the debate with its excesses that seemed a throwback to "yellow journalism."

Critics agreed on the problem—the commercial press was a danger to society. To the socialists, capitalism itself was the cause of all the distortions and lies in the press. To the progressives, the loss of individuality and the numbing sameness that chain journalism brought together with business efficiency endangered the public dialogue. To these people tabloids demonstrated the danger of excessive commercialism. In the 1920s the liberals joined the chorus of press criticism, asking for progressive reform, while the culture custodians were less vocal in defending the establishment.[2]

Defenders generally made the point that chain journalism provided strength for the press to fight against political evils, and the common syndicated matter served the positive purpose of linking a vast nation together. They argued that the notion of any one business or industrial power assuming repressive control of the press would not be tolerated by the people. They often chose to avoid direct confrontation with the liberal critics, letting extremist talk dissipate on its own. Since they saw no clear danger of widespread support for radical press reform and were not unhappy with the urban daily that had emerged after the flirtation with yellow journalism, they were content to leave the field to the public's good sense.

The earliest and most notorious critical book was *The Brass Check* by Upton Sinclair in 1920. It sold some 110,000 copies, according to its author who had personally paid for the publication.[3] Sinclair called the press a prostitute for business, charging that it suppressed news about labor and other powerless groups in the society, while it protected business and industrial interests, and covered up their scandals and embarrassments. Coverage of labor, industrial strife, and strikes were among the most unfairly handled, Sinclair claimed. This prompted Walter Lippmann to ask, "If the troubles of American journalism are Big Business, why does not the remedy lie in reading anti-capitalist newspapers?"[4]

Sinclair's book is not easy reading. The author spends the first two-thirds of the book repaying the editors and publishers who had offended him during the previous twenty years as he had attempted to get his early works of poetry, fiction, and opinion published. The final section gets down to specific journalistic cases, with examples culled from the previous two decades used to paint the picture of a conspiratorial press dynasty intent on destroying individual freedoms and undermining the social welfare. Sinclair's remedies included some that were already a part of contemporary discussion, such as the endowed newspaper and a reporters' union, but a unique proposal was a requirement that all news interviews be checked with their sources for accuracy prior to publication.[5] As critics scathingly pointed out, Sinclair made many charges and few useful suggestions.

Sinclair's "extraordinary diatribe was something to take with several grains of salt," snorted Frederick L. Allen in the *Atlantic Monthly*. The country had been "fed to repletion with supposed conspiracies of radicals, Bolsheviki, Jews, and so forth, and we are happily beginning to acquire some common sense."[6] Allen said these misrepresentations by Sinclair and other critics of the press proved "not that there is any conspiracy among newspaper men to withhold the truth from the public, but merely that newspaper owners, editors, and reporters are fallible; actuated too often by self-interest; too often ready to take the 'practical' view of things and to see on which side their bread is buttered; too often inclined to fight by illegitimate means what they dislike; and too often subject to those surges of mob-feeling that lead men to pillory those whom they detest."[7]

Sinclair said he knew he would be an attractive target for the critics because he was a poet and was lumped together with other eccentric artists. But his own retelling of fights with editors and publishers portrays an arrogance and a tempestuous personality. More importantly, Sinclair's writing was so filled with unsubstantiated charges that respectable editors had reason to be wary of publishing them.

Editor-critic H. L. Mencken viewed Sinclair's book as a "simple, clear, bold and idiotic" remedy for the evils of the press. "What ails the newspapers of the United States is the fact that their gigantic commercial development compels them to appeal to larger and larger masses of undifferentiated men, and that truth is a commodity that the masses of undifferentiated men cannot be induced to buy," he said. The causes of that are deep in the "psychology of Homo boobus," he pointed out.[8]

## IMPROVE THE REPORTER

The controversy over Sinclair himself, said Dean Eric Allen of the School of Journalism at the University of Oregon, kept the book from raising the questions in any effective way. Said one critic, newspaper editors could easily pass Sinclair off as "having a big head" and "striving for notoriety" and being "warped by his zeal for socialism," thus justifying their ignoring the charges he raised.[9] And much of the professional response to critics like Sinclair was just that.

But one thoughtful analysis of Sinclair's book was published in the *Journal of Political Economy*. Its author, Curtice N. Hitchcock of the University of Chicago, said that the professionalism of journalism was the "most promising means of countering the problems of daily journalism."[10] Just changing the political system, as Sinclair and others wanted, would not necessarily produce a better system for the press, said Hitchcock. The issue was not freedom of opinion, but "free access to all the important facts on which opinion is to be based." This meant that reporters had to be better educated, and editors had to be more discerning in their work. The nature of reporting and editing is a complex and highly organized business, Hitchcock explained. It demanded "intelligence, intuition, highly technical training and an enormously wide background of knowledge."[11]

He called for improvements in the education and training of the journalist that would create a journalist with "capacity for scientific analysis and critical judgment" and the ability to recognize and reduce to a minimum the cultural bias in his own reporting.[12] In the promotion of a real set of professional standards of training, ideals, and ethics, and in a required minimum standard of education "lies the real hope of newspaperdom—the building up of an ideal, not of propagating ideas for a new social order." His ideal reporter would work to disseminate the truth, leave members of the community free to form their own opinions, and regard community service as more important than the "scoop." Journalists would become more specialized in particular fields in order to do a better job of reporting a complex, modern society, he predicted, and with the increased professionalism the "problem of control" would become "less pressing."[13]

A "newspaper conscience" was needed, Professor Alfred H. Lloyd told a group of journalists. Newspapers were very unsettled, he noted, like the rest of society, with the idealism first aroused by the war dissipated.[14] The press was influential and powerful, he said, but not trusted and respected. The reasons included advertiser influence, venal sensationalism, fabrication, invasion of privacy, suppression of some news, and general conservatism. The argument that "newspapers only give the public what they want" was specious, he charged, because the newspapers decide what to print and catch the public "off guard" when people are relaxed. But the press pries into private life claiming a "right to know" that is really "a right to pry."[15]

Lloyd, a philosophy professor at the University of Michigan, charged that the newspaper was controlled by "the crowd mind," not by individuals of independence or personal responsibility and conscience. An editor was responsive to the "ideas, judgments, and purposes that are more atmospheric than personally his own, and publishes a great deal of "special interest publicity as news."[16] Worse, the press treats "individuality as exploitable, sensation, humor, derision—a foil to exalt the normal and conventional and commonplace," which encourages people to accommodate and comply, rather than to assert themselves. "Democracy that does not foster real leadership is riding to its own undoing," he warned.[17]

He said his central criticism of the press was its "conservative commercialism," which has allowed the press to "grow fast and run wild like a prodigal son." He advocated instead, "enlightened philosophical pragmatism," sober honesty, moderated partisanship, little publicity, and work for the social good. The growth of professional organizations, press associations, and standards would help create the newspaper conscience he believed was needed but missing.[18]

## THE PROBLEM IS AMERICA

There was some truth to Upton Sinclair's charges about the American press, agreed Professor Nelson A. Crawford of Kansas State Agricultural College, because some news is manufactured, suppressed, distorted, and colored by publishers' wishes. But the real concerns, he said, were "ignorance and fear." Newspapermen were not well educated, they did not care enough to look up things, and they made mistakes. Their editors demanded good stories, not knowledge, Crawford explained. Reporters "might be liberals, but they write to please their bosses." This results in a conservative slant, because "publishers are afraid of the herd, and defer to it by respecting a long list of taboos that are dogmas of American faith."[19]

Crawford, who wrote the first text on journalism ethics, said America was in an "end justifies the means" and "right or wrong, my country" mood that encouraged newspapers to play down problems in order to boost the positive side. Reporters are told to be truthful and fair, but they learn on the job to respect their employer's taboos and to tone down their individuality so they will not lose their jobs. "This develops a cynical attitude on the part of reporters, who come to regard their job as doing what it takes to sell newspapers."[20]

In Crawford's opinion, the Wilson administration had encouraged this tendency by giving the public only the facts it needed to help win the war. That unwise practice of concealing the facts reveals a lack of belief in popular government, he said, and it had continued after the war. A popular government, he insisted, should provide the public with "all available facts, clearly and objectively, because without facts, people could not challenge the government and would be swayed by prejudice."[21]

Crawford, too, was encouraged by the feeling among newspaper men and women that organization was desirable. He saw this as a chance to set some standards for entrance to the profession and to adopt a code of ethics that would guide the performance of daily journalism. "Schools and departments of journalism were implanting ethical principles in their students, and this would help future generations of journalists. But the American people still had to be released from the hopeless forces of ignorance and fear."[22]

There was a growing recognition that access to information was "one of the indispensible conditions of freedom," as Lippmann had argued.[23] The public was used to talking about the importance of free opinion, but F. L. Allen observed, "still more vital is to have the facts on which to form this opinion." Most people get those facts from the daily newspaper, and that meant that "all unsigned news" should be "presented as accurately and impartially as humanly possible," he said. The "cardinal rule of newspaper ethics" was that "what is presented as sheer fact should be accurate and without bias...."[24]

Bias was difficult to avoid, Allen admitted. Witnesses disagree on what they have seen, language and emphasis colors reporting of an event, reporters are in a hurry and they know too little about many subjects they report. There was even "some deliberate distortion and falsification," not, Allen said, in a "conspiracy to withhold truth from the public, but because people were fallible and motivated by self-interest." Reporting was getting better and more ethical, he believed, because reporters were better educated.[25]

The solution was to develop better reporters, people who were sensitive to accuracy and who would raise the standards of performance, and a better public that would demand better newspapers and be better critics. William J. Abbot, editor of the *Christian Science Monitor*, agreed with that view and thought that a better class of newspaper readers who wanted clean and constructive newspapers was already there and was growing. Those readers wanted a "complete daily survey of international current events rather than hasty reports of unusual happenings." They asked for "carefully matured stories by men with precise knowledge of their subjects," less crime and trivia reporting, and more world news and news of educational, ethical, reform, and economic movements. Advertisers, too, had started to demand "clean, constructive newspapers" in which to place their ads.[26]

## BIAS-FREE JOURNALISM

The notion that what was needed was objective, bias-free journalism for discerning readers was common to many of the statements by the critics of the early 1920s. The basic idea was not really so new, but the use of the term "objective" to describe it with the supporting arguments as articulated in Walter Lippmann's book, *Public Opinion*, was. Bruce Blivin, editor of the *Atlantic Monthly*, agreed on the new standards for journalism, but he thought technology, not reader demands, had made the difference. As he pointed out, fifty years earlier the newspapers were run by owner-editors, and advertising was of minor importance. Reporters then were eyewitnesses of events and tried for a "literary effect" with their writing. The paper was essentially a "personal, human, and local product."[27]

The newspaper of 1923 had been altered by inventions that made large circulation and increased advertising and syndicated material readily available, Blivin explained. Afternoon papers that captured women readers for the shopping advertisements put a premium on haste, tabloid summaries, pictures, flabby language. The rivalry had moved "from the editorial to the business office"—over circulation, instead of news. The result, Blivin said, was "not an editor's notion of a good paper, but a circulation manager's notion of a good seller."[28]

Daily journalism relied on similar copy produced by chain newspapers and feature syndicates and wire services, publicity copy and fluff, and reporters were more removed from the sources of their news, Blivin said. Quantity was valued over quality, the press competed with movies and radio, and with entertainment, and that meant the "bad newspapers were flourishing." Vulgarity need not become a permanent condition, said Blivin, but people would have to do something about it. He wanted a return to the higher standard of journalism represented by the *New York Times*, the *New York World*, and the *Christian Science Monitor*, and he urged community leaders to "abandon their laissez-faire attitude toward journalism" and demand higher standards and to sabotage the inferior papers by refusing to read them.[29]

Oswald Garrison Villard, the respected editor of the *Nation* for 26 years, and Don C. Seitz, business manager for 25 years at the *New York World*, stirred up still more controversy with their press criticism. Villard penned a series of profiles of editors, publishers, and newspapers that ran in his magazine during the early 1920s in which he praised the good and lambasted the bad examples. These were republished as a book, *Some Newspapers and Newspaper-Men*, in 1923, prefaced by his own philosophy of journalism that had grown out of a 105-year family tradition. Villard's lists of heroes and scoundrels sounds much like the traditional views handed down in American press history: mixed feelings about Pulitzer, high praise for Samuel Bowles, E. L. Godkin and Adolph Ochs, and spirited denunciation of Hearst and Frank Munsey. Villard wished for an Institute of Journalists that would enforce standards against the scoundrels in journalism, and deplored the willingness of people to abandon principle and write for the Hearst press for money and notoriety.[30] Professor James Melvin Lee, director of the Department of Journalism at New York University at the time, found Villard's work riddled with errors and biased by unethical treatment of many of the subjects. It was "not the book of constructive press criticism that was sadly needed," he said.[31]

## GUARDING THE LIBERTIES

Don Seitz's six-part series in *Outlook* magazine in 1926 caused more concern among the contemporary newspaper editors, perhaps because he had so long been associated with the *World* and spoke authoritatively as a respected insider. The editors considered but rejected making a public response to his charge that the press had lost its prestige as the special guardian of all liberties and had become just another corporation after profits, destroying individuality by creating newspapers that were "standardized like Ford cars."[32] Perhaps the editors didn't want to stir up more controversy over charges many recognized were uncomfortably close to the mark.

Few of the newspapers were owned by their editors, Seitz pointed out, and most of the work was done by hired men with "little individuality or community concern." The old editors had been influential and had used their press as a "watchdog that barked"; new editorials lacked influence because they had no force behind them, no potential purpose, no punch.[33] The greater a newspaper's circulation, Seitz explained, the weaker its editorial policy. As newspapers get rich, owners get timid. Reporters degenerate into "legs" that run after news to be styled by rewrite men in the office. This increases efficiency, but kills reporter individuality, he said.[34]

Should newspapers that had become primarily entertainment still be subsidized by low postal rates? Seitz wondered. Their mission was information and education, but the press had become lazy and fat during the war. The public was expressing growing distrust. Seitz had discovered that people believed newspapers were "in the hands of the advertisers, that opinions were modified or corrupted." He thought a return to "individual enterprise and unrelenting competition in the pursuit of news" was a good place to being repairing the damage.[35]

The war had encouraged the use of press agents, Seitz noted, and press agentry had become a "profession," better paid than reporting and attracting graduates from the journalism schools. But publicity was insidious. "Sugar hides the pill," and readers don't know the self-interest that is hidden behind the story. It was really free advertising, he said, and it was up to the reporters to dig for the facts so that readers would not be misled.[36]

A historian who turned her attention to the newspapers, Lucy Maynard

Salmon, published two lengthy, detailed studies, *The Newspaper and the Historian* and *The Newspaper and Authority* in 1923. In the latter she discussed contemporary press criticism and attempts to regulate the press. All kinds of restrictions had been made, she explained, but even without them the press could "still be fettered by its own low standards, timidity, irresponsibility, failure to respond to social needs."[37]

"True press freedom lies only within the keeping of the press itself," she declared. She challenged the press to correct the things the public was complaining about, including: excessive use of publicity handouts; excessive concern with the superficial aspects of life; lack of concern about ethics; too much pride in getting a scoop instead of accurate and thorough news coverage; misleading and pernicious ads; and abandonment of the public interest for profit and competition.[38]

## THE TABLOID MENACE

The tabloid newspapers, which sprang up in the 1920s, garnered the harshest criticism over their reporting of lurid criminal trials and use of faked photos. Here was an enemy that conservatives and liberals could agree upon. The Hall-Mills murder case, revived through the journalistic investigations of the *New York Mirror*, a Hearst tabloid, made front-page sensations. So did Peaches and Daddy Browning's annulment case and the electrocution photograph of Ruth Gary Snyder. New Yorkers were agog as the papers covered what seemed to be a run of sleaze and gore.[39] The small size of the tabloid newspaper and its emphasis on large pictures and big type headlines dramatized the underside of life in a way that outraged critics.

The *New York Daily News* introduced tabloid journalism to New York City in 1919, as a convenient modern format for busy city dwellers. It was in the London picture newspaper tradition of Alfred Harmsworth (later Lord Northcliff). By 1924 there were three competing tabloids in the city, representing almost 1.6 million circulation.[40] Critics analyzed their popularity. Some thought it was the small size, which made easy reading on the subway. Others said the pictures and breezy style attracted the marginally literate reading audience. Still others pointed out that sleaze need not be the identifying feature of the tabloid, and that the size and emphasis on pictures could just as well be used for socially valuable news.

A debate on the issue was staged for *Forum* magazine, with Villard on the attack and Martin Weyrauch, an editor of the tabloid *New York Graphic*, on the defense. Tabloids "pander to sensationalism and the prurient," charged Villard, "and have no sense of civic or social duty to the community." Similar charges had been made against the yellow press, he reminded readers, but those had turned increasingly sober and responsible and had not sunk "to quite such depths of vulgarity, sensationalism and frank description of crime and degeneracy, as do the tabloids of New York to-day."[41] He brushed aside as threadbare the argument that the tabloids merely supplied what people want. That had been used for "every stooping to the gutter to win circulation since modern journalism began," he charged.[42] Villard referred to a recent study that showed that tabloids gave almost as much space to crime and divorce as they did to all the general, foreign, and local news. He worried that they were attracting a new lot "of mentally underdeveloped citizens who would otherwise never see a newspaper at all." He still thought newspapers should educate and help improve citizens, not just make money.[43]

The *Graphic*'s Weyrauch countered with a defense right out of the days of sensationalism—tabloids were a symbol of progress, as inevitable as jazz and expressive of modern America. They were read by all levels of the society because they offered brief stories that held the reader's interest. Other papers were "musty," but the tabloids were full of human interest. They had been a constructive force helping labor and relating to the humanness of their readers, he said. They were successful because they were not above the heads of the readers.[44]

## OUT OF CONTROL

The tabloid's all-out coverage of the case of "Daddy" and fifteen-year-old Peaches Browning's marriage annulment trial raised public ire. The free press should not "pander to easy circulation," said *Editor and Publisher*. Most of the papers had not fallen for the "lurid, faked-up babbling smut" available during the Browning case, it editorialized, and the obscenity laws should be applied to those that did.[45] They were.

A vice society had already brought the *New York Graphic* to court for its reporting of lustful matters and for doctored photographs, but the case was dismissed. The New York Society for the Suppression of Vice had recommended a ban on reporting of lurid court testimony, but defenders pointed out that obscenity laws already on the books had only to be enforced.[46] A regulation to censor this court testimony was proposed in New York. Press reports from around the nation in *Editor and Publisher* showed that reporting in the Browing case had "passed beyond all limits of decency," and tabloid journalism was becoming a menace to the morals of the nation.[47]

The New York State Crime Commission issued a forty-page report on the subject and suggested censorship might "not be the worst of evils."[48] The trade journal agreed about the problem, but opposed censorship. It charged that the Commission was trying "to smash the mirror" that reflected the ills of society. Laws on the books already used against indecency in the theater should be applied to the newspapers, it thought.[49]

## BALLYHOO DRAGS PRESS DOWN

The most extensive contemporary study of the tabloid era was in Silas Bent's *Ballyhoo*, parts of which were published in *Harper's* magazine in 1927. "Ballyhoo" was born in the Spanish-American War and "became grotesque" during World War I, Bent charged. It was "the circus barker calling his wares," offering entertainment, sports, propaganda, romance, sex, crime, and escapism.[50]

"A great newspaper must be the lengthened shadow of a man," Bent said, but American newspapers had not realized that. As in other industries, standardization of the product provided great economies and higher profits. But it is the "personality and individuality" that create the conscience of newspaper publishing.[51] Changes in journalism, Bent observed, had come from factors outside; the main factor in newspaper consolidation was the advertiser who does not want to "spend money for overlapping circulation."[52] He wondered whether the chains would use their financial independence to speak out with hard-hitting editorials and accurate news, or whether they would be weak and indolent. This would be a key question on the minds of many press critics in years to come.

Bent agreed with Wilcox and Lippmann that reform had to come through greater responsibility by editors, better education of journalists, more self-criticism, and acknowledgment of errors. He worried over the public's apathy. The press had a special position as a "public utility" that acted "as a censor of government and a surrogate of popular liberties," while it afforded "prompt, accurate and unbiased information," the raw material of public opinion. It "was burdened with a special responsibility for the general well-being of public morality and the harmonious operation of democratic government."[53]

He warned that if the press did not acknowledge this responsibility, the government could subject it to "regulation and inspection," as done for any public utility, and there would be "little hope of protection under the First Amendment." Freedom of the press was not guaranteed "on the basis of being a good business."[54]

Newspapers can't print "all the news. They have to select," Bent said, "with the public interest in mind." To a newspaper reader it sometimes seemed that the freedom of the press was a freedom for the press to "invade his personal privacy, print his picture without his consent, dump onto his doorstep filth collected from the courts, and ballyhoo for the aggrandizement of its own treasury, prize-fighters, channel swimmers, football players, chorus girls and aviators." Bent said that the reader didn't see this freedom being used to "defend unpopular views, criticize elected officials, excoriate individual abuses and improve the public welfare." He warned that readers would not champion their newspapers until the newspapers "mend their ways." Moreover, he said, "it has itself to blame for public lethargy when its privileges are curtailed. This lethargy will be responsible if its privileges are abolished."[55]

## THE LINDBERGH LEGACY

The kidnapping of the Lindbergh baby in the fall of 1932, and the trial two years later of Bruno Hauptmann, gave this flamboyant press an unparalleled opportunity to milk gee-whiz emotions and engage in amateur detective work that made great copy, even if it impeded police work. Had the press hindered the police in finding the baby? Had the press been partly responsible, therefore, for the murder? Had the press inflicted unnecessary pain and suffering on the parents and driven them from the country? Critics raised all these questions and more.

As Bent put it, the press "outdid themselves and one another in verbosity and vulgarity. All the legitimate news could have been told adequately in three-quarters of a column of space; instead, day after day pages were devoted to it." Newspapers all over the country "were flooded with balderdash." The Associated Press sent out 10,000 words daily on the Lindbergh story. Hearst's International News Service sent 50,000 words the first day.[56] Though the baby was known worldwide within hours, and the press promoted its own attempts to help locate the baby and his kidnappers as a public service, Bent saw this as feeding the public's "voracious and quite insatiable" appetite. He called it "one of the ugliest phases of daily journalism, for it sets up a sort of circular hysteria between newspaper men and newspaper readers."[57] He concluded:

> Charles A. Lindbergh has suffered more, probably, than any other citizen at the hands of newspaper men. They capitalized for revenue only (their revenue) a stunt flight to France, they built up around his personality a myth which he had never been quite free to dissipate, they outrageously invaded the privacy of his honeymoon and his married life, and now they have made more difficult, if not impossible, the return by kidnappers of his son to Mrs. Lindbergh's arms. Colonel Lindbergh has an ugly score against the daily press.[58]

Bad as the reporting was, the press lost no opportunity in castigating its competition, radio, for poor performance as a prime source that was feeding misleading information and false rumors.[59] At the same time, newspapers realized the radio coverage promoted newspaper circulation. The story had universal appeal and each story fed the desire for more. Most responsible editors agreed that the press had behaved "very badly." Publisher Frank Knox, of the *Chicago Daily News*, said that the reckless and heedless capitalizing on the story for circulation "is a calamity to the press," and has earned "unquestioned disgust of thinking people everywhere."[60]

The greedy arrogance and insensitivity of the press invited legal controls. Privacy was threatened, said Mitchell Dawson in the *Atlantic Monthly*, when the press hounded unfortunate victims to gain profits. "Must we move backward, then, to some form of official censorship?" He believed it remote that the American press would be censored, but this was the case in other countries. The alternative, he said, was "development of a professional spirit among news agencies" so that the press itself would set limits on reporting tactics and reporters were trained to respect human life and dignity.[61]

The press must not have been listening, because during the Hauptmann trial the courtroom became a public spectacle. Criticism mounted, demanding restraint on the press and respect for the accused and for the victims. A two-year study by the press and the American Bar Association was begun just after the trial; it proposed seven specific recommendations for press trial coverage.[62] The candid camera, the photo-news magazine, and inexpensive listening devices newly on the market promised to add to this continuing controversy over the public and private life of American celebrities.[63]

Tabloid era criticism declined in a few years, when it became apparent that the new "jazz style" in journalism would not replace the omnibus big-city daily. A few tabloids would remain and some would still grow, but evidently there was a limit to the audience for daily sleaze. Splashy elements of the tabloid style would adhere to the standard daily press, just as yellow journalism had modernized newspaper design. But yellow journalism and tabloid jazz journalism went beyond acceptable limits and tested the public's tolerance. Notions that reporters should be professionals and that reporting should educate, be fair, factual, and "objective" were more frequently articulated in the 1920s, as critics inside and outside the press agreed on the need to raise the standards and performance of the press.

## NOTES

1. Patrick Jay Daley, "Radical Currents in Twentieth Century American Press Criticism: Notes for the Future," Ph.D. diss. (University of Iowa 1983), Chap. 7.
2. The concept and term "custodians of culture" is elaborated by John Tomsich in *A Genteel Endeavor*, p. 194. See my Chap. 1, n. 8.
3. Upton Sinclair, *The Brass Check: A Study of American Journalism*, 8th ed. (Pasadena, Calif.: printed by the author, 1920), 440.
4. Walter Lippmann, *Public Opinion* (New York: Macmillan, 1922/1961pb), 336–67.
5. Sinclair, *Brass*, 404.
6. Frederick L. Allen, "Newspapers and the Truth," *Atlantic Monthly* 129 (January 1922): 50.
7. Allen, "Newspapers," 50.
8. Leon Harris, *Upton Sinclair: An American Rebel* (New York: Crowell, 1975), 180.
9. Eric Allen, "Review of 'The Brass Check,'" *Editor and Publisher* (8 January 1921): 1.

10. Curtice N. Hitchcock, review of *The Brass Check, Journal of Political Economy* 29 (April 1921): 337.
11. Hitchcock, review, 339.
12. Hitchcock, review, 340.
13. Hitchcock, review, 347.
14. Alfred H. Lloyd, "Newspaper Conscience—A Study in Half Truths," *American Journal of Sociology* 27 (September 1921): 198.
15. Lloyd, "Conscience," 203.
16. Lloyd, "Conscience," 205.
17. Lloyd, "Conscience," 206–09.
18. Lloyd, "Conscience," 208.
19. Nelson Antrim Crawford, "The American Newspaper and the People: A Psychological Examination," *Nation* 115 (13 September 1922): 251.
20. Crawford, "Psychological," 251.
21. Crawford, "Psychological," 251.
22. Crawford, "Psychological," 253.
23. F. L. Allen, "Newspapers," 44.
24. Allen, "Newspapers," 46.
25. Allen, "Newspapers," 52–53.
26. Philip Schuyler, "Willis Abbott Visions a Press Devoted to 'Good News of the World,'" *Editor and Publisher* (12 July 1924): 3.
27. Bruce Blivin, "Our Changing Journalism," *Atlantic Monthly* 132 (December 1923): 744.
28. Blivin, "Changing," 745.
29. Blivin, "Changing," 750.
30. Oswald Garrison Villard, *Some Newspapers and Some Newspaper-men* (New York: Knopf, 1923).
31. James Melvin Lee, review of *Some Newspapers and Some Newspaper-men, Editor and Publisher* 17 November 1923: 12.
32. Don C. Seitz, "The American Press," six-part series, *Outlook* (6 January–3 February 1926): 6 January, 21.
33. Seitz, "Press," 6 January, 21.
34. Seitz, "Press," 6 January, 22.
35. Seitz, "Press," 10 February, 209.
36. Seitz "Press," 10 February, 210.
37. Lucy Maynard Salmon, *The Newspaper and the Historian* (New York: Oxford University Press, 1923), 428.
38. Lucy Maynard Salmon, *The Newspaper and Authority* (New York: Oxford University Press, 1923), 467.
39. John D. Stevens, "Social Utility of Sensational News: Murder and Divorce in the 1920s," *Journalism Quarterly* 61 (Spring 1985): 54.
40. Oswald Garrison Villard and Martin Weyrauch, "Are Tabloids a Menace?" *Forum* 77 (April 1927): 493.
41. Villard, "Menace," 485.
42. Villard, "Menace," 486.
43. Villard, "Menace," 489.
44. Villard, "Menace," 501.
45. Editorial, "Censorship or—?" *Editor and Publisher* (5 February 1927): 34.

46. "Vice Society Hales N.Y. Graphic to Court," *Editor and Publisher* (12 February 1927): 5.
47. "Shadow of Censorship Menaces Press: Many Editors Revolt at Browning Smut," *Editor and Publisher* (5 February 1927): 1.
48. "N.Y. State Committee Hits Crime News," *Editor and Publisher* (9 April 1927): 35.
49. Editorial, "A Strange Report," *Editor and Publisher* (9 April 1927): 48.
50. Silas Bent, *Ballyhoo* (New York: Boni & Liveright, 1927), xiv–xv. A later book, Simon M. Bessie, *Jazz Journalism: The Story of the Tabloid Newspaper* (New York: Dutton, 1938) may be more thorough.
51. Bent, *Ballyhoo*, 265.
52. Bent, *Ballyhoo*, 261.
53. Bent, *Ballyhoo*, 371–72.
54. Bent, *Ballyhoo*, 371–72.
55. Bent, *Ballyhoo*, 379.
56. Silas Bent, "Lindbergh and the Press," *Outlook* 160 (April 1932): 212.
57. Bent, "Lindbergh," 212.
58. Bent, "Lindbergh," 240.
59. John F. Roche, "False Rumors and Demands for Press Silence Complicate Lindbergh Kidnapping Story," *Editor and Publisher* (12 March 1932): 1. See also: "Editors Differ on Kidnap Broadcast," *Editor and Publisher* (19 March 1932).
60. "Has the Press Hampered the Search for the Lindbergh Baby?" *Literary Digest* 114 (30 April 1932): 34–35.
61. Mitchell Dawson, "Paul Pry and Privacy," *Atlantic Monthly* 150 (October 1932): 394.
62. "Regulation of Trial Coverage Urged in Bar Association Report," *Editor and Publisher* (18 September 1937): 5.
63. Meyer Berger, "Surrender of Privacy," *Scribner's* 105 (April 1939): 16–21.

# CHAPTER 7

# Reach for the High Ground: 1923–1929

Reform of American journalism should come from within. The journalists themselves have the power to sustain the role of the press as a popular educator and an important force for the betterment of society. Many critics inside and outside journalism had been saying that for decades, and by the early 1920s there was organized response. The spirit of professionalism pervading the new schools and departments of journalism led to textbooks and seminars linking the practicing journalists with the academy. State associations of journalists formulated codes of ethics, and in 1923 the metropolitan daily newspaper editors met to create the American Society of Newspaper Editors (ASNE). There was a willingness to engage in self-criticism and push toward codifying the best journalistic values and standards that had emerged, even though the codes were voluntary and the principles covered a range from practical to moral.

The modern newspaper was a technological wonder, manned by impersonal swarms of "leg men," "rewrite men," "copy editors," and a few "sob sisters," all rushing to get the latest news into print ahead of the competition. Contact with the local community had become quick and impersonal; the professionals seemed to be all over the city but not of it. Circulation and advertising profits dominated the thinking of most of the newspaper owners. Reporters learned how to behave on the job, or rather, they learned what they could get away with as long as they fulfilled the command of "get the story, or don't come back." The scoop, the story, the chase, was the thing. People became stories, a means to an end. That end was ever-greater profits.[1]

When this free-for-all behavior exceeded the community's tolerance, public criticism escalated and found support among many responsible editors, journalists, and educators. At about the same time, the scientific spirit of inquiry began to dominate in the educational institutions, and journalism schools adopted the social science mode of academic research. At some urban newspapers, codes of ethics, mottoes, or pledges provided standards to be followed. The strident voices of national critics and the leadership of national professional associations began to replace the influence of community monitoring for the metropolitan press.

Casper S. Yost, chief of the editorial page at the *St. Louis Globe-Democrat*, was one of the concerned editors. He said that he called a meeting of four other editors in 1922 to see if they too would support forming an organization that would develop a stronger professional spirit and raise the professional and ethical standards for journalism. They agreed, and held the first session of ASNE the following year in the nation's capital city. Their first project was writing a code of ethics or canon, which was adopted by the 107 members at that 1923 session.[2]

Yost, the first president, described the need for ASNE. Editors had become "anonymous beings, subordinating their identities to their institutions," he said. The days of personal journalism, when individual editors expressed the views of the paper, were gone. The newspaper had become an institution and editors "served it and passed on." We have been "too deeply absorbed in our individual tasks and obligations to pay much attention to our profession as a whole," he said, "or to permit much contact with our kind." He likened the editors to monks in their cells, and he warned that editors needed to mingle, develop professional solidarity, and to discuss the "mature problems of their profession."[3]

In his presidential address Yost lamented that journalism was almost "bookless," and he exhorted members to develop that needed body of professional literature. He believed the group also should respond to "unjust criticism" as well as build public confidence by establishing "definite standards of journalistic conduct . . . a code of professional ethics by which public and profession could measure their conduct."[4]

From the start, ASNE formed committees around the topical professional issues, including ethics, press law, syndicates, publicity, journalism education, and reporting. They invited top political and journalistic leaders to address their sessions, and usually met with the President of the United States in an off-the-record session near the end of each national meeting.

## A CANON OF ETHICS

When the *Canons of Journalism* were presented to the membership by H. J. Wright of the *New York Globe*, who had been given the task of developing them, he explained that all existing codes of the state journalistic associations had been consulted in order to make one that covered all the key points.

Wright worried that the editors might think the code "bombastic and self-righteous," but he wanted the public to see that journalists were taking themselves seriously and waking up to their responsibilities as the chief institution through which public opinion is formed.[5]

The code, which emphasized the journalist's support of freedom of speech and press and bound members to work for accuracy, truth, decency, and fairness, was well received. There was considerable debate over the matter of enforcement.[6] One group believed that the only way the code would have meaning was for the organization to be able to expel members that violated its tenets. "Lacking teeth, it is a beautiful gesture that is perfectly meaningless," said Bayard Swope of the *New York World*.[7] Others said that journalists who lived by freedom of speech should not censor anyone else. In the end they decided against a grievance board, but authorized their board of directors to handle problems of professional misconduct. This became a problem and an embarrassment for ASNE in its first decade.

Already in 1924 one of their members, Frederick G. Bonfils of the *Denver Post*, was under scrutiny for possible misuse of his newspaper in connection with the Teapot Dome scandal. The ASNE board voted to expel Bonfils, but Bonfils threatened to sue each board member. The *Canons* had not been made a part of the ASNE Constitution; thus they could not be enforced by the organization. That made each of the directors personally responsible for the expulsion, ASNE's legal counsel explained.[8] The board dropped its action; Bonfils resigned in 1927. But the matter simmered, provoking acrimonious sessions until 1932, when the opposing sides ironed out their differences. They agreed that ASNE should be able to expel a member, but that individuals should have an opportunity to appeal. To date ASNE has never expelled a member.[9]

## SENSITIVITY TO CRITICISM

The American press has always been thin-skinned. As the institution that shines the light of public scrutiny on all other members and institutions in society, the leaders of the press generally have been unwilling to lay aside a double standard of little or no comment about press behavior. As some editors have admitted, criticism is often deserved, but much of it that gained the most public attention came from people with causes of their own to promote, contending political ideologies, or personal grudges. A common institutional response was to ignore the outside critics, label them cranks or kooks, and wait for it all to blow over. But criticism from the leading press institutions was given serious attention, so professional organizations and schools became potentially important sources of self-criticism for the institution.

"The period of 1918 to 1923 ranks as one of abnormally persistent, searching and severe criticism of the American press," said Paul Bellamy, chair of ASNE's integrity committee in 1927. "It poured upon us in a perfect flood from magazine, periodical and platform—it seemed novel, fresh, interesting. Everybody noticed."[10]

But with economic prosperity, people became more satisfied and cared less about improving public or government institutions. They wanted to be entertained. Bellamy saw a new source of criticism emerging from the public officials, "who attempted to feed colored news to newspapers or news services through publicity."[11] He urged ASNE to commend Don R. Mellett of the *Canton Ohio Daily News* for his courageous fight against crooked politics in his city, and called his murder "the most outrageous assault on the integrity of the press." Mellett had exposed connections between city officials and organized crime, and as a result the governor had removed Canton's mayor from office. Mellett was shot one night as he parked his car in his garage; a few months later the town voted the mayor and his associates back into office.[12] ASNE had to "repulse attacks from without," said Bellamy, and "clean up from within." Crooked newspapers and grafting reporters hurt the press. We must "move to a higher standard of conduct."[13]

## CALL FOR SELF-CRITICISM

Outside criticism encouraged insider scrutiny of the press and a search for models and standards. Dean Eric W. Allen, president of the American Association of Schools and Departments of Journalism, was encouraged by the developments of 1923. As head of the University of Oregon's School of Journalism and an advocate of professionalism, he led a study of British and European newspaper organizations. There was a "faint suggestion detected here and there of a new attitude" toward journalism on the part of the newspaper worker, he said.[14] "If there is any one thing the American newspaper has needed and needs today, it is a spirit of searching, yet unexcited self-criticism. If there is anything that this stormy petrel of the professions has never had, it is just that. Vituperation from without; passionate, yet none too sincere, rebuttal from within—these do not constitute an atmosphere in which good critical thinking is likely to be done."[15]

American journalism lacked a professional tradition, Allen explained. It had a short history, lacking established traditions against which to judge the successful and responsible as well as the quacks. "The cub reporter is still initiated into a world of moral and intellectual confusion, where it is almost impossible for him to discover what are the higher professional aims of his calling," he said. Success seemed to be conspicuous attention and large circulation, Allen observed, instead of contribution to the public good.[16]

Allen called for informed criticism from scholars as well as from newspaper people that would better the press and help it develop a sense of proportion. "As effective criticism develops within the profession and true standards are set and recognized by newspaper men, it will become easier to separate the wheat from the chaff in what the critics say, and the candid friend speaking from the outside will find a certain uncomfortable welcome from the profession if he is speaking the truth." Allen asked journalism schools to look on the press as an institution that is an important social force and to educate professionals who will be more self-critical.[17]

This theme was sounded in the 1927 ASNE meeting by Senator James A. Reed (D–Missouri), who said that "no class of men is charged with so high a responsibility as you gentlemen who sit before me today. You can make war and you can make peace."[18] But he cautioned them to think about the consequences of their decisions as they considered sensational stories. The public has no other source of public opinion but the press, and "public opinion is the creator of the state and the prophet of the future," so the press should perform with "care and circumspection."[19]

*Detroit News* editor Malcolm W. Bingay followed with similar sentiments, declaring that "the curse of American journalism is a lack of introspection."[20] We should consider Edmund Burke's description of the press as the "Fourth Estate" more powerful than the other three estates, and we should not lose sight of the obligation that goes with that. The press has to train reporters not only in academic and professional subjects, he suggested, but also in manners, morals, ethics, and courtesy.[21]

"Blessed be the critics of newspapers," declared Paul Bellamy, managing editor of the *Cleveland Plain Dealer*, in his 1924 ASNE presidential address.[22] The newspapers needed to be treated "to a dose of their own medicine," he declared. The public is the daily judge of the press, but newspapers were more apt to hear about it when the reaction was unfavorable. And "they were hearing it now."[23] He listed several examples: *The Brass Check* was getting a lot of attention; and H. L. Mencken in his *Smart Set* magazine said the average newspaper was even worse than Sinclair said it was; a speaker at the University of Missouri's recent Journalism Week had charged that newspapers were "driven by ham-minded merchants" without standards, and several other critics believed newspapers were subservient to business interests.[24]

Three main charges typified all the criticism, Bellamy noted: first, business office control; second, overemphasis on sex, crime, and trivia; and third, poor newswriting. Recent studies showed that labor news and reporting about Russia were biased and distorted. "These are serious charges," said Bellamy. "Democratic society can't endure unless we are well informed. To present a true picture we must consider the average man."[25]

"Crime news is not overcovered," Bellamy explained, not when you measure the column inches devoted to it. But he agreed that newspapers did fail to get the news of government and were plagued by press agents. Despite these problems, he thought that news personnel were much better than they had been fifteen years ago (more were college educated).[26]

ASNE's Committee on Integrity of the Press was established to examine unfair criticism and counter the errors. But the committee quickly realized that this was a tough assignment. It tried to find a way to respond without appearing to want to close off the public discussion. In 1928 ASNE demonstrated its openness to criticism by inviting a panel of distinguished leaders from several fields to flail away at the assembled editors.[27] A lawyer, doctor, pastor, and politician told the ASNE exactly what they disliked about the newspapers. The session was preceded by a long session on the need for greater moral responsibility for the press, especially in reporting crime and cheap sensations. Fred Fuller Shedd, chairman of the ASNE Ethical Standards Committee and editor of the *Philadelphia Evening Bulletin*, had already set the theme with his declaration that cheap sensations sold papers but also "produced cheap thinking and cheap expressions of thought and consequently cheap moral conduct."[28]

Attorney Clarence Darrow led off the critics' session with the charge that the contemporary newspaper was a purely "commercial enterprise," no longer interested in ideas, and that it was part of an age that thinks of "nothing but money."[29] An idealistic editor would go broke, he speculated, in the "present scheme of things." What he wanted was thorough reporting that would get all sides of the issues, not play up sensations or impute motives to people. He asked newspapers not to be "in such haste to get out the news" because it created errors. The clever, sophisticated, skeptical, and intelligent newspapermen, he observed, were "too lacking in high ideals in a business filled with temptations but as such were in tune with the spirit of the age."[30]

Medical doctor Joseph Collins saw publicity and crime reporting as the major problems, and thought too little reporting dealt with the "great questions of the world—science, world hunger, birth control, longevity, and mental hygiene." The editors should raise the question "Where are we going?" even though the people were "emotionally sterile and unwilling to take risks." It was the newspapers that could shape opinion and be an influence for the public good.[31]

A Methodist pastor, the Reverend Ralph W. Sockman, attacked the overuse of publicity, propaganda, and sensationalism. Maryland Governor Albert C. Ritchie charged that the press was too cynical about men in public life, making their life difficult, discouraging others to seek this as a career. The press was hypocritical. It "professed to report and reflect public opinion" but was really creating the public appetite for news. It was a profitable business that was unwilling to admit its errors or accept the responsibility that came with great power.[32] "America's greatest contribution to the cause of human freedom is our doctrine of the freedom of the press—free even to abuse its freedom," said Ritchie. It was a freedom to think and print the news, but that carried with it "the highest obligations of responsibility."[33]

The critical session was wrapped up by Silas Bent, former journalist and author of *Ballyhoo*, who affirmed the need for press responsibility. "There is no visible evidence that editors are getting out the kind of newspapers people want," he charged. "Newspapermen have deceived their public and betrayed it." Bent was ashamed of his profession and could not reconcile the "selling of news like hooch" with the personal character of the editors he knew. Newspapers are big, profitable, and independent, he summed up, and now "they must become responsible."[34]

A cynical rebuttal to the critics by ASNE member William T. Ellis captures the essence of insensitivity and arrogance abroad in the profession. He said that Mr. Darrow had arraigned journalism and "engaged in character invectives," while the medical doctor gave a psychological "dissertation on life and said we are all getting crazier." The preacher, he went on, acted like he was at his first fair, and "Mr. Bent, our wailing Jeremiah, presented facts that are not facts."[35] It was an experiment in public criticism that would not soon be repeated by ASNE, although the group continued to respond to criticism at their meetings and in their newsletter. One action they took was to join with the American Bar Association to work on standards that would lead to responsible reporting of crime, taking into account the rights of the accused and the public interest in the news.[36]

## CHAIN PROBLEM

One frequent target of attack was the growth of chains of newspapers under a single, nationwide ownership and the potential damage to diversity of opinions, corporate suppression of news, standardization of contents, and absence of community involvement in the news.[37] Said Roy Howard, partner and business manager of the Scripps-Howard newspapers: "Standardization is not a negative . . . it provides a better product for more people . . . contributes to the development of a true American homogeneity."[38]

Howard explained that the costs and complexity of modern newspaper production had created the syndicates and chains, and that those provided access to the "best minds in America" by the smallest towns across the nation. "The passing of personal journalism is not a great calamity," he noted, even though the press had lost some of its "picturesque character." He thought the contemporary newspaper had better editorials, more tolerance, better news, and better leadership.[39]

Not all American newspapers were losing influence, he said. The only loss of influence was at newspapers "edited by demagogues seeking to inflame public opinion and stampede mass action for their own aggrandizement, and newspapers willing to prostitute themselves in the service of vested interests and public exploiters."[40] The successful newspapers of the future, Howard predicted, would be those devoting more energy to enabling readers to "think intelligently for themselves instead of attempting to do their thinking for them." He said that people no longer tolerated corrupt newspapers nor venal chains, and that "editorial judgment, news judgment, unselfish and effective public service will be the key elements of successful newspapers . . . not mere dollars."[41]

The same issue was discussed by Colonel Frank Knox, general manager of the Hearst newspapers and president of ASNE, in 1929. He told members that the chain was "necessary and inevitable growth for newspapers," similar to the growth in other areas of business. He believed that newspapers did respond to pressure from readers who wanted a complete newspaper. A new generation of readers wanted "to pick and choose" from the "latest and best of everything."[42] The newspaper was a cog in a big merchandising machine, Knox admitted. Advertisers wanted to reach large numbers and disliked the many competing newspapers with overlapping audiences. The newspaper was responding to these pressures, he explained, and was reaching the women who did 80 percent of the buying of goods sold. Newspapers were grouping and sharing to "rationalize the costs," but this was not a menace.

Knox believed it actually provided "greater independence and freedom for the press." The chains had more resources. This would be a menace only if the chains "bind themselves to unselfish and un-American ambitions." On the contrary, chains could "bind the nation together and make it truly united, less sectionalist," said Knox. Howard, speaking from the audience, added that chains "just grew . . . were here to stay . . . were sound economic operations and not a menace. He pointed out that his editors were stockholders and had more local autonomy than any other group.[43] Those defenses would become more familiar as the monopoly trend rolled on in post–World War II America. It is a classic linking of the myth of American individualism and freedom with free enterprise and its promise of voluntary corporate responsibility. It asks for the audience's trust without offering any means of accountability. The tactic is popular with political leaders who play on such resonant American themes that guarantee an emotional response.

## ACCREDITING THE SCHOOLS

Criticism from inside and out kept debates at ASNE lively, and these issues were also reflected in the professional and popular magazines. ASNE built on the growing interest in professionalism to press for adoption of codes of ethics, ways of raising the status of journalists, and improvement in the quality of journalism education. They looked into the experiences of other countries with journalistic institutes, guilds and unions, and matters of setting standards and licensing recognized journalists. Most successful, perhaps, were their efforts in education.

ASNE from its earliest days expressed concern over the varied quality of education offered in the new journalism schools and departments. The editors were not only interested in developing good future employees, but saw the importance of journalism education in raising the quality of journalism in the country and its standing as a respected profession. President Yost had asked for greater cooperation between the professionals and the schools in his first address. He noted the need for professionals to teach and provide visiting lectures in the schools, and he was already worried about the number of students being attracted away to publicity work.

In 1928, 18 of the 53 schools and departments of journalism had formed the American Association of Schools and Departments of Journalism (AASDJ), and were informally considered the Class A schools. Overall, journalism education in 35 states enrolled 5,526 students during 1926–27, about 40 percent of whom were female. There were 430 teachers, including 55 females, and they averaged six years of newspaper experience and eight years of teaching. The ASNE report cited Columbia University, the Universities of Missouri, Illinois, Oregon, and Wisconsin as the leading schools, pioneering curriculum, scholarly associations, writing textbooks, and conducting research.[44] Typical courses in these premier pioneer schools included: news writing and editing, law of the press, history of journalism, and ethics of journalism. Students did three-quarters of their work in general academic liberal arts subjects.[45]

There was also a strong feeling that journalism, like law and medicine, should become graduate education. Columbia converted to a graduate program, and some other schools added a fifth-year M.A. degree. During these years, competing philosophies emphasized the trade school versus the broad liberal arts education as journalism struggled for professional and academic acceptance. Journalism educators devoted their annual meetings to a variety of projects that would enhance professional education and improve methods of teaching. In 1921 they invited the Carnegie Foundation to make a study of the teaching of journalism, as it had for law and medicine. They reacted to critics like Mencken who charged that the journalism schools were "too easy."[46]

A small tempest was raised by Lawrence Abbott, contributing editor of *Outlook*, who attacked the "mediocre journalism schools" as trade schools and advocated a liberal education for those contemplating journalism careers. He was forced to publish a retraction after reading the principles and standards adopted by the AASDJ. Abbott admitted his surprise and pleasure at learning that social sciences, humanities, and natural sciences were all required for a B.A. in journalism, and he found the standards "admirable."[47]

AASDJ also advocated standards for the teachers, establishing five years of professional experience as a minimum for full-time teachers. At one point the group proposed giving each graduate an identification card that affirmed that the student "was adequately prepared to engage in journalistic work." This action would serve as a temporary measure, until the schools and professionals worked out formal accreditation.[48]

By the end of the 1920s the teachers believed they had accomplished much on the road toward standardizing the quality of instruction in college journalism. The twenty-one member schools of AASDJ voluntarily followed a list of fifteen criteria set for the group. Professor Willard G. Bleyer of the University of Wisconsin is credited with the one-fourth journalism and three-fourths liberal arts formula that journalism schools have generally followed in setting graduation requirements since the 1920s. He also led the development of scholarly research and doctoral study in journalism, and the accompanying development of scholarly publications.[49]

## LICENSING REVIVED

The journalism educators apparently did not take up the matter of a formal mechanism for monitoring the profession, perhaps believing that raising the educational level and inculcating high standards in the young would be effective in stopping this line of criticism. But there were still some individual educators who would support a kind of licensing system that would put journalists on the same level as lawyers and doctors.[50] Talcott Williams, Columbia University's first dean of the journalism school, believed that journalism training was developing just as law had developed. College men had been in journalism since the 1870s, and in another sixty years, he thought, would have specified training requirements, including number of years in professional work, education, and a form of comprehensive examination.[51]

Bleyer agreed that in order to have "intelligent, competent and reliable journalists," it would be necessary to have "standards for admission and standards of practice," but he noted that newspapers solidly opposed the licensing proposals. He told the Inland Daily Press Association in 1924 that journalism would be a profession, not a game or a trade, and that it was already "emerging from the apprenticeship method into the professional school method of training its recruits." The same development had taken place in other professions, but so far there were no definite requirements for admission to the practice of journalism. "Anyone may become a reporter."[52]

The growth of the middle class and the culture of professionalism was a mid-Victorian achievement, according to Burton J. Bledstein. The professional person gains status and autonomy through the mastery of a field of expertise that separates him from others. The professionals guard the boundaries of their specialty with licensing, regulation of standards, punishment for infractions, and scrupulous absence of public criticism of their peers. They maintain the ethic of service and practice a detatched manner that allows them to offer advice and objective solutions without emotional involvement.[53] Journalism's obvious lack of perfect "fit" to the professional standard would cause it continued troubles as it pursued that goal. A system of licensing is "not only feasible but is necessary," Bleyer said, supporting a similar statement by William Allen White, the nationally acclaimed small-town publisher-editor. "Journalism today is the only unorganized profession." Professional status would provide a greater feeling of solidarity among all newspaper writers and editors, improve salary scales, and attract men of ability and public respect, he explained.[54]

But Lawrence W. Murphy, of the University of Illinois, made a serious licensing proposal and found it raised strong hostility. He devised a two-day examination and tested twenty-five advanced-level journalism students and local newspaper reporters. The test covered journalistic practices, history, literature, sociology, economics, and political science.[55] He thought the examination could be used to establish a category of specialized reporter, educated and prepared to undertake specific categories of reporting, but not to bar unlicensed writers from general reporting, or society or feature writing.[56]

The next year, however, Murphy chaired the Illinois Press Association Committee on Education, which introduced a licensing proposal in the state legislature. That proposal required five years of experience for those presently working in journalism and a combination of education plus experience for those in school. The Illinois Press Association would certify the journalist's professional standing, and that would keep control within the profession and not put it in the hands of the state. The purpose, according to Murphy, was to "preserve all the good features of the licensing system without sacrificing freedom of the press or placing the press in the hands of politicians."[57] It failed. *Editor and Publisher*, which first found merit in the idea, by 1926 was strongly opposed to placing journalists under the control of state press associations and/or government.[58]

## TEACHING APPLIED ETHICS

The ethics books and courses that flourished in the 1920s were favorably received as a mechanism for raising the standards in journalism. Ethics were discussed in professional and academic groups and in their journals. A special issue of the *Annals of the American Academy of Political and Social Sciences* was devoted to the ethics of the professions, and journalism was included.[59] Five books on journalism ethics appeared in the decade, and their approach was to make journalistic ethics a matter of individual, personal responsibility, as Clifford Christians points out in his study.[60]

Mencken observed that it was good that journalistic soul-searching was going on, but he wryly observed that the journalist is "still a hired man . . . (while) a professional is answerable for his conduct to his peers. The journalist is in between." Mencken said that codes of ethics would be accepted, as long as they did not hurt profits, but journalists would still have no control over their salaries, would still compete in the market, and be subject to firing. Journalists were mostly uneducated men, their ignorance dragging down American journalism, Mencken believed. They needed to work on education, language, editing, accuracy, and performance standards—"clean house before they can dignify their trade."[61]

The most complete and often-quoted text on journalistic ethics was published in 1924 by Nelson A. Crawford, head of the Department of Industrial Journalism at Kansas State Agricultural College. *The Ethics of Journalism* opened with a discussion of the public charges against contemporary journalism and the public's belief that the newspaper was not fulfilling its function, not telling the truth, and was suppressing news to help political parties or advertisers. Crawford examined these familiar charges and offered some technical and practical explanations and defenses. The text poses a wide variety of ethical cases, choices, and possible solutions for readers. It represents the best thinking on the subject in its day, and is noteworthy, too, for its early and thorough discussion of the concept of journalistic objectivity, which had become the accepted standard.

"The public wants objective facts presented in an unbiased manner," Crawford said.[62] He saw "objectivity in the dissemination of the facts as the primary ideal of the press." He thought everyone was in agreement with the philosophy, but the practice was another matter. Science had made great advances and the speculative method had been abandoned in favor of the investigative method.[63] The press should follow that model, "striving for proportion and balance," trying to be fair and following an objective vision and agreed-upon rules about the practice of journalism. Crawford referred to Lippmann's study of public opinion, and he approved of the idea of independent and impartial fact-finding agencies to serve as intelligence bureaus for the press.[64]

## NATIONAL STUDY PROPOSED

Crawford advocated some form of entrance standards for professional journalists, and he asked for a national study of the press. Criticism of the press by people "strongly opposed to the press draws little sympathy or attention to improving conditions . . . and doesn't provide much evidence to support the conclusions." What was needed was a large, "endowed study that would be made by a representative committee of fair-minded analysts who were familiar with journalistic practices and would cover various sections of the country and types of newspapers."[65]

In the meantime, Crawford worked to introduce ethics into the journalism schools and advocated curricula that supported professional ideals. He advocated an end to faculty censorship of student newspapers, replacing it with instruction that developed responsible student editors. Students, he pointed out, might lack judgment, but "censorship was used to protect the schools and to keep the public from learning what was going on."[66]

Truth to Crawford was the highest good in society, and he referred to

Lippmann's notion of two environments to illustrate the importance of journalism's service to the truth. Lippmann had said there was a real environment and then there was the environment formed by the "pictures in our heads." Journalists provided most of those "pictures" for the public, and Crawford thought they had to work "to release the public from ignorance, inertia and fear." Opinions were merely opinions, but "journalists should provide the facts that are needed to test those opinions."[67]

Leon N. Flint's book, *Conscience of the Newspaper*, provided a good companion to Crawford's text, by offering case studies for discussion on each of the major ethical issues in journalism. He, too, argued for the independence of the press from political parties and advertisers, and advocated giving the public "what it needs." Journalism was something like a public utility, "not quite a profession and something more than a business," as he saw it. That meant journalism had "an implied contract to the people, to serve the community and the society."[68] But journalists were only partly responsible for the shortcomings of the press; "some of the responsibility rested on the public and required readers to react."[69]

Journalism in the 1920s, under heavy pressure from its critics, grew in importance and stature and strained toward the goal of professionalism, but fell short of reaching any consensus on the desirability or means of professional accountability. The thrust of the talk was to place the greatest hope on the professional organizations and schools that would inculcate and maintain the higher moral standards, set some rules for proper journalistic behavior, and enforce them through peer pressure and personal ethical behavior. There would be a cleansing effect on the entire institution, without sacrificing the precious freedoms of speech and press to any organized form of outside control. Journalism would remain part art, part craft, part profession. Flawed as that was, it seemed for the time to be the only way to balance the competing forces of the market place and democratic ideals. The public would provide external, informal monitoring. Faith in democratic ideology was still intact, but doubt was just around the corner.

## NOTES

1. A vivid portrait of the era is found in A. A. Dornfeld, *Hello Sweetheart, Get Me Rewrite!* (Chicago: Academy Chicago Publications, 1988), originally published as *Behind the Front Page* (1983). See also the fictional portraits in Howard Good, *Acquainted*: and my Chap. 1, n. 34.
2. *Problems of Journalism: ASNE Proceedings* (1923): 1–2.
3. *Problems*, 1923, 16.
4. *Problems*, 1923, 18.
5. *Problems*, 1923, 40–41.
6. *Problems*, 1923, 1–2.
7. *Problems*, 1923, 118.

8. "F. G. Bonfils, Denver Publisher Dies," *Editor and Publisher* (4 February 1933): 7.

9. *Problems*, 1932, 39. Personal correspondence from Lee Stinnett, executive director ASNE, 13 July 1989 to the author. In 1986 ASNE discussed a proposal to drop the code, but retained it. That same year SPJ, SDX voted to remove a censure clause in its ethics code. The debate was as divided in 1986 as it had been in the 1920s. See: "Journalist Groups Arguing Over the Need for Strong Ethics Codes," by Frank Sutherland, *ASNE Bulletin*, December 1987: 4–5.

10. *Problems*, 1927, 153. My search turned up 167 critical magazine articles in the 1910s, 153 in the 1920s, and 216 in the 1930s, with a decline to 100 in the 1940s. Bellamy's perception of growing criticism is probably correct, because there were also several important critical books and discussions in the professional and academic circles.

11. *Problems*, 1927, 155.

12. MacDougal, *Newsroom Problems*, 151. The Mellett Memorial Lectures began at the University of Missouri in 1929. Mellett was killed July 16, 1926.

13. *Problems*, 1927, 156.

14. Eric W. Allen, "Newspapers Need Criticism, *Editor and Publisher* (8 September 1923): 1.

15. Allen, "Criticism," 1.

16. Allen, "Criticism," 1.

17. Allen, "Criticism," 1.

18. *Problems*, 1927, 38.

19. *Problems*, 1927, 39.

20. *Problems*, 1927, 86.

21. *Problems*, 1927, 87–89.

22. *Problems*, 1924, 111.

23. *Problems*, 1924, 112.

24. *Problems*, 1924, 113.

25. *Problems*, 1924, 121.

26. *Problems*, 1924, 126.

27. *Problems*, 1928, 26.

28. *Problems*, 1928, 54.

29. *Problems*, 1928, 54–63.

30. *Problems*, 1928, 65–72.

31. *Problems*, 1928, 76–111.

32. *Problems*, 1928, 110.

33. *Problems*, 1928, 115.

34. *Problems*, 1928, 161.

35. *Problems*, 1928, 170.

36. *Problems*, 1927, 210.

37. Between 1910 and 1930 U.S. population and total daily newspaper circulation rose roughly parallel, but the number of one-newspaper cities rose from 20.6 percent to 57.1 percent in that period. The trend accelerated so that by 1976 only 2.5 percent of the cities had competing newspapers. Circulation in proportion to the population started a decline in 1960. National average (read yesterday) newspaper readership declined 12 percent between 1967 and 1985. (Gamst, Alldridge, and Bush, "Effects of Targeted Sales Messages on Subscription Sales

and Retention," *Journalism Quarterly* 64 [Summer 1987]: 463.) For about 50 years roughly every 3.6 persons subscribed to a daily newspaper. In 1989 only 51 percent of the population read a newspaper, down from 73 percent in 1967. See: Betty W. Cox, "Spoon-Feeding the Baby Boomers," *APME News* (15 June 1989): 3. Between 1910 and 1980 the number of dailies declined from 2,200 to 1,730. See: Emery, *Press*, 430, 436. But the critics' predictions were on target as Ben Bagdikian shows in *Media Monopoly* (Boston: Beacon Press, 1983, 4): 20 corporations controlled more than half the total daily circulation in the early 1980s and 50 corporations controlled most of the mass media outlets. That trend accelerated in the late 1980s with megamergers like Time Inc. with Warner Communications as media corporations extended their international services and range of operations.

38. *Problems*, 1927, 210.
39. *Problems*, 1927, 210.
40. *Problems*, 1927, 211.
41. *Problems*, 1927, 212.
42. *Problems*, 1929, 105.
43. *Problems*, 1929, 107, 109
44. *Problems*, 1928, 42.
45. Vernon Nash, *What Is Taught in Schools of Journalism*, Bulletin 29, #54 (Columbia, Mo.: University of Missouri, 1928).
46. H. L. M., editorial, *American Mercury* 2 (October 1924): 155–59.
47. Lawrence Abbott, "An Apology," *Outlook* (24 February 1926): 283–84.
48. "Five Years of Newspaper Experience Suggested for Journalism Teachers," *Editor and Publisher* (5 January 1929): 16. For formation of national council see: *Editor and Publisher* (28 January 1939): 8.
49. AEJMC, *75 Years*, 5.
50. For extended discussion of licensing see: Petersen, "Unthinkable."
51. Talcott Williams, *The Newspaper Man* (New York: Scribner, 1922), 123.
52. Willard G. Bleyer, "Bleyer Says Journalism is Only Unorganized Profession," *Editor and Publisher* (18 October 1924): 8.
53. Burton J. Bledstein, *The Culture of Professionalism* (New York: Norton, 1978), 87; and Jethro K. Lieberman, *The Tyranny of the Experts* (New York: Walker, 1970), 57–58.
54. Bleyer, speech, 33.
55. "Licensing Idea for Journalists Given Trial," *Editor and Publisher* (25 July 1925 ): 9.
56. "Licensing," 9.
57. "State Certificates for Newspaper Men Advocated by Illinois Press," *Editor and Publisher* (13 March 1926): 11. See also: my Chap. 5, n. 17.
58. Editorial, "Professional Status," *Editor and Publisher* (13 March 1926): 32.
59. "The Ethics of the Professions and of Business," Supplement, *Annals of the American Academy of Political and Social Sciences* (Philadelphia: AAPSS, 1922), Part VII: 169–87.
60. Clifford G. Christians, "Fifty Years of Scholarship in Media Ethics," *Journal of Communication* 27 (Autumn 1977). The books are: Nelson A. Crawford, *The Ethics of Journalism* (New York: Alfred A. Knopf, 1924); Casper S. Yost, *The Principles of Journalism* (New York: Appleton, 1924); Thomas A. Lahey, *The*

*Morals of Newspaper Making* (Notre Dame: University of Notre Dame, 1924); Leon Nelson Flint, *The Conscience of the Newspaper: A Case Book in the Principles and Problems of Journalism* (New York: Appleton-Century, 1925); and William Futhey Gibbons, *Newspaper Ethics* (Ann Arbor: Edwards Brothers, 1926).

61. Mencken, editorial, 155–9.
62. Crawford, *Ethics*, 39.
63. Crawford, *Ethics*, 99.
64. Crawford, *Ethics*, Chap. 11.
65. Crawford, *Ethics*, 164. See also: "Rockefeller Money Backs Scientific Probe of News Methods and Sources," *Editor and Publisher* (6 September 1924): 3, and Chap. 9 of this book.
66. Crawford, *Ethics*, 174.
67. Crawford, *Ethics*, 178.
68. Flint, *Conscience*, 129.
69. Flint, *Conscience*, 271.

# CHAPTER 8

# Propaganda, Publicity, and Public Opinion: 1911–1928

Along with concern about the growing commercialization of the press in the 1920s, critics worried about the power of propaganda as it might be used in peacetime by government and big business to mobilize masses. The war had accelerated the commercialization of the press; rising costs of newsprint and wartime shortages sped up the trend to newspaper chains and one-newspaper cities. Money-saving strategies like wire service news and syndicated features made for more homogenized newspapers. Free publicity releases could work in the same way, if they were used as fillers and not checked. Critics feared the loss of a diversity of voices, replaced by a glut of propaganda. Before World War I, it was widely believed that a public with access to the facts would promote enlightened government. After the war it was just as easy to believe that an irrational public could be victimized by emotions whipped up by the propagandist who propagated opinion as fact. Democracy was in trouble.

The nation and its journalists had responded quickly to President Woodrow Wilson's call to mobilize public opinion to support American entry into the war. The Committee for Public Information (CPI), led by George Creel, attracted many journalists, publicists, artists, photographers, and filmmakers to the cause. Many of the men who would develop the American public relations profession and many critics of that profession forged their opinions in the experience of developing propaganda for the home front and abroad. The CPI, for example, employed Ivy Lee and Edward Bernays, both pioneers in public relations, as well as Walter Lippmann, Charles Merz, and Will Irwin from journalism. As Schudson sees it, the reporters learned that "facts themselves are not to be trusted" and could just as easily be used to create illusions.[1]

Some CPI press agents came from the earlier tradition of theatrical promotion of shows, performers, and circuses, and they knew the public's attention could be gained by stunts and sensations. They knew, too, how to create sensations that would find their way into the news pages. The journalists, on the other hand, worked in a tradition that separated fact from opinion, reserving the latter for the editorial page, while still allowing opinionated sensationalism and muckraking. Wartime propaganda could equally be justified by patriotism and national security. That was not the problem—peacetime propaganda was.

It was time to restore the "free play of public opinion," *New York World* editor Frank I. Cobb told the Women's City Club of New York in 1920.[2] Cobb said there had been none for five years because of the war, government censorship, and propaganda. Private propaganda had taken on a new phase, he warned, functioning not to tell the whole truth but to tell the truth that is "of greatest benefit to their clients." Such propaganda was flooding the newspapers, he said, so that readers couldn't tell what was truth and what was half truth. It was creating a "terror of mass thought" demagoguery.

Cobb insisted it was the newspaper's duty was to furnish raw materials for public opinion, but news of social unrest, strikes, and economic conditions were going unreported, Cobb charged. "The gravest duty that confronts the American press today is to bring these vast questions that have come out of the war into the forum of public discussion."[3]

"News that was tainted at the source" was another editor's worry. "The real menace of propaganda is the discovery by governments and other interested agencies that this extension of advertising—for that is what propaganda essentially is—can be readily utilized to sway and control democratic masses," warned Robert Herrick. He predicted that government would use it to confront the electorate, that the liquor forces would use it to link prohibition with Bolshevism, and that every great "interest" would organize its own form of "special pleading." The techniques, he explained, were misrepresentation, suppression, distortion, and direct falsehood. But Herrick hoped that propaganda would eventually kill itself by its own excesses and truth and democratic ideals would win.[4] Herrick was right—after the war, special pleading became a growth industry renamed "public relations."

On the press table at the National Press Club in Washington, D.C., according to journalist Roscoe Brown in 1921, were piles of press releases "like a free lunch counter," and they spread like "parasitic fungi" carried by the press agent. One Washington editor said he received the equivalent of twenty-four full newspaper pages of press releases daily; another estimated that there were 1,200 publicity agents before the war.[5]

Press agentry was changing newsgathering for the worse, Brown charged, keeping reporters away from sources, making them lazy, and turning newspapers into "retailers of ready-made intelligence . . . less of news than what somebody wishes to be considered news."[6] Executives were refusing to be interviewed; businesses found they could get their message directly into the newspapers through their puffery. According to Brown, "The essence of journalism is its autonomous expression of itself as an interpreter of society." The public expects what it reads in the newspapers to be the result of the newspaper's "independent outlook on the world in the capacity of a public watchman. That is its profession; that is its trust." Brown warned that the newspaper's distinction and claim to be the Fourth Estate would be lost if it became the mouthpiece of "irresponsible agents of propaganda."[7]

## CAMPAIGNING AGAINST FREE PUBLICITY

The newspaper publishers were already in the fight. The 1909 American Newspaper Publishers Association's (ANPA) convention had formed a Committee on Free Publicity to scout out and publicize to its members all known press agents and their tricks for getting free coverage.[8] The publishers' main concern was the loss of advertising to successful publicity campaigns that planted newspaper stories to attract audiences and businesses otherwise reached by advertising.

"A few purist editors have protested, all along, at this tainting of the stream of pure news," said Irwin. "However, the situation did not greatly agitate the newspaper publishers until its business aspect dawned on them."[9] The publishers circulated lists of agents and tried to get their members to boycott advertising from agencies that furnished publicity for their clients. In 1917 ANPA voted that free publicity in return for advertising contracts was "illegal and unethical," but some newspapers persisted in the practice.[10] Sports, amusements, and the auto industry were particularly successful in placing free publicity, as were some public utilities and businesses. The battle continued into the 1930s, when ANPA finally had to limit its efforts to fighting the most flagrant abuses, according to Ed Emery's study of the publishers association.[11]

Will Irwin, whose concern had been deepened by his experience in propaganda work during the war, wrote a two-part series on the subject for *Collier's* in 1923. "The public must understand this new era in journalism in order to deal with it," he said.[12] He speculated that editors who once tried to keep their news columns "clean and colorless" in order to influence readers through their editorial pages, now doubted that they had any power to influence public opinion. They had learned that the real power was in the news columns, said Irwin. This was where Americans gained their "pictures of the world," so influencing the news had become the new way "to mold public opinion." But the problem was, Irwin explained, that the public was unaware of the tainted quality of the news columns.

Truth, lies, and half-lies helped Germany prepare for and conduct the war, Irwin recalled. Even the peace treaty reporting was influenced by publicity agents. The new method of managing the news was cheaper and more effective than bribery or creating your own newspaper. "Get at the sources of the news —and slant it," Irwin said. And Americans had quickly learned to employ these tactics in wartime reporting. Irwin was worried that publicity efforts in the United States and abroad were being snatched up by peacetime business and government. "Nearly a thousand bureaus of propaganda had established their headquarters in Washington alone" by 1920, he observed. Newspapers had been raided of some of their best talent; publicity had attracted reporters by offers of better pay and higher status.[13]

*Editor and Publisher* joined a campaign uniting business, advertising, and publishing groups against publicity agents, targeting 1926 as the year to rid the industry of industrial press agentry, "the most destructive factor in advertising practice." Their editorial charged that press agentry created "artificial news," misused the editorial columns, and was a corruptive influence in the newspapers that lent credence to the charge that newspapers were "kept" by the corporations. Newspapers had to stop offering puffery for lucrative advertising contacts:

> The press, which has put the patent medicine faker out of business; which supports an international fight for truth in advertising; which is on an ethical pedestal before the American people; the press which has developed power to create consumer demand for merchandise in such volume that retailing has become in our day a relatively simple operation; the press which is jealous of its good name can in 1926 clean its own household of a scandal which cries aloud in every city and town on the map.[14]

Don Seitz, who had left the *New York World* to join *Outlook* magazine, carried the fight to the popular magazine audience the same year. Seitz had compiled a list of 1,400 press agents and had advised other publishers about them several years before the war, but his efforts had little impact. In fact, he was chagrined to note that business was elevating publicity to the "rank of a profession" and even graduates of the Pulitzer School for Journalism were joining the ranks.[15]

Editors should refuse the publicity stuff; they were partly to blame for the situation, Seitz said. Reporters should dig and discover the false leads and errors. The newspaper should be "shamed" back "into doing its own work— enterprise reporting, with unrelenting competition in the pursuit of news." This could help restore the newspaper's independence and individuality and the public's confidence.[16]

By 1929 there was a public relations course at Columbia (not in the journalism school), and in 1927 the public relations agents were starting their own professional organization in an attempt to "clean up the evil practices in publicity."[17] Opposition had not stopped publicity, nor tamed it very much, and the warnings were passed on to later generations of students and novice reporters.

## UNDERSTANDING PUBLIC OPINION

The whole question of how public opinion was formed and how it functioned in society was engaging the early social scientists of this period. Sociologist Charles Horton Cooley, for example, offered a theory in 1909 in his important work, *Social Organization*. He said the process of a group making up its mind was like that of an individual. "Public opinion is not a mere aggregate of separate individual judgments, but an organization, a cooperative product of communication and reciprocal influence." Public opinion results from giving time and attention to a question, searching for pertinent ideas and sentiments, and working them together into a whole. Individuals know what they think, Cooley said, and they are aware of the thoughts of others, as ideas and sentiments are exchanged and "poured into the general stream of thought." Then these ideas of communicating minds become a single organizing whole, a unity "not of one identity, but of life and action, a crystallization of diverse but related ideas," he theorized.[18]

Cooley made a distinction between a "true or mature opinion" and a "popular impression." The mature opinion requires "earnest attention and discussion for a considerable time, and when reached is significant, even if mistaken." Popular impression was "facile, shallow, transient, and fickle," usually related to matters of temporary interest. He believed that the mature public opinion was "nearly always superior" to the thoughts of any one of its members, and that group opinion was always subject to change and discussion in the society. It takes time to arouse public opinion, he observed, and "you cannot do it upon more than one matter at a time."[19]

The leaders of a society take the initiative in defining and organizing the public mind, he explained, and the public did not deal with the details of public business, but could "change direction, standards and policy." The masses, in Professor Cooley's view, "gave momentum and general direction to progress," leaving the particulars to be handed to leaders and trained experts. He did not, as so many popular writers of the day did, think democracy was endangered by being ruled by "the crowd, swayed and moved," and out of control. Rather, he said, healthy democracy is a "training in judgment and self-control as applied to political action," and the disturbances of "contending passions" provide confidence and understanding of the basic stability of things.[20]

The earliest and most widely applied analysis of public opinion and the press in modern America came from Walter Lippmann, a Harvard philosophy graduate and cofounder of the *New Republic*, in a series of books, *Liberty and the News*, *Public Opinion*, and *The Phantom Public*.[21] Lippmann, who had worked with the CPI on the peace conference in Europe, was troubled by manipulation of information that pretended to be news. He saw a danger to democracy and wondered if the way people were informed was part of the problem. Lippmann said the 1919 public had to deal with questions "more intricate than any that church or school had prepared them to understand," and that they were increasingly baffled because "the facts are not available." People were being fed rumors and guesses and propaganda in an attempt to "manufacture consent." This corruption of the news information process presented a "crisis" for Western democracy and journalism, he explained, because democracy required reliable information on which an informed citizenry could act.[22]

Corruption was not the only cause, Lippmann pointed out, but there was plenty of it. He blamed modern journalism for putting the national interest ahead of the truth, presenting readers with what was patriotic, but not necessarily the truth. This tendency had been increased during wartime and Lippmann and others worried about its peacetime continuation. "Public opinion is blockaded," he said. "For when a people can no longer confidently repair to 'the best fountains for their information,' then anyone's guess and anyone's rumor and each man's hopes and each man's whim becomes the basis of government." Lippmann warned:

> All that the sharpest critics of democracy have alleged is true, if there is no steady supply of trustworthy and relevant news. Incompetence and aimlessness, corruption and disloyalty, panic and ultimate disaster, must come to any people which is denied an assured access to the facts. No one can manage anything on pap. Neither can a people.[23]

Lippmann believed there "can be no higher law in journalism than to tell the truth and shame the devil."[24] In modern society the problem is, he explained, that the world has become so complicated that it defies any individual's "power of understanding." The individual knows little of the world firsthand. News comes from a distance, "helter-skelter, in inconceivable confusion; it deals with matters that are not easily understood; it arrives and is assimilated by busy and tired people who must take what is given to them."[25]

The reliability of news is also limited by the use of "eye-witness testimony" and "privileged informants." For example, releasing tidbits of information and scraps of gossip to the press had been common practice at the Peace Conference after World War I, and the world waited to learn the results of the negotiations in sessions closed to reporters.[26] The process of news dissemination was difficult even under the best conditions. Foreign news was limited by the cost of transmission and by the knowledge of reporters and editors handling it. Since the war, a new and dangerous element had been added, and that, warned Lippmann, was the intentional distortion of international news by means of propaganda, especially from governments in the troubled areas of the world.

"The ordering of news is one of the truly sacred and priestly offices in a democracy," according to Lippmann:

> For the newspaper is in all literalness the bible of democracy, the book out of which a people determines its conduct. It is the only serious book most people read. It is the only book they read every day. Now the power to determine each day what shall seem important and what shall be neglected is a power unlike any that has been exercised since the Pope lost his hold on the secular mind.[27]

Because both the editors and their readers have "little real knowledge of people and affairs beyond their own experience, they can easily be the victims of agitation and propaganda," Lippmann reasoned. "The quack, the charlatan, the jingo, and the terrorist can flourish only where the audience is deprived of independent access to information. When all the news is second-hand, where all testimony is uncertain, we are responding to opinions and assertions, not what is," he said. Where people are bewildered and acting like a crowd "under the influence of headlines and panicky print, the contagion of unreason can easily spread through a settled community."[28]

## OBJECTIVE INFORMATION

War and revolution, according to Lippmann, are founded on censorship and propaganda and are "supreme destroyers of realistic thinking." To restore the nation's sanity, Lippmann said, it would be necessary to return to "objective information."[29] Readers must be given the evidence, be able to detect lies, test the validity of news. It was crucial to define liberty of opinion in terms of access to truthful information, he suggested, not only in terms of contending opinions.[30]

This thinking led Lippmann to suggest improvements in the news process. Newspapers should retract errors and publish the names of staff writers and editors. Courts of honor, where editors could be questioned by their accusers on matters of accuracy and misrepresentation, was another possibility. He thought reporters for large news organizations "might be required to have a diploma from a journalism school," but this could cause other problems, he admitted.[31] The best idea would be to "bring into journalism a generation of men who will by sheer superiority, drive the incompetents out of business." Then journalism would increase in prestige and dignity, and "cease to be the refuge of the vaguely talented."[32] Journalists need sophisticated and inquiring minds, he believed, and they should treat newsgathering more as a science, knowing how to weigh evidence, understanding the role of public opinion in society, and being attuned to the values and suggestive meanings of the words they use. News should "enable mankind to live successfully toward the future."[33]

The idea of impartial, scientific information bureaus to analyze and provide news of government in an objective and unbiased form was an important Lippmann proposal. He knew many would think this "too limiting and arbitrary," but he worried about a greater problem. "The real enemy was ignorance. Democracy would degenerate into dictatorship to the Right or Left" if it did not become genuinely self-governing. That meant the news business had to have "men with a new training and outlook" who sought the truth above all else.[34]

Lippmann soon realized that the political scientists had not yet examined the formation of public opinion, so he left his editing job to write *Public Opinion* in 1922. In it he proposed: "We define first and then we see."[35] He explored the role of stereotypes that pattern thoughts, allowing people to make quick sense of the world. Stereotypes contain a grain of truth, along with prejudices and suspicions, he explained. They allow people to avoid the challenging ideas that do not fit their preconception. Newspapers relied heavily on stereotypes for quick characterization of people and issues, and since most people received their news of the world from newspapers, the democratic process was in danger if the pictures in people's heads did not correspond to reality.[36]

Lippmann realized that representative government would not work without access to the facts, and relying on the journalistic process was not enough. What was needed were independent, scientific information bureaus that could furnish the facts on which others might base their opinions. He had earlier demonstrated the flaws in fact-gathering in a study of the *New York Times'* coverage of the Russian Revolution. He and Charles Merz had found that the *Times* was a victim of habitual thinking and traditional practices that led to errors and bias by overreliance on biased official sources.[37]

Lippmann took over the editorial page direction for the *New York World* soon after completing his book and continued to study the process of public opinion formation, but in a darker mood. Lippmann seemed to have become disillusioned about the public, which he explained in the next book "does not really make up its mind" on the issues, but rather can say "yes" or "no" only as issues are raised and articulated by informed insiders. As Ronald Steel points out, Lippmann here "came fully to terms with the inadequacy of traditional democratic theory."[38] Lippmann had earlier shown how difficult it was for one person to be well informed on the world's problems. In this work he saw that the public had to rely on specialists and functionaries and got involved only at a late stage in the debate.

The press still had a vital role in the process, because it was the press that brought the "informed insider opinions" to the public's attention. The press determined the public agenda for attention. The popular press does this, Lippmann said, in an article published about a decade later, and it is "the first politically independent press which the world has known."[39] But, he warned that it carried with it the "seeds of its own dissolution," because it tries to attract the largest mass attention daily by means of dramatic human interest items. It will eventually exhaust the readers.[40]

## A NATIONAL STUDY

Concern about the modern press—its news sources, news gathering methods, and the rising influence of propaganda—was strong enough to generate proposals for a national study of the subject in 1924. *Editor and Publisher* announced that Rockefeller money would back a "scientific probe of news media and sources," led by Professor Herbert A. Miller of Ohio State University. According to the story, a group of scholars had met at the American Sociological Society two years earlier and was seeking the assistance of the Social Science Research Council.[41]

The plan was to look at "worldwide collection and dissemination of current news and opinion and the formation of expression and attitudes on international affairs." The role of propaganda and press agents in international reporting was a key element in the study. The researchers hoped for support from ASNE, which had been contemplating its own investigation of the profession. They thought the high-level scholarly research support would also get support of newspapermen in a "good faith effort."[42]

Just how deeply the Rockefeller Foundation was committed to the study was revealed the next week. Ivy Lee, publicity agent for the Foundation, said it had provided only $2,500 for a first planning session. The projected study would cost $170,000 and would not be funded by the Rockefeller Foundation. Miller expressed disappointment over what he thought was a firm commitment. It would be two decades before an independently funded national study of the press would be undertaken.[43]

## PROFESSIONAL PUBLIC RELATIONS

Press agentry had functioned effectively for the wartime CPI and had bred a first generation of professional publicists. Best known was Edward L. Bernays, who developed campaigns for support for Lithuania and for the War Department's drive to employ ex-servicemen. With his colleague and wife, Doris Fleishman, he came up with the title "counsel on public relations" to describe the postwar commercial work they did—"giving advice to clients on their public relationships, regardless of whether such advice resulted in publicity."[44] The term "counsel" came from the law, and was intended by Bernays to convey the professionalism he wished to see develop in the field, and also to differentiate it from the old and discredited publicity and propaganda labels.

The man who would be called the "father of public relations" carried on the battle against negative attitudes about publicity held by newspaper people and others through his personal contacts, newsletters, and books. He had been impressed by Lippmann's *Public Opinion* and by other new studies of crowd instincts and mass behavior. But none of these directly dealt with Bernays' interest in the private use of publicity to form public opinion. So Bernays set out to define the working practices and standards for modern public relations.[45]

*Crystallizing Public Opinion* appeared in 1923, and in it Bernays gave the positive side of the new profession. "The rise of the modern public relations counsel is based on the need and value of his services," he said.[46] Once business leaders could say "the public be damned," but that is no longer possible, said Bernays. The modern public demanded information and made up its own mind. But at the same time, society was so complex and disconnected from individuals that someone was needed to bring specialized information to the public. Bernays saw this as the job for public relations.

As he envisioned it, the public relations counsel's job was essentially one of analysis and advice giving. He had to understand the way in which public opinion was formed, to be able to read the popular feelings and attitudes of the public and groups, and to develop the best means of reaching the desired public with the client's message. The press could not and should not do this, Bernays, pointed out, but the press could amplify the message and put it into circulation.[47]

The public and press jointly created public opinion, Bernays said. The press "had to compromise between giving the public what it wants and what it should have," just as effective leaders had to grasp "what the public would accept and where it wanted to be led." Many overlapping groups fought for public approval; it was the counsel's job to get the client's message the best possible hearing.[48]

Bernays expanded his ideas in 1928 in a book on propaganda, in which he separated propaganda from public relations. Propaganda was the "conscious and intelligent manipulation of the organized habits and opinions of the masses." Those who "manipulate this unseen mechanism of society constitute an invisible government which is the true ruling power of our country...."[49] In theory, each citizen makes up his own mind. In reality, each citizen chooses from a "narrowed field of alternatives" presented by leaders via the media. Public relations, on the other hand, would have to operate within an ethical framework, and Bernays suggested that framework would include not serving competing clients, honesty in messages, not fooling the public, and making clear identification of the sources of all published information.[50]

Bernays explored the different media available to the public relations counsel. It was easier to place ideas and suggestions in magazines than in newspapers, he said, because the former had no "obligation to reflect the news." Radio and movies offered the great potential of bringing "standard-ized values to the society." Propaganda and publicity were going to stay, he was certain. He urged the budding public relations counsel to study public opinion formation, psychology of influence, and the media in order to become successful.[51]

Bernays was correct; his new profession would experience enormous growth in the twentieth century, but its relationship to the news media would remain in tension. Although the two professions are symbiotic, their essential differences of purpose and allegiance separate them. The war between them ended in a truce that left each side wary. Reporters and editors were supposed to check out the press releases, but often used them whole. Public relations people became more adept at managing their clients' images and reputations, while trying to raise their own from "flack" to professional. In 1939, *Editor and Publisher* began including public relations as a regular department.

The criticism of publicity and propaganda during the 1920s raised the issue of deceptive information parading as news and emphasized the need for skeptical reporters and editors who would have to reassure the public that its interests were still being served, even as journalism became more dependent on public relations in a complex world of big government and big business. The term "propaganda" inherited intensely negative and manipulative con-notations, whereas public relations became more respectable as a part of modern business, just as Bernays had proposed.

Scholars have generally placed the rise of journalistic objectivity as an accepted professional norm in the 1920s, the same time during which press criticism revolved around the dangers associated with publicity and propaganda and the manipulation of public opinion. Contemporary observers realized that mass public opinion was fed by many sources, not all of them healthy for the public well-being; publicity was forced to adopt more ethical professional practices. Journalists in this era were stressing the importance of fair, honest, and impartial reporting so that readers might make up their own minds about the issues. They were on guard against propaganda in the news, but acknowl-edged the reality of public relations as a fixture in modern society. The ideal of objective reporting suited the professional spirit of the modern journalist and of the times. It was democratic, scientific in spirit, and open. Publishers found that it was a style that made friends and offended few readers. It had the flexibility to serve both the private and the public good, or so it seemed, and that made it very attractive.

## NOTES

1. Michael Schudson, *Discovering the News: A Social History of American News-papers* (New York: Basic Books, 1978), 141.
2. Frank I. Cobb, "Frank I. Cobb Urges the Restoration of the Free Play of Opinion," *Editor and Publisher* (8 January 1920): 6.

3. Cobb, speech, 29.
4. Robert Herrick, "The Paper War," *Dial* 66 (8 February 1919): 114.
5. Roscoe C. E. Brown, "The Menace to Journalism," *North American Review* 214 (November 1921): 510.
6. Brown, "Menace," 611.
7. Brown, "Menace," 618.
8. Emery, *ANPA*, 127; and Will Irwin, "The Press Agent, His Rise and Decline," *Collier's* 48 (8 December 1911): 24.
9. Irwin, "Press Agent," 24.
10. Emery, *ANPA*, 129.
11. Emery, *ANPA*, 130.
12. Will Irwin, "If You See It in the Paper, It's—?" *Collier's* 72 (18 August 1923): 11.
13. Irwin, "See It," 27.
14. Editorial, "Do It!" *Editor and Publisher* (2 January 1926): 24.
15. Seitz, "Press," Part 6, 210.
16. Seitz, "Press," Part 6, 210.
17. "Planning to 'Professionalize' Press Agentry," *Editor and Publisher* (2 April 1927): 9.
18. Charles Horton Cooley, *Social Organization: A Study of the Larger Mind* (New York: Scribner's 1909/1925), 122. For a discussion of Cooley's impact on communication theory see: Daniel J. Czitrom, *Media and the American Mind from Mass to McLuhan* (Chapel Hill: University of North Carolina Press, 1982).
19. Cooley, *Social*, 128.
20. Cooley, *Social*, 148.
21. Walter Lippmann, *Liberty and the News* (New York: Harcourt, Brace & Howe, 1920); *The Phantom Public* (New York: Macmillan, 1930 ed.); and *Public Opinion* (New York: Macmillan, 1922/1961).
22. Walter Lippmann, "Journalism and the Higher Law," in *Liberty and the News*, 4–5.
23. Lippmann, "Higher Law," 11.
24. Lippmann, "Higher Law," 13.
25. Lippmann, "What Modern Liberty Means," in *Liberty and the News*, 38.
26. Lippmann, "Modern," 43–44.
27. Lippmann, "Modern," 47.
28. Lippmann, "Modern," 56.
29. Lippmann, "Modern," 57.
30. Lippmann, "Modern," 68.
31. Lippmann, "Modern," 74, 81.
32. Lippmann, "Liberty and the News," 82.
33. Lippmann, "Liberty," 89.
34. Lippmann, "Liberty," 104.
35. Lippmann, *Opinion*, 81.
36. Lippmann, *Opinion*, 31.
37. Walter Lippmann and Charles Merz, "A Test of the News," *New Republic* 23 (4 August 1920): 1–42.
38. Lippmann, *Phantom* 53; and Ronald Steel, *Walter Lippmann and the American Century* (London: Bodley Head, 1980), 214.
39. Walter Lippmann, "Two Revolutions in the American Press," *Yale Review* 20 (March 1931): 437.

40. Lippmann, "Revolutions," 439.
41. William T. Ellis, "Rockefeller Money Backs Scientific Probe of News Methods and Sources," *Editor and Publisher* (6 September 1924): 3.
42. Ellis, "Scientific," 26.
43. "Rockefellers Disclaim Press Probe—Lee," *Editor and Publisher* (20 September 1924): 10. Charles Merriam, a professor at the University of Chicago and chairman of the Social Science Research Council, was one of those supporting the Rockefeller request. He later served on the Hutchins Commission. This article says the idea for the study originated in a *Christian Century* editorial.
44. Edward L. Bernays, *Biography of an Idea: Memoirs of Public Relations Counsel Edward L. Bernays* (New York: Simon & Schuster, 1965), 288.
45. Bernays, *Memoirs*, 290–91.
46. Edward L. Bernays, *Crystallizing Public Opinion* (New York: Horace Liveright, 1923), 34.
47. Bernays, *Crystallizing*, 52–57.
48. Bernays, *Crystallizing*, 112.
49. Edward L. Bernays, *Propaganda* (New York: Horace Liveright, 1928), 9.
50. Bernays, *Propaganda*, 45.
51. Bernays, *Propaganda*, 156–59.

# CHAPTER 9

# The Objectivity Standard: 1920–1948

Strangely enough, the term "objective reporting" did not appear in the public discussion of American journalism until the 1930s when it met its first test. Most journalists supported a standard of fair, accurate, and unbiased reporting and a firm separation of the news pages from the editorial voice of the newspaper. Partisan bias and personal interests of publishers were still in place in some major newspapers. Objectivity ruled in most places, but it became a constraint for the Washington and foreign correspondents in the 1930s as events swept forward and required a better grasp of economics, social reform, and international politics. These correspondents and some editors pressed for a loosening of the bonds to permit something they called "interpretive" reporting, which would allow background, explanation, and analysis within the news report.

William Rivers in *The Opinionmakers* fixes the date that he and other observers attached to the failure of objective journalism:

> Then came the New Deal, and suddenly news reporting seemed inadequate. Some correspondents say they can fix on the exact time when "the old journalism" failed: the day in 1933 when the United States went off the gold standard. Vainly trying to report that cataclysmic and baffling change, they appealed to the White House, and a government economist was sent over to help. Then the correspondents tried to explain the new facts of economic life to the American people in the economic specialist's idiom, almost disastrously.[1]

Professor Curtis MacDougall of Northwestern University had incorporated "interpretative" reporting in this 1932 college text, *Reporting for*

*Beginners*, and gave the second edition of the book in 1938 the title *Interpretative Reporting*. He and Professor Kenneth E. Olson, then at the University of Minnesota and later dean of the Medill School of Journalism at Northwestern, were early exponents of the new reporting approach. Olson worried about the public's loss of confidence in the press in the 1930s as the press and its public parted ways. The nation had made a social revolution and had a new conception of the role of government, he asserted, but most of the press remained in the conservative camp with other leaders of American capitalism in business and industry. Conservative papers reached 95 percent of the population and had 81.2 percent of the daily newspaper circulation, he said. But the people resented the "exploitation" by past leaders and could no longer believe a press that did not understand or promote the general public interest. Olson pointed out that organized labor had long experienced press bias, and the last presidential election had shown that the New Deal had been "discredited by large sections of the press."[2]

The newspapers, according to Olson, were not giving the readers an understanding of their world, and those readers were turning to the newly successful weekly newsmagazines where explanation was offered. "Readers can't be treated as children looking for entertainment," he warned, but they must be given analysis and interpretative reporting. He urged other journalism teachers to place greater stress on "social responsibility" and ethics in order to educate young people who would build better newspapers.[3]

Most daily newspapers and the wire services then and now adhere to a standard of objective reporting for daily news, allowing reporters more freedom in feature writing, specialty areas, columns, and sports. A reporting text defines the standard:

> Objectivity means the coverage of news on the basis of its facts and its importance, apart from the views and selfish interests of the reporters and editors dealing with it, of the newspaper publishing it, and of the community of readers supporting that newspaper and its staff. It means seeing the truth as a thing in itself, a thing that stands by itself regardless of what you may think of it or how it may affect you. It means that news facts have a real existence of their own and in themselves.[4]

But newspapers in the 1930s that were still personally owned and directed by old-style opinion leaders, like Colonel Robert R. McCormick of the *Chicago Tribune* and William Randolph Hearst of the Hearst chain, were known for political bias and special likes and taboos that influenced news coverage and treatment as well as dictated the editorial page and editorial cartoon selections. Readers of these publications knew the bias and either liked it or adjusted for it. The McCormick and Hearst daily newspaper circulation in this period totaled about five million, roughly 15 percent of the total daily news circulation in major cities.[5] There was also political analysis in the newsmagazines, and in a growing body of signed political columns appearing in most newspapers.

Ordinary reporters and correspondents were restrained to reciting the facts, getting both sides and using sources to make the points and offer opinions. Reporters were told to stay out of the story and to let the reader be the judge. But sometimes this meant that the reader had to compare the news reports against columns and editorials and try to figure it out. More likely, they just skipped it and waited for later developments. Reader surveys typically showed the editorial page had the lowest rating of all and the comic pages the highest. The issue in the 1930s was whether explanation, analysis, and background could be handled with the high regard for accuracy and truth that guided objective reporting.

## THE OBJECTIVITY STANDARD

Scholars differ on just when and why objective reporting became the professional standard in American journalism—possibly because it is so hard to find any discussion of the term before the 1930s. Yet the standard seems to have been developing since about the mid-nineteenth century. Journalism historian Frank Luther Mott believed that there had been a gradual raising of standards of performance that put "getting it right" at least as high as getting the "scoop." He ranked the concept of the "objective news fact as a basis for reporting" as the sixth stage of news reporting in America. Mott thought it arose from publishers like Pulitzer insisting on accuracy, elimination of error and distortion, and "straight, clean reporting." When the ASNE 1923 ethics code branded partisanship in the news "subversive of a fundamental principle of the profession," he said, the objective news fact became the central tradition in American journalism.[6]

The concept rested on the idea that news was a timely report and that free and intelligent people in a democracy needed unbiased intelligence on which to base their views, Mott explained. The Jeffersonian principle was that given "prompt and proper information, the people guided by honest leaders will know what to do about it."[7]

Most scholars credit the mid-nineteenth-century wire services as early influences in the shift from partisan journalism to objective reporting. As one of Pulitzer's biographers put it, structural change made newspapers rely heavily on advertising lineage, and the widest possible circulation increased the pressure to avoid offending readers. Sticking to a "neutral rendition of the facts" was the answer. So, the ethical principle of objectivity was "at least equally motivated by commercial considerations."[8] Most press scholars agree with the view that the introduction of wire service news on a national scale influenced local reporting to follow the same factual, unbiased style.

Professor Richard A. Schwarzlose's comprehensive examination of the history of the wire services did not turn up any specific discussion of this matter in the personal papers of editors, the wire services, or contemporary printed sources.[9] He says, however, that wire service copy from the start (1846) "was objective by today's standards." At first it was stenographic accounts of legislative sessions or brief summary paragraphs of events. Space was limited and time was of the essence; reports were short, factual, and free of opinion. Whether this style was influential on the local reporting staff of the daily press is unclear, says Schwarzlose, because there is no supporting documentation.[10]

Scholars have tried to answer the question by using other research approaches. One widely accepted content analysis traced the decline of bias and the growth of wire service news in presidential campaign news coverage in Wisconsin between 1852 and 1916, and Professor Donald Shaw concluded that the sharp drop in bias between 1880 and 1884 was related to the increased use of wire copy. He speculated that local reporters "may have learned to write more unbiased political copy from imitating the relatively unbiased style of wire news."[11] The audience mix that resulted as more and more cities and towns were reduced to a single daily newspaper meant that the newspaper needed a broader and less politically controversial appeal. Another scholar tracked the growth of objective news reporting using content analysis, and he determined that 1905 to 1913 was the formative period.[12] Others emphasize the economic necessity argument, and Schudson, for example, added that a "distrust of facts," which had become ideological weapons in the hands of propagandists and publicists, encouraged the objectivity standard.[13]

## QUESTIONING THE STANDARD

By the 1930s objective news reporting was the accepted national standard. Not only did this harmonize with the recommendations of critics looking for the ideal newspaper, but it also suited the scientific spirit of the times and added some measure of respect and seriousness to the emerging profession. But the factual style was being tested by competing sources of interpretation and analysis. There was impressive work in documentary film, still photography, and radio that dramatized in pictures and sound the people and problems of the times. *Time* magazine's offering of the week's news in perspective was a success. The Depression made the terms of life serious; New Deal policies had to be explained, supported, and discussed. The very future of the democratic experience was being weighed and challenged in many forums. "The facts did not speak for themselves," as Ronald Shilen put it in his study linking journalistic objectivity to objectivity in other professions.[14] Although President Roosevelt objected to interpretive reporting and admonished reporters for using it, the reality of his administrative style with its off-the-record and background press conferences encouraged the Washington correspondents to write more interpretatively, Professor Betty Winfield has pointed out.[15]

## WHAT WAS OBJECTIVITY?

Walter Lippmann introduced the term "objective reporting" in his 1919 essay "What Modern Liberty Means," and seems to have been the first to discuss objective journalism in his 1920 book, *Liberty and the News*.[16] Nelson Crawford's widely used 1924 journalistic ethics text propagated the ideal. Crawford states that the "fundamental function of the newspaper is to disseminate the objective facts concerning matters of public concern."[17] The ability to "present news objectively and to interpret it realistically is not a native instinct in the human species," Lippmann realized. That comes from one's culture and knowledge of the past. The development of professional schools preparing journalists would be essential for this new, objective journalism. "Journalism has not been a profession, and could not be one until objective journalism was created," and "until the journalists would consider themselves devoted, as the professionals ideally are, to the service of truth alone."[18]

Because the "health of society depends upon the quality of the information it receives," journalism should be a "post of peculiar honor." Lippmann thought the increased prestige would come through professional training where "the ideal of objective testimony is cardinal." Scoop mentality and cynicism should be replaced by "patient and fearless men of science who have labored to see what the world really is." Good reporting, therefore, required the "exercise of the highest of scientific virtues," including assessing credibility of statements, probabilities, and statistics. He imagined that academic preparation for this would include study of types of witnesses, sources of information, tests of credibility, precise word usage, logic, politics, and sociology.[19]

Lippmann's good reporter needed a trained intuition based on experience and a "general sense of what the world is doing." He clearly would not serve any cause, but should make use of explanations based on objective realities and analysis. The introduction of professionally educated journalists with these standards of reporting would drive out the bad, and journalists would be doing their job of "seeking the truth, revealing it and publishing it."[20]

Crawford described the current standards for journalism as "the doctrine that the dissemination of objective facts is the primary if not the exclusive function of the press, and that all other possible functions should be subordinated to this." This doctrine was rooted in Jeffersonian theory, which, Crawford said, had been modified by the urban experience. In the city the problems were more complex and voters had less access through personal observation or investigation to the objective facts. So, Crawford explained, the public was beginning to expect the newspaper to do that for them. More and more believed that "the fundamental function of the newspaper is to disseminate the objective facts concerning matters of public concern."[21]

"The only chance for actual popular government is for all the available facts to be given to the people clearly and objectively. The people may not always be wise, but they can gain no wisdom save through experience," Crawford said. The public no longer tolerated distortion and political bias. The press, according to Crawford, "faced a formidable task of convincing a public that it was a serious public institution acting on their behalf." Newspapers had improved greatly, he thought, and would improve still more "were the ideal of objectivity more tenaciously and realistically held by journalists."[22]

Objective reporting, modeled on the processes used for scientific inquiry in the natural sciences, was initially promoted, if not in name, at least in essence, in the early twentieth-century journalism schools and departments, in early reporting textbooks, and gradually in research findings. It was implied, if not stated, in the early codes of ethics adopted on state and national levels.

Editorial pages and political columns, of course, were not eliminated by objective news reporting, nor did the style infringe on the creative liberties taken in feature, sports, and entertainment writing. Objectivity also frequently was strained in the news reporting of political campaigns, which caused a large part of the press criticism of the 1930s and 1940s. As the discussion over objectivity and interpretation warmed up in public, the definitions of objectivity also appeared.

In 1931, when he was editor of the *New York World*, Walter Lippmann told a Yale University audience that American journalism was on the verge of its third and greatest epoch, one that relied on objective facts. The third revolution that Lippmann anticipated was emerging from "the search for a more reliable and responsible press," set in motion by the "profound revulsion" among educated people and newspapermen that the war propaganda had let loose.[23] The press had first been based on partisan opinion, then on mass opinion. Future journalism would be "even more independent . . . less temperamental . . . more a liberal profession." It would deal with the news objectively and use "trained intelligence." It would allow room for "originating minds," but would not be subservient to the whims of the public, Lippmann predicted.[24] He added:

> The new journalism is even more independent than the popular commercial press which it is crowding into a corner. For it has just as broad a base in the number of its readers, and because it obviously enlists a more sustained attention it is more profitable as an advertising medium. Its real independence lies, however, in the fact that it is not only so self-sufficient, that it can be free of hidden control, but that since the commodity it deals in primarily is the approximation to objective fact, it is free also of subserviency to the whims of the public. The strength of this journalism will, I think, be cumu-

lative because it opens the door to the use of trained intelligence in newspaper work.[25]

The old journalism was "a romantic art dependent on the virtuosity of men like Bennett, Hearst, and Pulitzer," he observed. The new was less temperamental and more professional. "For the ability to present news objectively and to interpret it realistically is not a native instinct in the human species; it is a product of culture which comes only with knowledge of the past and acute awareness of how deceptive is our normal observation and how wishful is our thinking." Journalism "could not be a profession until modern objective journalism was successfully created," he declared, and this new professional journalism was devoted to "the service of truth."[26]

## THE CALL FOR INTERPRETATION

The public was demanding "papers of more substantial worth and less provincially local in their point of view," said Frank Gannett, president of The Gannett Company, responding to Lippmann's address. The principal function of newspapers was to supply news of the world, but "there was a growing need for newspapers to get beyond the local stories and provide background and interpretation on topics of major interest and consequence to the whole country."[27]

The new managing editor of the *New York Times*, E. L. James, agreed that the complexity of the international situation and the gravity of affairs both at home and abroad required unbiased news, with interpretation in foreign news to provide the background.[28] The newspaper publishers heard their association president, Harry Chandler, in 1932 urge newspapers to greater responsibility. "These are the times when the conduct of a daily newspaper ceases to be a commercial enterprise. It becomes a stewardship that often involves great self-sacrifice and great courage." The Depression had doubled the responsibility of the press, he said. "The collapse of an inflated era of spending has suddenly sobered them. . . . They want bread and butter—and facts."[29]

President Franklin D. Roosevelt disagreed. He opposed reporter interpretation, believing it was a dangerous mix of fact and opinion. The press and radio should just supply citizens with the information, the facts, so they can make up their own minds, he said, in 1939. The government should supply the facts to make this possible, he added.[30] One biographer of Roosevelt believes the president had developed this view of objective reporting early in his career and that it was based on Jeffersonian ideals. Others suspected his animosity toward several conservative newspaper publishers was the reason.[31] But, whatever the president's motives, the actions of the New Deal and its large publicity apparatus not only provided Americans with much interpretative matter but also caused reporters to see a need for it. Speaker after speaker at gatherings of professional journalists and editors in the 1930s worried about the public's dissatisfaction with the press.[32] At the same time they believed that the public had grown more serious and discriminating and was asking for explanation, which was readily available on radio, and in magazines, and news weeklies.

## CHANGING THE STANDARD

The standard of the last generation was "outdated," announced Herbert Brucker, journalist and teacher at Columbia. A new conception of news was needed, one that would provide "a connected, smooth running account of the day's happenings." It would include context and background. Explanation, according to Brucker, was not argumentation; it had always been part of the foreign and political correspondence. Now, he advocated applying this to other news. "If the newspaper sticks to surface fact, it dodges a measure of its responsibility." He thought the newspaper should be more like a daily magazine and should learn from the ratio commentary and *Time* magazine, which had pioneered "the new style of interpretive journalism for a 'news hungry public.'"[33]

Brucker later expanded his remarks in two books, *The Changing American Newspaper* (1937) and *Freedom of Information* (1949; started in 1940). He pointed out that we live in two worlds—one personally experienced and one vicarious. The media have to be adequate to the task of making the worlds beyond the personal known and understandable. Information provided the general public had to be free of partisan or other special interests, and this information "helps us link our two worlds."[34]

The old theory of the free press had become remote to the twentieth century because of economic, technological, and social changes. It was too simple to make advertising the villain, he said. People and government no longer had a two-way relationship, he explained, and the press had to be the "third leg of the triangle" that battles with the government on the citizens' behalf. He warned that the press had become a remote institution like government, and citizens no longer identified with it. They saw it as "big, powerful," with its own interests and motives. That was the key to citizen distrust of the press, Brucker felt. The New Deal came along and brought "what the common man wants," he said, but the press "speaks to other interests."[35] Liberals, said Brucker, think the press does not serve all the people, and conservatives think the people are deluded by the New Deal.[36]

Brucker found the endowed or adless newspaper unworkable, because each included some form of control of the press. The answer was "objective reporting, America's special contribution to journalism." The objective press "is the most man can ask of his press and his information system. The basic task is simply to tell him honestly what is happening out of eyesight and out of earshot, so that the picture of the world in his head will bear at least a working resemblance to the great world in which he lives."[37] Brucker thought objective reporting would somehow guarantee a diversity of voices in the press, even though monopoly ownership was causing others to expect even more uniformity.

## FOURTH ESTATE IDEAL

"To say that objectivity came about just because it was a search for circulation and advertising is cynical and reflects the curent world view," he declared. "It overlooks the spirit" of the nineteenth-century editors who had "ideals as well as interests in profits."[38] Objectivity had grown without law or compulsion, Brucker explained, to become a "powerful tradition" that keeps "most reporting free of bias, separates news from opinion" and is the "force that will carry us forward toward the ideal Fourth Estate." He suggested the critics should appreciate objectivity and press for more. It was not that the newspapers "were defeated in the FDR elections," but that they "helped to elect him by means of their objective news pages."[39]

Brucker rejected solutions that would revive partisan papers or adless newspapers. He saw the *Chicago Tribune* and the new adless *PM* as the extreme edges of newspapering. What was needed was interpretation and explanation in the news, done in the "spirit of scientific inquiry and in the search for truth." He said that the "system works because there are publishers with vision and standards," and he urged people to keep up the pressure on newspapers owners and editors to keep newspapers fair and objective and devoted to the public service.[40]

The daily newspaper would not be allowed to neglect the growing role of interpretation with spokesmen like Herbert Brucker and Lester Markel around. Markel, Sunday editor of the *New York Times* since 1923 and originator of the Sunday "Review of the Week," told his twenty-fifth anniversary audience that newspapers had "abdicated to radio and the newsweeklies" in certain areas. Newspapers had to take back the function of "interpreting as well as presenting the news," Markel warned. Government, radio, and schools all had a role in educating the citizens, he said, but "only 25 percent of those who vote are well-informed," and that was dangerous to democratic society. "In these days when international news is of such surpassing importance, it seems to me that what is needed is the kind of interpretive review-of-the-week that the *New York Times* attempts to do," but he admitted small newspapers did not have the resources.[41]

W. M. Kiplinger, then a Washington-based business writer, pleaded for interpretation as a "more advanced form of news reporting" that may be difficult but "not impossible" for reporters to do. Seasoned reporters could be trusted to interpret the news because they were often closer to the details than editorial writers, he argued. He urged that student journalists be instructed in interpretive reporting and the critical judgment needed for the explanation and analysis that it required.[42]

The dilemma facing journalists was succinctly put by radio news analyst Elmer Davis:

> The good newspaper, the good news broadcaster, must walk a tightrope between two great gulfs—on one side the false objectivity that takes everything at face value and lets the public be imposed on by the charlatan with the most brazen front; on the other, the "interpretive" reporting which fails to draw the line between objective and subjective, between a reasonably well-established fact and what the reporter or editor wishes were fact. To say that is easy; to do it is hard.[43]

Theologian Reinhold Niebuhr urged the press to provide "more than isolated facts" about the world. "Interpretation of the facts" was needed because the general reader lacks general knowledge about foreign affairs that would place "isolated facts into a proper setting." People of the world had to understand each other, friend and foe, he said, warning that America would not remain free "if the rest of the world was enslaved."[44] Journalism's responsibility would be to present the facts, Niebuhr asserted, even when they run "counter to our presuppositions" and to provide citizens with the "fullest possible knowledge of all the facts and factors in the world situation" in a conscientious way and without financial sacrifice, but this would take "moral and political imagination."[45]

## CRISIS FOR OBJECTIVITY

Objectivity continued to raise questions for reporters. The 1950s reporting of Senator Joe McCarthy's crusade against communism, and the 1960s and 1970s controversial war in Vietnam and civil rights protest movements, revealed new inadequacies in the American reporting style. The McCarthy era provoked journalistic soul searching that became a benchmark for the profession. Most of the public agony over McCarthy's tactics naturally centered on the Senator himself and the cold war public's acquiescence or support of reckless disregard for the truth, lack of rights for the accused, and bullying by public officials protected by congressional immunity. The wreckage in shattered lives of individuals "tried" in congressional hearings and press reports showed how vulnerable journalistic objectivity was to manipulation by the demagogue. Liberal magazines and newspapers raised the issue. "For decades the American press has worshiped the God of objectivity," said one observer, Ronald May, in the *New Republic*. "This seemed to keep voters informed on all sides of the question until the invention of the technique of the big lie. Under this technique a public official can use totalitarian methods —knowing his utterances will be reported straight and that the truth will never catch up with his falsehoods."[46]

May pointed out that the splendid technology of radio, high-speed press, airmail, and television gave the "widest possible distribution to the big lie in the shortest possible time."[47] Editors were alert to the danger, he said, and some played down stories that were obvious lies; a few criticized McCarthy directly and then became victims of the senator's smear counterattack, which moved the spotlight to the hapless critic who had set out to warn the public. McCarthy had learned early in his career what made headlines, and how to release news close to deadline to limit journalists' time to check the story. He could accuse and offer no evidence, and the press would think a fair job of reporting was done by quoting him accurately. It took some time for the press to realize it had become a victim of cold war hysteria.

This first major crisis for objectivity "was credited largely to the assumption that journalists are not obligated to write what they can demonstrate as true and significant unless it comes from the mouth of authority," observed Ben Bagdikian, press critic.[48] In the aftermath of Edward R. Murrow's exposé of the senator's tactics on the March 1954 CBS television "See it Now" program, and the ensuing Army–McCarthy hearings and Senate censure, journalism professionals tried to deal with the failure of their ideal. It was agreed that explanation could be added to provide evidence or facts that refuted official charges, to do a kind of "instant analysis," but this was neither very widely done nor as useful as was hoped. It often took too much time to check out the assertions and provide evidence. The journalistic institution did not then and still has not faced the real culprit—the pervasive nineteenth-century scoop mentality that makes journalists' and editors' blood cascade at the thought of beating their rivals. Being right provides no such rush, nor does it attract hoards of loyal readers or viewers. Given the problems with objectivity, some critics have advocated scrapping it altogether and returning to forthright acknowledgment of reporter opinion, participation, or political bias in the news.[49] They would welcome more color and personality in the writing, but of course, others see this as inviting bias or fiction.

Certainly in the early twentieth century, objective reporting was seen as a positive and responsible answer to the criticism of sensationalism, propaganda, and invasion of privacy. It fit the requirements critics had in mind for an ideal newspaper. It served the newly emerging professionals as a noble and altruistic standard, in line with other professions like law and medicine. The publisher, too, was pleased because it offered a noncontroversial mode of reporting that served ever-larger audiences, and still allowed for agrument and opinion in the separate editorial pages.

Objective reporting, however, when shorn of its implied moral responsibility and devotion to truth and Jeffersonian democratic ideals, can degenerate into the mindless stringing together of facts by skilled practitioners. This "false" objectivity allowed reporters to disregard ethical concerns and the human impact of their stories, or whether the stories were worthy of printing in the first place. All that rote application of objectivity required was to stick to the rules of quoting everyone and attributing all opinion to credible sources. The reporter stayed out of the story. The reader was left to figure out what it meant. Sometimes it was a puzzle.

The press adopted interpretive reporting, or news analysis, during the New Deal years, and offered weekend pages of reporter-written news analysis and background in the quality newspapers. Curtis MacDougall's popular college reporting text was promoted by his publishers as the first to "anticipate the new trend in journalism toward interpretation and comment," and the first to provide "background and training necessary for the rapidly growing field of news interpretation."[50] Editors made an effort to teach readers to notice the difference between standard reporting and the interpretation by labeling articles as "news analysis" or "background." That was supposed to signal that an article lay somewhere in the gray area between objective reporting and personal opinion. But necessary explanation and background also were woven into hard news dispatches, and only rarely then boxed for emphasis. Mostly, readers had to be alert.

Professor Bill Rivers pointed out that interpretive reporting had the positive effect of placing "a high premium on several varieties of expertise" in reporting.[51] In that way interpretation can be regarded as another step along the road to professionalism in journalism, because it offers greater freedom and more responsibility to the individual journalist. But interpretive reporting is still no safeguard that assures diversity of views in the reporting, because it has the same cultural biases that pervade all the nation's news. Readers still need to proceed with caution, with intellect engaged.

## NOTES

1. William Rivers, *The Opinionmarkers: The Washington Press Corps* (Boston: Beacon Press, 1965/1967), 42.
2. Kenneth E. Olson, "The Newspaper in Times of Social Change," *Journalism Quarterly* 12 (March 1935): 13.
3. Olson, "Change," 19.
4. Neil MacNeil, *How to Be a Newspaperman* (New York: Harper & Row, 1942), 25.
5. Emery, *Press*, 5th ed., 428–30. (See Chap. 1, n. 2.)
6. Frank Luther Mott, "Development of News Concepts in American Journalism," *Editor and Publisher* (28 February 1942): 36.
7. Mott, "Development," 36.
8. George Juergens, *News from the White House: The Presidential-Press Relationship in the Progressive Era* (Chicago: University of Chicago Press, 1981), 6.
9. Personal letter from Richard A. Schwarzlose, 25 May 1989, to the author.
10. Richard A. Schwarzlose, *The Nation's Newsbrokers*, Vol. 1 (Evanston: North-

western University Press, 1989), 181; and personal correspondence noted above.

11. Donald L. Shaw, "News Bias and the Telegraph: A Study of Historical Change," *Journalism Quarterly* 44 (Spring 1967): 3–12, 31.

12. Harlan S. Stensas, "Development of the Objectivity Ethic in U.S. Daily Newspapers," *Journal of Mass Media Ethics* 2 (Fall/Winter 1986–87): 55.

13. Schudson, *Discovering*: 122.

14. Ronald Shilen, "The Concept of Objectivity in Journalism in the U.S.," Ph.D. dissertation (New York University, 1955).

15. Betty H. Winfield, "F. D. R. Wins (and Loses) Journalist Friends in the Rising Age of News Interpretation," *Journalism Quarterly* 64 (Winter 1987): 706.

16. Walter Lippmann, "What Modern Liberty Means," *Liberty and the News* (New York: Harcourt, Brace & Howe, 1920).

17. Lippmann, *Opinion*, 18–19: and Crawford, *Ethics*, 37.

18. Lippmann, "Revolutions," 440.

19. Lippmann, "Liberty," 82.

20. Lippmann, "Liberty," 104.

21. Crawford, *Ethics*, 37.

22. Crawford, *Ethics*, 99.

23. Lippmann, "Revolutions," 439.

24. Lippmann, "Revolutions," 440.

25. Lippmann, "Revolutions," 440.

26. Lippmann, "Lippmann Sees Passing of Popular Press," *Editor and Publisher* (17 January 1931): 41.

27. Frank E. Gannett, "Sensational Newspapers Near End of Vogue Here and Abroad, Gannett," *Editor and Publisher* (18 April 1931): 30.

28. John W. Perry, "Scope of U.S. Journalism Widening," *Editor and Publisher* (April 1932): 7.

29. Harry Chandler, "Our Day of Responsibility," *Editor and Publisher* (April 1932): 7.

30. Graham J. White, *FDR and the Press* (Chicago: University of Chicago Press, 1979), 129.

31. Richard W. Steele, *Propaganda in an Open Society: The Roosevelt Administration and the Media 1933–1941* (Westport, Conn.: Greenwood Press, 1985).

32. *Problems*, 1933, 62.

33. Herbert Brucker, "The Glut of Occurrences," *Atlantic Monthly* 156 (August 1935): 204.

34. Herbert Brucker, *Freedom of Information* (New York: Macmillan, 1949), 32.

35. Brucker, *Freedom*, 70.

36. Brucker, *Freedom*, 228.

37. Brucker, *Freedom*, 252.

38. Brucker, *Freedom*, 266.

39. Brucker, *Freedom*, 272.

40. Brucker, *Freedom*, 281.

41. "Lester Markel Thinks Press Neglects Interpretive Role," *Editor and Publisher* (3 April 1948): 61.

42. W. M. Kiplinger, "Interpret the News," *Journalism Quarterly* 13 (September 1936): 291.

43. Elmer Davis, *But We Were Born Free* (New York: Bobbs-Merrill, 1952), 175. Davis was director of the Office of War Information in World War II.

44. Reinhold Niebuhr, "The Role of the Newspapers in America's Function as the Greatest World Power," *The Press in Perspective* (Baton Rouge, La.: Louisiana State University Press, 1963), 41, 44.
45. Niebuhr, "Role," 49.
46. Ronald May, "Is the Press Unfair to McCarthy?" *New Republic* 128 (20 April 1953): 10–12. May coauthored with muckraking journalist Jack Anderson the book, *McCarthy the Man, the Senator and the Ism*, (Boston: Beacon Press, 1952).
47. May, "Unfair," 12.
48. Ben Bagdikian, *Media Monopoly*, 183.
49. Theodore L. Glasser, "Objectivity Precludes Responsibility," *Quill* (February 1984): 103–107.
50. Curtis MacDougall, *Interpretative Reporting* (New York: Macmillan, 1938); and advertisement in *Journalism Quarterly* 15 (March 1938): 71.
51. Rivers, *Opinionmakers*, 47.

# CHAPTER 10

# A Waning Influence: 1930–1939

Press criticism in the New Deal era is so mixed with political and social criticism that it is difficult to distinguish whether people were unhappy with the press or with the society it reported. Underlying this discussion is a tacit understanding that the essential power of the mass press was access to the mass public. Who was going to wield that power, and with how much or how little governmental influence, was the real question.

What Alexis de Tocqueville admired in America's decentralized tradition of strong community ownership of local newspapers that he said caused "political life to circulate through all parts of that vast territory" was rapidly changing.[1] Chains (two or more newspapers under one ownership), often with outside ownership, were replacing the homegrown product. Concentration of regional groups or national strings of newspapers under a powerful press baron with definite political views and ambitions had caught the public's attention. Chain ownership between 1923 and 1930 grew at a rate of about one million circulation per year, so that by 1923 one-third of all subscribers were reading chain newspapers. By 1935 40 percent were doing so, but chains were concentrated in the largest cities, so the large circulation represented only 7.87 percent of the total *number* of daily newspapers.[2] Chains were developing sound business management and were making journalism a profitable business, changing the structure of the American press. It was still too early to tell whether the need to serve the masses would restrain the chains from slanting the news to wield power for the owner, his political party, and special friends. It was possible, however, that the Scripps and Gannett models, favoring local political independence as long as the operation maintained a profit, might be the dominant form of organization. The old adage of "not messing with a man who buys ink by the barrel" seemed more apt than ever in this politically heated era.

New Deal rhetoric claimed that 85 percent of the daily press was against the President. Later studies put the anti–New Deal press closer to 60 percent of the total number of newspapers.[3] Could objective reporting be working? Was the press bias against the New Deal on the editorial page not enough to counter the factual news coverage? Where did that leave the so-called editorial page leadership? Faltering or failing, according to the liberal critics.

Press criticism reflected the 1930s social and political schisms. There are two competing visions of the press in modern America. In one, the press is an idealized Fourth Estate, serving the public, educating the citizens and watching a potentially corrupt government on the public's behalf. The other, older vision, is of an advocacy press, challenging the social order, aiding democratic revolutions, crusading, using the power of the pen against the power of the sword and big government. In the 1930s both visions were invoked in the debate as the press stubbornly fought to limit big government, retain press freedoms and to engage in fierce partisan infighting, frequently in opposition to the majority public opinion. Press criticism was equally polemic. The progressives saw danger in a newspaper industry dominated by selfish business interests that threatened to become as intolerant and arrogant as big government. Conservatives saw potential government censorship, control, and interference with the press embedded in the new social policies. Journalists and journalism educators, who had been working steadily to raise the level of journalism to the status of a profession, were squeezed from both sides. Professionalism suffered a loss of momentum in this decade, despite efforts to expand journalistic objectivity with "responsible interpretation" and to pursue "professional accreditation" of the journalism school curricula.

## PUBLISHERS AND THE NEW DEAL

Early in the 1930s, when most newspaper publishers banded together to oppose New Deal legislation that could improve working conditions and pay and open the way for union organizing in the newsrooms, journalists were forced to face the reality of their terms of employment. They were hired hands, as critics at the end of the nineteenth century had already pointed out, not autonomous professionals. Their bosses could and did hire and fire them at will. This change in attitude among journalists made possible the first successful efforts to organize reporters and other nonmechanical employees into the Newspaper Guild, a labor union that would fight for better pay and negotiate conditions in their behalf. For the past two decades, American journalists had mulled over the virtues of a national professional association versus a labor union. Other special-interest groups representing reporters, editors, honor students, college men and women, and public relations practitioners had formed, but a single attempt to forge a national professional association for all journalists had failed.[4]

Now dead was the notion of licensing. There seemed to be no way to counter the argument that any form of regulation on who could and who could not write for the press was an infringement on freedom of the press and would restrict access to the press on the basis of examination or college degree criteria. A 1931 proposal to certify "the capability of journalists" through qualifying exams given by the newspapers and admission to membership in a national Institute of Journalism, a variant of the British model, went nowhere. Its formulators intended it as a means for raising standards and increasing the sense of social responsibility by newspapers without actually resorting to licensing.[5] Chilling examples of the abuse of reporter licensing in totalitarian nations in Europe added weight to the argument. The Newspaper Guild, moving to become a union rather than a professional association, adopted the position that journalists were skilled craftsmen rather than professionals. This further weakened the drive for a professional association, though it strengthened union negotiating power.

Reporters, editors, and individual newspaper management teams might establish codes of ethics and journalistic performance, but these were only voluntary. Publishers might or might not agree with such codes. There was no universal standard nor was there any enforcement mechanism except the bosses' right to hire and fire and the employees' right to stay or quit. It was questionable whether or not an aroused public could offer any real protection for a virtuous journalist who was in opposition to his or her employer. If organized, this public might deplete circulation and advertising support, though this tactic became less tenable in the growing number of one-newspaper towns. Readers were more apt to grumble and "read around" the political bias in their local papers. When polled, a majority of readers (even in 1938 when President Roosevelt thought his press relations were at their worst) thought that the newspapers they read reported the news fairly.[6]

There was a sense among journalists of all political temperaments that the press had become a faceless institution run by anonymous corporate executives and boards of directors. Although talk of responsibility and ethics had increased in press circles since the turn of the century, it quickened when the conservative press was pitted against a powerful, popular New Deal government.

## INVITING CRITICISM

Marlen E. Pew, editor of *Editor and Publisher*, praised ASNE's promotion of ethical standards. He characterized 1930 as a time "reeking with doubt and insecurity," when newspaper ethics were being tested in the "general worship of profit and success." Pew declared: "The newspaper is more than a business" and has a "stewardship to serve the public interest." He urged editors to work to rid their profession of the overuse of publicity "puffery," ballyhoo, and stunts, and instead to revive enterprising reporting and revitalize the editorial pages. Newspapers should celebrate honorable public service and the free spirit.[7]

ASNE was in its eighth convention in 1930 and wrestling with enforcement of its own code of ethics, but it still sought the opinions of American cultural leaders. One such, known for his hostility to journalism education, was University of Chicago Chancellor, Robert M. Hutchins. He scolded the editors for not introducing him as a lawyer and for printing his middle initial wrong in the program. Then he launched into a recital of personal grievances over press treatment, finishing with his prepared remarks. He said that the press was comprised of "individuals weak in mind and low in character, and totally defective in that scientific spirit, which should be the principal trait of all great men." The press was important in molding public opinion, but if the public had to "rely on the press to educate people it would take a long time."[8]

ASNE sought out "helpful criticism," but Hutchins' outburst was extreme. It does illustrate the attitude held by many contemporary cultural leaders toward the daily press.[9] Two years later journalism Dean Carl W. Ackerman of Columbia University tried to sum up press criticism as it could be gleaned from leading citizens. He had a list of nineteen charges from this "intelligent minority" that said they had high regard for individual newspapers but had many complaints about the press in general.[10] Their complaints were familiar: news promotes special interests and sensationalism, makes heroes of criminals, invades personal privacy, is subservient to political parties, is not impartial and often deliberately false, conceals the truth, and does not provide a comprehensive account of what is happening. As Ackerman explained, "What our critics desire is a superhuman institution." But he believed the criticism had merit and must be considered by the leaders of the daily press. A press dedicated to public service would do much to counter these charges, he said.[11]

President Roosevelt had received bipartisan newspaper support in his first campaign and for his handling of the banking crisis, but it was not long before some major newspaper leaders became vociferous critics or even vitriolic enemies. University of Wisconsin journalism professor Willard G. Bleyer explained, "The four years of the Depression have demonstrated more clearly than ever before the fact that the fortunes of newspapers as private business enterprises are inextricably bound up with the success or failure of modern capitalism."[12] Circulation and advertising depended on the business climate, he said, and yet publishers believed the press was exempt from New Deal legislation like the National Industrial Recovery Act (NIRA). The NIRA proposed developing codes for all industries, covering such items as wages, hours, union organizing, and fair work practices. The newspaper publishers opposed NIRA, arguing that the code was a form of unconstitutional license.[13]

Robert R. McCormick, publisher of the *Chicago Tribune* and head of the ANPA Freedom of the Press Committee, led the publishers' protest over modest opposition that the Association should not use the issue of free press to excuse meager wages, excessive hours, and child labor. The ANPA persevered and forced FDR to accept language in a special code for newspapers that stated that the code did not "invalidate the First Amendment to the Constitution." FDR spluttered, "pure surplusage," but he signed anyway.[14] The Act was overturned in 1935 by the Supreme Court on the grounds that it usurped powers delegated to the states.[15] But because of the NIRA and the publishers' response, the Newspaper Guild of America was successfully organized in 1933 and attracted substantial support.[16]

The Guild movement, according to Professor Bleyer, "will mean an entirely new status for the profession of journalism."[17] Although few publishers openly opposed the Guild, there were reports of reprisal against organizers. Bleyer predicted that the formation of the Guild would accentuate the "dual character of the newspaper" and the problem growing out of it.[18] It would pose the professional ideal against the older craft tradition, he said, and the professional ideal would become "tarnished" as reporters and editors learned that their wages were "far below" those of the mechanical skilled trades. Bleyer concluded that the events of 1933 had sharply focused the problem.[19] He was noncommital on the licensing issue except to say that licensing could "elevate greatly the status of the profession," but would violate the constitutional right for anyone "to write what he pleases in a newspaper, within the limitations of the law, regardless of his qualifications to do so."[20]

An official history of the ANPA points out that the publishers feared that President Roosevelt's legislative program would abridge free press rights, if not impose direct controls on the press. The ANPA fought the New Deal in the name of guarding free speech against restrictive governmental actions. Emery says that the publishers opposed the American Newspaper Guild on the same grounds, speculating that Guild members might color the news pro-labor.[21]

But to some observers, ANPA was using press freedom as a cover for economic self-interest. Later research showed that most Washington correspondents (63.8 percent) thought the publishers' free press argument had been a ruse.[22] An apathetic public might not rally to the defense of newspapers in times "when freedom of the press is actually threatened with invasion," warned Gerald W. Johnson, editorial writer for the *Baltimore Evening Sun*. Instead, a public cynical about press freedom might allow policies that abolished that freedom and thus endangered the whole society.[23]

## THE POLITICAL BIAS COMPLAINT

President Roosevelt and others frequently charged the newspapers with political bias in their reporting. Although later studies have shown that these charges were greatly exaggerated at the time, there were enough clear examples of bias to make the case emotionally convincing. One study found that nine of the daily newspapers most regularly read by President Roosevelt were most fair in their news reports and that bias tended to be localized or mostly in the anti–New Deal Hearst papers, the *Chicago Tribune*, and the like.[24]

The first election of President Franklin D. Roosevelt in 1932 and the gathering of Republican opposition to the New Deal alerted many to the realization that "the press and the public were going in different directions," said Clark McAdams, a former editor of the *St. Louis Post-Dispatch*. He argued for a return to "free news . . . undoctored by the bias of any editor or publisher." The mission of the newspaper should be "to tell people the truth," he declared. "There has never been a time when truth was more important to the well-being of the people than it is today"; the papers were engaged in large-scale editorializing and doctoring of the news. Readers were forced to learn about Washington, he warned, through syndicated columns "not strained through the prejudices of proprietors and news editors."[25]

If the newspaper was no longer trusted by the New Deal and much of the public, radio seemed to offer a good alternative. The president could speak directly to the people, without newspaper reporters and editors handling his words. In fact, FDR suggested that only radio and film provided educational and informative matter, thus exemplifying the true role of the press in a democratic society. At one point he even warned radio listeners that they did not need newspapers to help them make up their minds.[26]

The New Deal had public relations officers in all government agencies to explain the new laws and policies and to offer context and background information; they always managed to get the government's explanation of events into the news pages for an information-hungry public. One scholar of this institution says that FDR did not want a watchdog press, but, rather, a managed one, and he effectively created the "foundation for a modern presidency" with his executive publicity office.[27]

Arthur Krock, a political columnist and member of the editorial board of the *New York Times*, pointed out that under FDR the publicity apparatus started by President Woodrow Wilson had "come to full flower" and was used to "channel publicity." Access was limited to public relations officers, and that made it easier for the administration to cover mistakes while promoting successes. But even so, Krock agreed that the President was justified in doing what all presidents have done in complaining about "unfairness and inaccuracies" of certain writers, editors, or publishers. That was "the only kind of censorship possible in this country."[28]

Press criticism during FDR's first two terms was characterized by one side charging that the press was coloring and manipulating the reporting of government activities, while the other countered that the New Deal was doing the same thing through its use of radio and publicity. President Roosevelt sometimes attempted to enlist the sympathy of the Washington correspondents by telling them that he understood that they might be trying to get out the accurate story but that their bosses were changing things back at the office.[29]

Roosevelt's antipathy toward the press is well known and has been the subject of several scholarly studies. As Graham White points out, the President had bipartisan support at the beginning of his administration and retained support (with some criticism) of the Scripps-Howard newspapers, of the *New York Times*, the *Washington Post*, and key publishers like J. David Stern of the *New York Post*, Marshall Field, and William Allen White. Joseph Patterson, publisher of the *New York Daily News* remained a loyal supporter until 1941 when he did an about-face on the issue of lend-lease. Colonel Robert R. McCormick and William Randolph Hearst were bitter enemies of FDR, and the Luce publications were sometimes hostile or critical.[30] White charts the President's support from the press as running from over 50 percent in favour of his domestic policy to 72.8 percent for his foreign policy in 1939. The domestic policy support declined in 1940 to 30 percent, but foreign policy support rose after 1940 and the bitter third term reelection.[31]

Another FDR target was the political columnist. By 1938, 112 of them addressed an audience of about seven million readers. Although the President had good relations with a few of them, he thought that the columnists were generally ill-equipped for political analysis and endangered the tradition of objective journalism.[32]

## THE WANING POWER THEME

Following the 1936 reelection of Roosevelt to a second term, liberals raised the "waning power of the press theme." The President's 60.8 percent share of the popular vote seemed to justify the "loss of power" slogan hurled at the conservative publishers. The perceived power of the press to influence voters seemed to have melted away, and some doubted that such power ever really existed. The real power of the press, in fact, was to tell the nation through the news columns what its government was doing and thinking, they pointed out. Citizens could continue to show their independence at the polls, and that was as it should be.

*Commonweal* charged the newspapers with manipulation of the news in order to oppose the President on "purely business grounds," and warned that newspaper ownership was dangerously concentrated in few hands.[33] The *New Republic* in an election study concluded that the press was "unrepresentative of its readers because its business leaders were too far removed" from the readers and this gave them little influence. The *New Republic* editorialized that radio competition was not a worry, nor did an endowed or reform journalism seem to solve the issue of unrepresentativeness. The remedy, it said, was reader refusal to subscribe.[34]

The *Literary Digest* summarized the situation, saying that circulation was rising as was advertising, but the press was troubled because "66, 80, 85 or perhaps 90 percent of the newspapers have been wrong on the election." The article pointed out that the waning power theme had been around since late in the nineteenth century. "But since November 4, the yammer has been wide-spread, the ubiquitous bogey-man of the press, 'Mr. Waning Power,' has been traveling the countryside. His cronies today are said to be the radio, newsreels, magazines. It is they who are aligned against the Fourth Estate, alarmists cry."[35]

The "half-heartedly pro–New Deal *New York Times*" estimated that President Roosevelt had the support of 40 percent of the nation's press circulation, the *Digest* reported. Other sources find large support from the radio audiences. But, a CBS representative said, "neither newspapers nor radio can swing an election. They merely focus public opinion," and radio's influence depended entirely upon the speaker's "voice, personality, and what he says."[36] William Allen White, editor-publisher of the *Emporia Gazette* and regarded as an elder statesman of small-town publishers, told the *Digest* that he had worked months "in vain for the Republican cause and might just as well have been on a vacation." He was sure newspapers no longer had influence, and unsure they had ever had political influence.[37]

## NO RESPECT FOR JOURNALISTS

Several popular books criticized the press in the late 1930s, a sign to some of the sharp increase in press criticism.[38] George Seldes, Ferdinand Lundberg, Silas Bent, and Leo Rosten all published such books and magazine articles. A sharply worded battle between publisher Frank Gannett and Interior Secretary Harold Ickes highlighted the debate at the end of the decade. In general, the critics on the left continued the attack on commercialization, while those on the right defended the freedom and independence of the press from government control.

Best known and most prolific of the critics was George Seldes, whose books *Freedom of the Press* (1935) and *Lords of the Press* (1938) were on the best-seller lists of their day, even though they were assailed by some critics and ignored by many others. Seldes was often regarded as one of the "cranks" who enjoyed sniping at an institution that had nurtured him as a cub.[39] He worked for the *Pittsburgh Leader* and covered World War I in Europe for the *Chicago Tribune*. He remained in Europe as the *Tribune*'s chief correspondent until returning to Chicago in 1927. His views did not mesh with publisher McCormick's and he left the paper the next year. Seldes had decided that the press was neither noble nor free, and that it had sold out to the advertisers and big-money interests; he was ready to name names and cases. His books did that, but they also offered reforms that seemed far-fetched in their time though they was later considered pioneering.[40]

In *Freedom of the Press*, Seldes used muckraking journalistic reporting in the tradition of Sinclair and Irwin to attack the major problems besetting the press. He saw the threat to press freedom emerging more from the growing dominance of business in journalism, and viewed self-censorship as catering more to advertisers than emanating from government pressure. He attacked the Associated Press, the *New York Times*, and the Hearst press for unfair reporting and he worried about their undue influence in journalism. He dug into the influence on the press from the utilities, the oil industry, and others, and he blasted the pernicious growth of propaganda and publicity. He rebuked the press for failing to report courageously and honestly about the 1929 stock market crash and the Depression, and for not covering the medical research linking cancer to cigarettes.

Seldes agreed with Lippmann that the press needed better trained newsmen—professionals who adhered to an enforceable code. The old ideas of the endowed press and the adless newspaper had not really offered much, Seldes admitted, because the purely commercial, sensational press could always drive out the good newspapers by offering "enticing goods at cheap prices." Competing publications with alternative views—such as the labor press, and radio, which had direct access to the home—would help the general improvement, but Seldes believed that the biggest improvement had to come from the publishers themselves. If they would just "put their news editors free from outside control . . . publish in strict accordance with the *Canons of Journalism* and code of ethics and their own consciences . . . that would produce a free newspaper." The economic freedom of the newspaper workers, Seldes believed, would insure their spiritual freedom, and would thus be uplifting for journalism as a whole.[41]

In *Lords of the Press*, which he dedicated to the American Newspaper Guild, Seldes chastised the ANPA for fighting labor, holding secret meetings, and campaigning against the New Deal. He said the foreign correspondents, Washington press corps, and reporters in general had become "servants" of the press lords, kept down by low pay, and lack of independence and respect. Seldes attacked the press lords individually and collectively, reiterating the charges that they used the press as an instrument to further their own interests with little regard for public service. Seldes wanted the public to get involved in order to force a stop to "red-baiting" in the press, by ceasing support of the "colored, biased, perverted" papers and placing their support behind the "honest newspapers." The "most effective weapon," he believed, was organized public protest. He also called for a government investigation of the press, and urged the press to expose the truth about consumer products, such as autos and cigarettes, to publish Federal Trade Commission reports and labor news, and to give equal space to political party news.[42]

Reviewers were not kind to Seldes, but the public purchased his books. Some reviewers feared punishment if they praised his work, and one did lose his job because of a favorable review. Many remained silent even when the

*New York Times* and the *New York Herald Tribune* refused to run ads for *Lords of the Press*. The book still sold 150,000 copies.[43] *Editor and Publisher* charged that Seldes was "still fighting press abuses that were common on the newspaper of his cubhood."[44] His examples did span a few decades, but most of his cases were uncomfortably current. Dennis and Bertrand praised Seldes' muckraking techniques but thought the old-fashioned writing style probably had not appealed to a new generation of readers. Nevertheless, reviewers agreed that Seldes deserved to be regarded as the father of American press criticism, that his ideas had been picked up later by others, and that many of his predictions had proven to be right.[45] Seldes influenced another generation of critics, including A. J. Liebling and I. F. Stone, who read some of his eighteen books, articles, and the newsletter, *In Fact*, which was published from 1940 until 1950. The review carried on his crusade and critiques of the press and once attracted 100,000 subscribers, but it gradually lost its edge. Seldes learned after closing the publication that some funding had come to his publication from the Communist Party through an associate, but he could proudly say that the Party had never been able to dictate his views.[46]

Silas Bent was still engaged in press criticism in the 1930s. He published *Newspaper Crusaders*, where he championed the need for crusading as a "normal, routine activity" of newspapers and called for a strong editorial page.[47] Another former journalist, Ferdinand Lundberg, linked the newspaper dynasties to the top capitalists in business and industry through club memberships and boards of directors, and published his findings in a muckraking analysis, *America's 60 Families*. He said American journalism was "bought and paid for by the wealthy, fanatics, some professional politicians, and chain press lords" at the service of economic and political power.[48] Freedom of the press, he charged, is "largely theoretical," because dissident groups are forced out of business by the rich and powerful.[49] The real threat, as he saw it, was not from government but from the concentration of power and money in the hands of a few families who pose the "danger of a dictatorship from the right."[50]

## PUBLISHERS SET THE TONE

Journalist Leo C. Rosten took a different approach to press criticism in *The Washington Correspondents* in 1937, using the research methods of social scientists to examine the persistent charge of political bias in the Washington press corps. He learned that the Washington press corps was composed chiefly of middle-class, youthful rebels against symbols of authority, but these "rebels" were stable, highly skilled, and moral people with an "unarticulated" code of ethics. These correspondents had learned to work in modern Washington "awash with news agencies and public relations staffs generating hundreds of handouts daily and making effective use of the press conference to seize headlines and the initiative in defining the New Deal's programs."[51]

These Washington correspondents confirmed the contention that they were well aware of their newspaper's defined policy to be objective and equally aware of the way stories were played back home, depending on views of the publisher. Rosten said Washington correspondents did not get direct orders to slant their reports, but policy was maintained through such subtle channels as choice of personnel, socialization of values, an approval or disapproval of work, getting good news space, or having stories played down or killed for policy reasons. Reporters learned to adjust, and by the time they were sent to Washington, they had learned that objectivity "was impossible" anyway.[52] The publisher "sets the tone" for the newspaper, correspondents believed, and they themselves were clear about their roles as employees, Rosten said.[53] These middle-class correspondents had a more liberal personal view of society than their bosses and sometimes fought the urge to take a stand, letting a protective cynicism cover their idealism.[54]

Because American journalism had no standard for supervision of its publishers, Rosten said, its performance and character had become dominated by the business ethic. Those norms for journalists that emphasize individualism and personal responsibility "are extolled at a time when social responsibility is the key approach." Organizations like the American Society of Newspaper Editors and the Newspaper Guild lacked the authority of national professional groups like those in Britain, which provided a strong counterforce, he pointed out.[55] "Until people in this country get it well into their heads that journalism is a profession that must be licensed and controlled, as the medical and legal profession are licensed and controlled, there can be no freedom of the press that is not liable to abuses . . . ," he said, quoting William Allen White.[56]

In the meantime, Rosten concluded that the danger was that people could be misled and manipulated by newspapers that were not held publically accountable. "The newspaper is a school, dispensing facts. It is the crucible in which political ideas are resolved, the opinion-making institution which disseminates the symbols of political life and assigns moral values."[57] The press had become an informal "house of lords," he agreed, warning that "newspapers get the reporters they deserve, and the public gets what the publishers make possible."[58]

## ICKES VERSUS GANNETT

Most publishers did not get publicly involved in disputes over press standards, so when Interior Secretary Harold L. Ickes and publisher Frank Gannett faced off on the NBC radio program, "America's Town Meeting of the Air," their debate attracted more than a little attention. The topic was: "Do we have a free press, or don't we?" Participants were asked to discuss how public opinion functioned and was formed in a modern world of propaganda, radio, movies, and a monopoly press. Secretary Ickes tore into the abuse of freedom exercised by a few powerful publishers and their financial interests, including advertisers. Gannett, owner of a chain of nineteen newspapers and three radio stations, and considered even by Ickes as "above average among American publishers" defended the free and unshackled press, but Ickes charged that even Gannett papers served special interests.[59]

Gannett responded that the American press was "emphatically free, as historically understood—free from governmental domination and censorship. Given this freedom, one need fear no other form of press control," he declared. He further maintained that the freedom to report on government, to criticize it, and even to include bias in the news, "was a freedom for all." He urged critics to look at the entire press, rather than isolated examples, before they made their charges.[60] "The publisher who habitually suppressed important news would sign his own slow death warrant," Gannett pointed out, because the competing newspapers, radio, and magazines would spread the news he tried to hide. Ickes and FDR were not suppressed by the press, Gannett observed, and the current "hue and cry" against the press he thought was a response to the press's opposition to the "packing of the Supreme Court."[61] Gannett said there were rumors that the President was planning to "do" something about the press. "Any newspaper that opposes the Administration" is in danger of prosecution, he warned, and this situation spelled an end to free speech and would promote government propaganda.[62]

Ickes responded that the press was a "thin-skinned lot" unable to take criticism.[63] *Editor and Publisher* finally called the story "tiresome" and blamed the "communists and their volunteer aides" for keeping press criticism in vogue.[64] When Ickes published *America's House of Lords* late in 1939, the book offered little that was new about the danger of business domination of the press, but he did suggest the following: elimination of advertising, expanded columns of letters and opinions, ample corrections of newspaper mistakes, and equal space to both sides in major political controversies. He wanted healthy press criticism. "All of us—publishers, editors, public men, and average citizens—should ever remember that eternal truth is the result of eternal vigilance—and of plain speaking."[65]

## THE VALUE OF CRITICISM

Professional journalists passed resolutions for improvement of the press in the late 1930s. It was no comfort that many critics were "critics for a cause they want us to join," or were critics who want to change society and saw the press as a "drag on social change," said ASNE's 1938 president.[66] He urged that the press remain free to criticize government and not be subservient to it. Newspaper performance had improved; decent newspapers subscribed to codes of ethics and printed both sides of issues, but radio news offered strong competition.[67]

William Allen White, incoming ASNE president, saw the country under FDR in the middle of "something approaching a class struggle" between a planned economy and capitalism. The country and the leadership were thinking in workingman terms, while the newspapers were thinking in middle-class terms. That, White observed, made the press unpopular, but he believed the press had been fair in reporting the latest presidential campaign.[68]

Grove Patterson, an ASNE founding member and editor of the *Toledo Blade*, said he had "heard more criticism of the press" in the last few years than he had heard in "all the preceding years" of his professional experience. "People say you can't believe what you see in the newspapers," he said, and that worried him. Patterson urged ASNE to remind the public that what the press stands for is good taste and accuracy, not private profit. It was a "fundamental privilege of citizenship."[69]

After some discussion, ASNE passed the following resolution:

> We call upon all editors to recognize a growing criticism, to face it fairly, to set their houses in order, to be governed by good taste, by a sense of justice, by a complete devotion to the public interest, and to toil unceasingly to educate our readers to such a sense of the value of a free press in America that the citizens of this republic shall become the willing co-operators, the fellow warriors, in a never-ceasing fight for the maintenance of democratic institutions.[70]

But the next year, 1939, William Allen White was still worried about the level of press criticism and public mistrust. Newspapers are free from political party control, he said, but there is still editorial bias "infecting the news columns." And newspaper people have sometimes unconsciously sided with the property owners. "The critics are sore." The extreme right "calls the left Socialists and Communists, the left calls the right Facists, the middle is bewildered." White urged the press to print both sides and take a stand on the editorial pages, reserving their "steam" for Mussolini, Hitler, and Stalin. Now there was an even greater threat to democracy, he said, the probability of American involvement in the war in Europe, and with it a new threat to the free press.[71]

The press on the eve of a second World War was still troubled by the split between its publicly expressed ideals of a free press and the independent-minded citizens who were ignoring its political advice. The crisis had polarized society and the press and was already starting to escalate into the name-calling and scapegoating that would mark the postwar cold war era. Once the reality of war was faced, the press found a better enemy to combat on its own terms. The nation could pull together to fight the war and the press would be a formidable asset; it could lead the crusade for press freedom on a world scale.

## NOTES

1. Alexis de Tocqueville, *Democracy in America* (New York: Modern Library, 1981; original 1835).
2. William Weinfeld, "The Growth of Daily Newspaper Chains in the U.S.: 1923, 1926–35," *Journalism Quarterly* 13 (December 1936): 357–380.
3. White, *FDR*: 69, 159. This source analyzed press support during the presidential campaigns of the New Deal and found from 26 to 29 percent of the newspapers were officially Republican or Democrat; the rest were Independent or Independent-Republican or Independent-Democrat.
4. "American Journalists' Association Forum," *Editor and Publisher* (5 June 1920): 19. There were several articles about the British Institute of Journalists as a model for the U.S. See: "Institute of Journalists Called U.S. Need," *Editor and Publisher* (6 October 1928): 5; and "Bullen Tells How Institute Works," *Editor and Publisher* (30 December 1933): 7, 33.
5. M. V. Atwood, "Proposed Plan for Certifying to Capability of Persons in Journalism," *Journalism Quarterly*, 8 (March 1931): 25.
6. White, *FDR*, 77.
7. *Problems*, 1930, 29–39. Pew was editor of *E&P* from 1924–36, and often used his "Shop Talk at 30 Column" to raise criticism of the press. See: obituary, *E&P* (17 October 1936): 13.
8. *Problems*, 1930, 131–36.
9. In 1947, when the commission headed by Hutchins set forth requirements for a free and responsible press, a few editors recalled the incident and his long-standing animosity toward journalism and journalism schools, but this never became a major thrust in the journalistic response. For examples, see: *Editor and Publisher* (29 March 1947): 47; and *ASNE Proceedings* of 1947: 41, 46.
10. "Nineteen Charges," *Problems*, 1933, 53–54.
11. "Nineteen," *Problems*, 1933, 54.
12. Willard Grosvenor Bleyer, "Journalism in the U.S.: 1933," *Journalism Quarterly* 10 (1933): 296.
13. Emery, *ANPA*, 225.
14. Emery, *ANPA*, 225.
15. A.L.A. *Schecter Poultry Corp.* v. *United States*, 295 U.S. 495, 55 S.Ct. 837, 79 L. Ed. 1570, 97 A.L.R. 97 (1935); and *Panama Refining Co.* v. *Ryan* 293 U.S. 388, 55 S.Ct. 241, 79. L. Ed. 446 (1935). In the Schecter case the Supreme Court discussed the standard of delegation of power.
16. Isabelle Keating, "Reporters Become of Age," *Harper's Monthly* 170 (April 1935): 601–12.
17. Bleyer, "Journalism," 299.
18. Bleyer, "Journalism," 296.
19. Bleyer, "Journalism," 301.

20. Bleyer, "Journalism," 301.
21. Emery, *ANPA*, 218.
22. Leo C. Rosten, *The Washington Correspondents* (New York: Harcourt, Brace, 1937), 217. See also: his articles "The Social Composition of Washington Correspondents," *Journalism Quarterly* 14 (June 1937): 132; and "The Professional Composition of the Washington Press Corps," *Journalism Quarterly* 14 (September 1937): 221.
23. Gerald W. Johnson, "Freedom of the Newspaper Press," *Annals of the American Academy of Political and Social Science* 200 (November 1938): 74.
24. White, *FDR*, 99–100.
25. "Win Public Confidence, Press Told," *Editor and Publisher*, 22 December 1934, 9.
26. Steele, *Propaganda*: 49.
27. Betty H. Winfield, "FDR's Publicity Foundation for a Modern Presidency," unpublished paper, History Division, AEJ Convention, 1981. The same author is preparing a book on this subject.
28. Arthur Krock, "The Press and Government," *Annals of the American Academy of Political and Social Sciences* 180 (July 1935): 167.
29. Steele, *Propaganda*, 41.
30. White, *FDR*, 78.
31. White, *FDR*, 78.
32. White, *FDR*, 28.
33. Editorial, "Public Opinion and the Press," *Commonweal* 25 (November 20): 1936, 85–86.
34. "The Press and the Public," *New Republic* 90 (17 March 1937): 78–91.
35. "Faith in Power of Editors Shaken," *Literary Digest* 121 (19 December 1936): 42.
36. "Faith," *Literary Digest*, 42.
37. "Faith," *Literary Digest*, 42.
38. See: Chap. 7, n. 10.
39. George Seldes, *Tell the Truth and Run* (New York: Greenberg, 1953), 42.
40. Everette E. Dennis and Claude-Jean Bertrand, "Seldes at 90: They Don't Give Pulitzers for That Kind of Criticism," *Journalism History* 7 (Autumn–Winter 1980–81): 84.
41. George Seldes, *Freedom of the Press* (New York: Garden City, 1937), 358.
42. Seldes, *Lords*, Chap. 3, 4.
43. Dennis, "Seldes at 90," 85.
44. Editorial "Welcome Criticism," *Editor and Publisher* (21 September 1935): 26.
45. Dennis, "Seldes at 90," 120.
46. Dennis, "Seldes at 90," 85.
47. Silas Bent, *Newspaper Crusaders* (New York: McGraw Hill, 1939), 279.
48. Ferdinand Lundberg, *America's 60 Families* (New York: Vanguard Press, 1937), 244. He had also published *Imperial Hearst* (1936).
49. Lundberg, *Families*, 286.
50. Lundberg, *Families*, 490.
51. Rosten, *Washington*, 5.
52. Rosten, *Washington*, 225.
53. Rosten, *Washington*, 234–35.
54. Rosten, *Washington*, 245.

55. Rosten, *Washington*, 299.
56. Rosten, *Washington*, 301.
57. Rosten, *Washington*, 302.
58. Rosten, *Washington*, 303.
59. "Ickes Charges News Distortion by Press in Debate," *Editor and Publisher* (21 January 1939): 4.
60. "Gannett Defends Press as Fair," *Editor and Publisher* (21 January 1939): 5, 29.
61. "Gannett Defends," 29.
62. "Gannett Defends," 29.
63. "Ickes Broadens Attack on Press in New Speech," *Editor and Publisher* (18 February 1939): 14.
64. Editorial, "Mr. Ickes Again," *Editor and Publisher* (28 January 1939): 32.
65. Harold L. Ickes, *America's House of Lords* (New York: Harcourt, Brace, 1939), 171.
66. *Problems*, 1938, 16.
67. *Problems*, 1938, 19.
68. *Problems*, 1938, 133.
69. *Problems*, 1938, 136–37.
70. *Problems*, 1938, 138.
71. *Problems*, 1939, 20.

# CHAPTER 11

# Press Freedom and the War: 1940–1946

In the early 1940s press criticism continued to stress the Depression-era 1930s issues, but the fear that the free press was in danger from governments at home and abroad gave the debate a new edge. Liberal critics continued to warn that the danger was from the business-minded leadership, standardization, and lack of diversity. The conservatives thought the New Deal might drift toward totalitarian supression, with wartime censorship as the first wedge. Both sides worried about wresting press control away from any form of censorship, voluntary or otherwise, as soon as the war ended. Editors and journalism teachers made early efforts to work for international press freedom for the postwar world.

The middle ground—made up of the editors, journalists, and some publishers and educators—pushed for a responsible tradition of news reporting that would remain above partisan battles, economic and other biases, and at last would elevate journalism to become a respectable and honored profession. They supported codes of ethics, accreditation of journalism education, and adherence to objectivity in reporting and in news interpretation.

The more the professional journalists and social scientists studied the modern press, the more they were able to clarify and understand its central role in society and its potential power in shaping public opinion and the public agenda for attention. The very formulation of freedom of the press in a democratic society contained within it the revulsion toward any mechanism to control speech and press. Those in journalism had to be guided by a higher goal than profit, sensations, and scoops. Serving the public interest was that higher goal, but people defined the public interest differently.

The spirit of wartime patriotism modulated press criticism temporarily.

Conservatives actively promoted the idea that press freedom was endangered by government. This was easily a popular view, regardless of political partisanship. A variation on this theme was the stress on the importance of continued press surveillance and criticism of the government. The familiar voices of George Seldes and Oswald Garrison Villard and Secretary Harold Ickes, joined by civil rights attorney Morris Ernst, continued in the 1940s to keep the liberal anti–big business press criticism issue alive, while Colonel Robert McCormick kept criticizing the Roosevelt administration for repeated attempts to control the press. It was fairly easy to ignore Seldes and Villard, but Ickes and Ernst commanded attention.[1]

## POWER IN THE MESSAGE

A trusted cabinet member, already known for his critical book on press lords, Ickes invited fifty-eight leaders from press and radio to join him in a book called *Freedom of the Press Today*. Press performance, he thought, needed attention and the press was too arrogant to open the subject. It was the citizen's "duty to criticize the press when it merits criticism," he said. But the press could snarl back at criticism, he warned, such as in the 219 editorials calling Ickes' criticism a "blast, attack or tirade."[2]

That arrogance, the commercial domination, and the business mentality of the press were serious problems. Ickes wanted a press free of control and open to all sides. Instead, his examination of press coverage of the 1940 election showed that the majority of pro-Republican newspapers allotted nearly six times as much space to the Republican challenger as to President Roosevelt, and that in Ickes' opinion 86.6 percent of those were biased. But the President had won a large majority vote supported by only 23 percent of the daily newspapers. This "reveals an unprecedented and progressively perilous situation requiring public consideration," he declared. The press had lost public confidence because it had come to represent a single class, Ickes charged.[3]

A *Baltimore Sun* editorial replied that Ickes' theory boiled down to this: "Any politician who can command the long-continued support or toleration of the readers, whether by corruption, demagoguery, or whatnot, is entitled to the support of the newspapers. And, by the same rule, any time-serving, popularity-seeking charlatan in journalism may wrap himself in the mantle of duty when he tramples upon conviction and scuttles headlines to the high tide."[4]

Frank E. Tripp, vice president and general manager of the Gannett Newspapers and a newspaperman for forty years, charged that Ickes' argument was self-defeating. "Can it be that your idea of a free press, one that you would like, is a press that the government could control as it does your pal, the radio?" he asked. Radio was restricted from expressing opinions because of licensing, Tripp pointed out, but newspapers could have opinions.[5] These opinions were published "by thousands of different individuals in thousands of different cities and villages in America. They are licensed by nobody except their readers," 42 million of whom pay daily to receive those newspapers.[6]

The value of an independent press, Tripp thought, was that it was free to speak its mind, "even against the tide." He would not want to go back to the old partisan press. He preferred an independent and open press that printed both sides, even "your stuff and that of all your pals." That was really Ickes' complaint, he believed—that the press did not express the opinions Ickes liked. "You are right about one thing, however," Tripp said. "That old-time ballyhoo about the 'power of the press' is the bunk. I hadn't heard of it for years. The power of the press is and always was nothing more than the delivery of the message. The power lies in the message itself. Americans get the message and think for themselves. They vote for the man they like, or they buy a can of beans the same way."[7]

The essayists who agreed to contribute to Ickes' book were mostly liberals, even though Ickes had encouraged wider participation by promising not to read any manuscripts before publication. The book covers much familiar ground. For example, Bruce Blivin, editor of the *New Republic*, said that sharp criticism from men like Sinclair, Seldes, and Lundberg, though "fiercely resisted and repudiated," had encouraged the press to remedy some of its faults. Journalists were better educated and the Guild encouraged self-respect by newspapermen, but the pressing problem remained domination of advertisers and big businessmen in chain journalism. Blivin thought there was too much standardization from technological advances, but hoped that facsimile newspapers transmitted by wirephoto to homes would lower costs and break the grip of monopoly chains. He expected better educated readers to demand better papers.[8]

## TRUTH WILL OUT

*PM*, the experimental adless newspaper started by Ralph Ingersoll in New York City in 1940, was an attempt to reach that special group of readers. Ingersoll's hopeful essay in Ickes's book, written during the newspaper's first year, describes the attempt to produce a newspaper that pursued the truth and was free from "antagonistic interests . . . advertising . . . financial control . . . politicians."[9] *PM* was capitalized by private stockholders and attracted a talented group of reporters and editors. It lasted only eight years. Ingersoll was editor for less than three years, yet he is credited with making a major impact on modern American journalism.[10] The paper was compartmentalized for easy reading, it covered neglected subjects like labor and consumer affairs, and it emphasized solid research and good writing. It blended elements of magazine journalism and daily newspaper reporting, and gave the tabloid format a fresh design and the feel of reading a daily news magazine.

The necessary 200,000 readers didn't materialize, recalled Ingersoll, sharing his disappointment and his "education" in 1963 with professional journalists: "I started a newspaper to correct all the abuses which I found so easy to inventory . . . we tried hard . . . but the newspaper we produced ended up by being even more opinionated than the newspapers we had dedicated ourselves to setting straight."[11] The truth "is difficult to arrive at" and can be served only "with discipline—in journalism as in science and the arts." Ingersoll was disappointed that the press was an "echo" of the popular voice, little willing or able to challenge the status quo.[12]

It hadn't been a complete newspaper, says Ingersoll's biographer Roy Hoopes, and it had problems with finances, lack of enough professional staff, and charges of harboring writers with communist ideas. Ingersoll's attempt was courageous and his defeat gallant, according to I. F. Stone, a former *PM* writer who later founded his own noted investigative weekly newsletter.[13] Ingersoll was trying to do the impossible—publish a newspaper in 1940 with magazine standards—the funding, the talent, and the readers were not there yet. Since then no one has tried to produce a newspaper in the United States that would cater only to an elite class of readers. The potential audience for such a newspaper is distributed across the nation, not just centered in New York City, so distribution costs without the heavy infusion of advertising have been considered prohibitive.[14]

Scripps-Howard columnist Raymond Clapper took up the case for press criticism in Ickes's book. It would be as healthy for the press as it was for politicians, he challenged. "No patent formula for improving newspapers is to be trusted except that of public criticism."[15] Laws don't work, and government newspapers would become propaganda, he explained. The only safe rule was "truth will eventually out" through the "boundless energy and enterprise of free newspapers." But each newspaper would be publicly judged on its merits. "Alert and discriminating criticism" by the public was an "old-fashioned remedy," but Clapper still found it "the best one for a democracy."[16]

Poet and Librarian of Congress Archibald MacLeish pleaded to keep the press open and free, even in wartime. The press is not by its "essential nature an instrument of illumination. . . . It can be used for truth against ignorance, or against truth and freedom." It was vital, he said, to keep the press free in wartime, even when there was a temptation to restrict content.[17]

One pessimistic view in the Ickes book came from Herbert Agar, editor of the *Louisville Courier-Journal*, who charged that the press in America was failing to justify itself as an institution allowed special privileges.[18] It was not just a money-making venture and should not "treat news as a butter salesman treats butter," or it would lose its protection.[19] It should be bringing enlightenment to people in troubled times, but Agar admitted this truth was not what people wanted to hear. The press was morally "unfree . . . timid . . . lacking in imagination." Ager challenged the press to live up to the responsibility of its public trust.[20]

A few years after Ickes's book, Oswald Garrison Villard reworked his earlier press criticism in a new volume, *The Disappearing Daily*. In it he said that a 20-year survey of newspapers in America had convinced him that they had been affected by the same tendencies as other businesses. The newspaper owners behaved like other community leaders. Newspaper costs and circulation were up, but newspaper individuality was down, and the public no longer trusted editorials that contained lies, bias, or propaganda, or suppressed facts, said Villard. The only hope for the press was to "bring to the editorial chairs men of fire and passion."[21] Even though the problems and causes were complex, the editor had a free soul and was free to fight daily for the betterment of the human condition, an ideal Villard found few could reach.[22]

## THE DIVERSITY ISSUE

A forceful case for diversity of opinion in the press was made by Morris Ernst, a noted First Amendment lawyer, prolific writer, and attorney for the Newspaper Guild. The shrinking number of newspapers, the growth of chains, and the interlocking ownership of newspapers and radio stations forecast a future of "concentrated control over the minds of 138 million people," he warned in 1946. He called for a national congressional debate on the issue, and said it was not too late to do something about "our vanishing freedom."[23] He advocated a joint Senate-House inquiry that would try to save the small daily, the weekly, the magazine, and the movie company and examine monopoly control of these media voices which were important educational forces in the society. Ernst advocated separating radio and press ownership, splitting movie companies from theater ownership, separating radio and television ownership from the networks, and divesting newspaper publishers from ownership of wood pulp, paper, and forests. He proposed tax relief for smaller newspapers to encourage them to stay in business. Furthermore, he said, limits on profits might enable more diversity of voices. The problem was that monopoly threatened diversity, and diversity was vital to the process of providing competing ideas and voices in the marketplace of ideas.[24]

Concentration of ownership had cut in half newspaper competition in ninety-two cities with 100,000 or more population, and one-quarter of those remaining were chain newspapers. The nation had fewer total newspapers, more chain ownerships, fewer local features and columnists, and more syndicated columns. A few voices reached millions, limiting the number of ideas circulating and giving undue prominence to those that were amplified.[25] The problem, Ernst said, was essentially spiritual. The public would be deprived of vital information and ideas, and finally "wake up to its mental starvation."

America had controlled interlocking directorates in other industries, Ernst pointed out, and he expected the same would have to be done for the mass media. Concentration of ownership may reduce costs for the owners, but it did not bring relief to consumers, he pointed out.[26]

Americans objected to government control of the press, Ernst acknowledged, but they also wanted diversity and competing opinions. "It makes little difference to the receiving public whether the absence of competition stems from government or from economic concentration of power." He believed in free enterprise, but he also saw the need to restore "our own marketplaces of the mind."[27] *Editor and Publisher* responded that Ernst's sweeping assumptions were debatable, and "so far the dangers from concentration were unproven." The reviewer thought that there was a limit to the number of newspapers that could survive, and that "mergers were better than subsidy."[28]

In its own count, *Editor and Publisher* found the number of daily newspapers had declined from a high of 2,166 in 1918 to 1,744 in 1944; the decline began tapering off in 1945. Total daily circulation of 45.9 million was the highest thus far in history. By looking at the economic stability of newspapers, the trade journal concluded that the public was getting more and better papers.[29] The magazine did not emphasize that while circulation was keeping up with the national population increase, only 8.4 percent of the towns with daily newspapers had competing papers.[30]

## VOLUNTARY CENSORSHIP

During the war, Republicans kept the pressure on the New Deal administration, and FDR did not hide his dislike for certain publishers, but both sides made voluntary censorship work. American newspapers and wire services expanded their overseas service, making up for the loss of European services cut off by the war. The few critical articles about the press centered on the themes of press freedom and concentration of ownership trends. In their professional annual meetings editors and journalists were quick to see governmental actions as direct or implied pressure, leading to some form of postwar control. McCormick led the publishers' battle against the Justice Department over the issue of whether the Associated Press was a monopoly and in violation of the 1890 Sherman Antitrust Act.[31]

McCormick was on the AP board of directors and he opposed giving an AP franchise to the pro–New Deal *Chicago Sun*, founded by Marshall Field in 1940. AP rules permitted a member to blackball a new applicant in his own city, and required a four-fifths vote of the total membership to override this. Field had helped fund the experimental *PM* in New York City, and now wanted membership in AP for his Chicago paper. It would put a potentially strong New Deal voice in a town dominated by the Republican *Tribune*. McCormick rallied support to veto the application, passing the word to colleagues that the Justice Department action was a pressure tactic in FDR's attempt to muzzle the press. The government brought suit and won.[32] In 1945 the Supreme Court held that these AP bylaws constituted unfair competition and AP had to change its rules.[33] The AP later had to modify its membership rules so that newspaper members could not blackball admission of their competitors. McCormick and his supporters charged that the government was trying to turn the AP into a public utility.

As the *Tribune*'s writer put it, they had been fighting the New Deal on free press issues since 1933 when the NIRA ended the brief honeymoon days of the Roosevelt administration. "If you abandon freedom of the press, you substitute tyrannical government . . . [and] the first thing to go is the free press."[34] The *Tribune* charged in early cold war rhetoric that Archibald MacLeish was laying secret plans to put pressure on the *Chicago Tribune*, the *New York Daily News*, and the *Washington Times-Herald* (published by the McCormick and Patterson families), and this action was supported by the "Communist press, Marshall Field press, *Time-Life-Fortune* axis and various Communist-front organizations."[35] McCormick said that since the government had not succeeded in its direct attack on the free press, it had begun using bureaucracy, stratagems, fifth columns, and "dropping parachute troops upon press freedom, under the guise of regulating labor conditions, preserving business competition, and superintending accuracy in advertising." He vowed to keep up the fight.[36]

John S. Knight, president of Knight Newspapers in Detroit, Akron, and Miami, and publisher of the *Chicago Daily News*, told several hundred Chicago businessmen that as president of ASNE he would lead American newspapers in the fight "to maintain freedom of the press, even if it takes every last dollar from their tills." The publishers had lost contact with the public mind, he said, and this had led to the election of the New Deal administration. Roosevelt had tried to make the press "the whipping boy of his administration" and the press was a frequent target of abuse from both top and "small fry politicians," but Knight believed the public would make up its own mind.[37] "Newspapers are the last line of defense in this country," he said. Radio exists on government license, and can't be too critical, he warned. "The Fourth Term means more socialism in this country, more absolutism and more of a labor government." He warned that more young people would have to be recruited to the Republican party or there would be a repeat of the last four elections.[38]

## WORLD PRESS FREEDOM

In 1944, with Roy Roberts of the *Kansas City Star* as president and Knight as incoming president, ASNE took up the theme of "responsible journalism." Knight had recently returned from several months in London working for the

American Office of Censorship. Knight warned that wartime censorship tended to "establish certain habit patterns dulling the enterprise of newspapers."[39] Over 250 of the 363 members attended and they voted to defend freedom of the press both during and after the war.[40] Wartime censorship and propaganda must cease and old-fashioned reporting and open sources must be restored, they were told.[41] The members pledged themselves anew to their 1923 Canons of Journalism and called for "fullest information consistent with security" to be given at the peace settlement. They agreed to work for "international agreements permitting direct communication between each and every nation in the world wherever feasible, eliminating conventions and customs."[42]

*Christian Science Monitor* Editor Erwin Canham challenged the group to restore news enterprise. "We are too soft," he said. It was not advertiser influence, but lack of editorial planning and follow-through with "imagination, persistence and courage" that were problems. There was a flood tide of investigation on the subject of press freedom, he said (the Hutchins Commission study was just under way), but Canham thought what was really needed was action. "We are the basic masters of our destiny . . . our way of keeping the freedom of the press is . . . to keep on doing our job and doing it better."[43]

Censorship and wartime reporting occupied several of the ASNE sessions, and later that year three emissaries began a "free press pilgrimage" to European nations that were still at war in order to promote a plan for the free exchange of information and views in the postwar era.[44] The trio was determined not to miss another opportunity like that offered at Versailles in 1919, and pressed for open press coverage of the forthcoming peace conference. The American press had already succeeded in forcing FDR to open up to the press a 1943 world food conference held in the United States, which the government had wanted to keep under wraps.[45]

These men and others would work spiritedly to bring to the United Nations an agreement that would "define world press freedom," but in the process they learned how vastly difficult it was to get even the narrowest agreement on such a vital matter by nations with differing philosophies. Margaret Blanchard has fully documented this struggle, which the U.S. trade press promoted enthusiastically.[46] The American editors appeared to relish the opportunity to strike a blow for press freedom on the grand scale when they had been so frustrated about this issue on the home front.

Kent Cooper, who ran the AP from 1925 until he retired in 1950, is credited with coining the phrase "right to know" in a 1945 speech. He said citizens should have access to the news, fully and accurately presented. "We can't have political freedom without respect for the right to know."[47] Cooper had started soon after American entry into the war to press for international agreements and support for the right to freedom of information. He had helped establish the International Press Institute in Zurich and the American Press Institute at Columbia. He fought against censorship and a controlled press, regardless of the political party in power, because he believed that "the right to know made this country strong." People would be more loyal and patriotic if they knew what was going on, he pointed out, and he worked to rid the nation of the hateful wartime practices of censorship and propaganda.[48]

Some critics pointed out, however, that these patriotic and noble efforts would also benefit the growth of the American overseas wire services like the AP, which had taken the wartime opportunity to expand globally. The decline of the European-based news cartels created an open market for information, so Cooper's crusade was good business as well as patriotic rhetoric.

The contemporary partisan debate on both sides was heavily larded with political self-interest, but what of the idealism of the 1920s that had led to the high-minded codes of ethics adopted by professional associations? These groups had grown in strength and structure and even during the war were working out methods of elevating the standards of professional journalism and academic scholarship. After an initial clumsy "class" ranking system for the schools, the professional and academic associations collaborated on developing an accreditation system early in the 1940s. Because the schools would be the major source of future journalists, both editors and educators wanted to influence their philosophy and programs. Journalism was a new discipline seeking to be taken seriously by other academics.

## SCHOLARLY VIEWS OF THE PRESS

*The Annals of the American Academy of Political and Social Science* devoted an entire issue in 1942 to "The Press in the Contemporary Scene," edited by Dr. Malcolm M. Willey (sociology) and Dr. Ralph Casey (journalism), professors at the University of Minnesota.[49] That journal had previously taken up the subject of journalistic ethics in 1922 and propaganda in 1935. Now the concern was over the freedom of the press, which the editors felt was under intense current discussion, but frequently not in the context of a democratic society. Because the press "played such a central role in the thinking of citizens, they ought to understand it better." So the journal took up the news process, responsibility, bias, political reporting, and propaganda. The articles were written before the United States entered the war.[50]

The newspaper was a business and a social institution, explained Willey; that understanding was basic. The newspaper served six functions—news, editorial, background, entertainment, advertising, and encyclopedic (including guidance and service)—he explained. Most of the press criticism focused "largely upon one function, to the general exclusion of the others." Newspapers may be serving all the needs generally well, even if there is a "deficiency in one area."[51]

Critics, he thought, were not realistic in their criticism of newspapers. Society was the problem. Willey explained that the modern newspaper reflected the relatively impersonal urban and middle-class society. This society wanted amusement and vicarious personal contacts through its newspapers. The society's preferences, not the reformers, determined the kind of newspapers that evolved.[52]

In a related essay Casey suggested that propaganda was probably credited with too much power. "Public opinion is probably more important," he said, "because more factors than propaganda are at work in forming one's opinion," including sex, education, culture, age, race, the event itself, and what we hear about it. Propaganda had been a "red hot" topic since the First World War and had been used by some to "besmirch the press," making the public think that news columns are "full of distortion and untruths," and that the helpless public is at the mercy of the "magical power of propaganda," said Casey. As long as the press has varied readers, he pointed out, there will be criticism of propaganda in the press. The key was to differentiate between the willful efforts of propagandists to shape beliefs and the genuine efforts of the press to get at all sides of issues in the news.[53] The best "check on propaganda" was news organizations with people of disciplined minds, mental alertness, moral courage, honesty, and dedication to the public interest. Casey said the number of "this type of newspaperman has steadily risen in American journalism in recent years."[54]

Other scholars analyzed the role of press, movies, and radio on mass behavior and on the propagation of values and moral codes. The press was beginning to attract serious study in the social sciences as well as in journalism schools and departments, and these early efforts turned research in the professional schools more toward the social and institutional and away from their early association with the humanities. While probing the social issues, this research about the press and other media in society was also often critical.

Robert Park, one of the first sociologists to analyze the urban press, said that "the power of the press is the influence that newspapers exercise in the formation of public opinion and in mobilizing the community for action." Park explained that the process started with criticism and unrest and ended by changing mores and law. Since the editorial pages were intended more for the elite and the news pages were more widely read, the news makes opinion in democracies, Park said. The press orients the public, helps bring about political power that "as it mobilizes the community to act, tends to terminate discussion."[55] Park, a former journalist, stressed the complexity of public opinion formation and the role played by the press. He agreed with Lippmann that in a democracy, "as long as the sources of news are not fouled by propaganda, it is possible for a people to preserve the liberties guaranteed them by the existence of a democratic society."[56]

Psychologist Gordon Allport and student Janet M. Faden looked at the psychological relationship between newspapers and readers. They proposed the notion that newspapers skeletonized an issue and "operated in a field of influence that is well-structured in a pattern of editorials, policy stories, propaganda, columns." Readers get fatigued and want closure, according to Ross' laws of social psychology. "The more intense a craze the sharper will be the reaction against it." Allport and Faden noted that editors tended to drop stories before they are really dead because "they sense" this public desire to end the tension. This is also reflected in the brief "waves of interest in governmental reform" by the general public, which wishes to return to more personal interests.[57]

The scholarly research and other criticism of the press was regularly reported in *Editor and Publisher*, which became increasingly concerned over the rising press criticism in the prewar era. "We are actually doing all our work behind a plate glass window on Main Street . . . and we owe the people a trusteeship and a responsibility that is shared by no other business, trade, or profession." After the materialistic 1920s and the Depression, editors were awakened to "their responsibilities," said editor Arthur Robb.[58]

The tone of comments by editors and publishers in the 1940s was optimistic. They thought newspapers were better than ever, had higher standards of reporting, and showed a sense of responsibility to the public. The Pulitzer prize jurors were impressed by the 1941 entries.[59] Editors anticipated postwar improvements, more competition and rising costs. Many agreed with Louis Seltzer, editor of the *Cleveland Press*, on the need for more able young men and women, more specialists who could write about business and medicine, more investigative reporters, and more local coverage containing "the juice of the communities in which they are published."[60]

A similar vision was shared by Erwin D. Canham, editor of the *Christian Science Monitor*. He told newspaper advertising executives that the complex modern world needed far more subject area specialists and more daily news magazine-style coverage with explanation. The "big news stories of the world can no longer be covered by a bright boy just off the police beat. . . . Joseph Pulitzer recognized this fact half a century ago when he projected his postgraduate journalism school. This trend will greatly intensify." But Canham reminded them that newspapers had to re-earn the trust of readers. Public trust and responsibility were the keys to the future.[61]

Radio's "instant news and living speeches" and the weekly news magazines' summarizations and interpretations, were providing new challenges to the daily newspaper, observed Felix Morely, editor of the *Washington Post*. The press can't sufficiently rival the speed of radio or the luxury of time at the news magazine, he said, but it could and should "emphasize better reporting, higher quality editorial pages and less dilution of the newspaper" with syndicated material. The temptation to use more features and syndicated news will deteriorate enterprise reporting and editorial commentary, he warned. There should be more self-criticism that asks if the American newspaper "is rising to its responsibilities, and if not, why not?"[62]

Outsiders, Morely said, think the newspaper is losing prestige. To counter that, Morley wanted the journalism schools to produce reporters who know something about the political and social institutions they report, "scholars in journalism" with "well-trained and well-disciplined minds. The half-baked method of newspaper production cannot continue," he warned, "unless we are willing to see our papers fill a progressively less important role in American society"[63]

## CITIZENS' COUNCILS PROPOSED

In 1946, in an attempt to help the press regain its lost prestige and reconnect with the readers, Dean Ralph L. Crossman of the College of Journalism at the University of Colorado proposed "citizens' councils" to help news executives discuss press behavior and policy. There was a "rising tide of dissatisfaction," he warned. The advisory council would be a means of bringing the critical citizens "into the organization . . . where the validity of criticism can be tested." Crossman also chastised the press for not living up to its public responsibilities and challenged journalism schools to teach students to be good and effective critics of the press.[64]

Also calling for more responsible journalism was Arthur Hays Sulzberger, publisher of the *New York Times*. He felt that the New Deal attacks on the press had undermined public confidence. He feared they would inspire efforts to restrict press abuses by laws or alternate forms of ownership. A better approach was to create "a responsible newspaper" that prints the news "without fear or favor of any party, sect or interest, and which admits that the manner in which it presents that news is a matter of legitimate public concern."[65]

As the war ended, journalists found common ground in the need for self-improvement and professional growth. The satisfaction they had over their important job of war coverage and the anticipation of America's new role in world affairs strengthened their self-confidence. President Truman did some carping about the press, but the momentum for self-improvement was already under way. The ground for reform was seeded with suggestions and standards that had been thoroughly explored by professional journalists, academics, and interested citizens. The values and practices of modern journalism had been forged, and a better educated public and a nation that would assume international leadership was anticipated. The press seemed to be a little further along the road to the ideal of responsible journalism.

## NOTES

1. George Seldes, *1,000 Americans* (New York: Boni & Gaer, 1947); and *The People Don't Know* (New York: Gaer & Associates, 1949).
2. Ickes, Harold L., *Freedom of the Press Today: A Clinical Examination by Twenty Eight Specialists* (New York: Vanguard, 1941), 7.
3. Ickes, *Freedom*, 10.

4. "Shop Talk at 30," *Editor and Publisher* (16 November 1940): 44.
5. Erik Barnouw, *A History of Broadcasting in the U.S.*, vol. 1, "A Tower in Babel," (New York: Oxford University Press, 1966).
6. "Election Proved Freedom of Press Tripp Says in Letter to Ickes," *Editor and Publisher* (16 November 1940): 3.
7. Tripp, "Letter," 29.
8. Bruce Blivin, "Balance Sheet for American Journalism," in Ickes, *Specialists*, 30, 37.
9. Ralph Ingersoll, "A Free Press—for What?" in Ickes, *Specialists*, 140.
10. Roy Hoopes, "When Ralph Ingersoll Papered Manhattan: The Saga of *PM*, a Revolutionary Newspaper," *Washington Journalism Review* (December 1984): 25.
11. Ralph Ingersoll, "Postscript to *PM*," *Nieman Reports* (September 1963): 22–24.
12. Ingersoll, "Postscript," 23.
13. Hoopes, "Papered Manhattan," 32.
14. New technology using satellite printing, and the global media conglomerates and market segmentation may provide a new potential for the 1990s.
15. Raymond Clapper, "A Free Press Needs Discriminating Public Criticism," Ickes, *Specialists* 85.
16. Clapper, "Discriminating," 93.
17. Archibald MacLeish, "The Duty of Freedom," Ickes, *Specialists*, 188.
18. Herbert Agar, "Rights are Responsibilities," Ickes, *Specialists*, 21.
19. Agar, "Rights," 22.
20. Agar, "Rights," 24.
21. Oswald Garrison Villard, *The Disappearing Daily* (New York: Knopf, 1944), 19.
22. Villard, *Disappearing*, 28–29.
23. Morris Ernst, *First Freedom* (New York: Macmillan, 1946), xii–xiv.
24. Ernst, *First*, 246–50. Both the Hutchins Commission on Freedom of the Press (1947) and the First Royal Commission on the Press (1947–49) in England considered these and other potential regulations that would enforce diversity in a rapidly monopolizing press industry after World War II.
25. Ernst, *First*, 71.
26. Ernst, *First*, 245.
27. Ernst, *First*, 270–71.
28. "Books in Review," *Editor and Publisher* (30 March 1946): 58.
29. "Shop Talk at 30," *Editor and Publisher* (21 March 1945): 68.
30. Emery, *Press*, 5th edition, 676.
31. The Sherman Act, 15 USCA 1–3.
32. Emery, *Press*, 5th ed., 514.
33. *Associated Press* v. *United States* (326 US 1, 65 S.Ct. 1416, 89 L. Ed. 2013 [1942]).
34. Philip Kinsley, *Liberty and the Press* (Chicago: Chicago Tribune, 1944), 73, vi.
35. Kinsley, *Liberty*, 74. MacLeish was an outspoken New Dealer and critic of the press. He was Assistant Secretary of State for Cultural Affairs from 1944–45.
36. Robert R. McCormick, "Bureaucracy is Greatest Threat to Press Freedom—McCormick," *Editor and Publisher* (28 September 1940): xiv.
37. "Knight Asserts Press Will Not Give Up Freedom," *Editor and Publisher* (9 December 1944): 16.
38. "Knight," *Editor and Publisher*, 16.

39. "Knight Discusses U.S. Censorship in London," *Editor and Publisher* (29 April 1944): 123.
40. *Problems*, 1944, 52.
41. *Problems*, 1944, 18.
42. *Problems*, 1944, 18.
43. "Canham Cites Enterprise," *Editor and Publisher* (29 April 1944): 19, 62.
44. They were: Wilbur S. Forrest, assistant editor of the *New York Herald Tribune*, Ralph E. McGill, editor of the *Atlanta Constitution*, and Carl W. Ackerman, Dean of the Columbia Graduate School of Journalism and a former journalist.
45. Robert U. Brown, "ASNE to Strive for Free Press Principle Internationally," *Editor and Publisher*, (29 April 1944): 17.
46. For a thorough discussion, see: Margaret Blanchard, *Exporting the First Amendment* (New York: Longman, 1986).
47. Kent Cooper, *The Right to Know: An Exposition of the Evils of News Suppression and Propaganda* (New York: Farrar, Straus & Cudahy, 1956), xiii. The concept of a right to know had been used earlier by other journalists including Julius Chambers in 1910. See my Chap. 5.
48. Cooper, *Right*, 314.
49. "The Press in the Contemporary Scene," *Annals of the American Academy of Political and Social Science* 219, special issue (1942).
50. "Contemporary," *Annals*, vii–viii.
51. Malcolm M. Willey, "The Function of the Newspaper," *Annals* (1942): 18–24.
52. Willey, *Annals*, 23.
53. Ralph D. Casey, "The Press, Propaganda and Pressure Groups," *Annals* (1942): 66–67.
54. Casey, *Annals*, 70.
55. Robert E. Park, "News and the Power of the Press," *American Journal of Sociology* 47: 1–2.
56. Park, "News and Power," 11.
57. Gordon W. Allport and Janet M. Faden, "The Psychology of Newspapers: Five Tentative Laws," *Public Opinion Quarterly* 4 (December 1940): 702–03.
58. Arthur Robb, "Shop Talk at 30," *Editor and Publisher* (19 October 1940): 44.
59. "Higher Journalistic Standards Reported by Pulitzer Judges," *Editor and Publisher* (24 May 1941): 9.
60. "Seltzer Sees Youth Needed to Revitalize Newspapers," *Editor and Publisher* (8 December 1945): 8.
61. "Canham Visions Trend to Daily News Magazine," *Editor and Publisher* (19 January 1946): 9.
62. "More Scholarly Newspapermen Needed, Felix Morley Says," *Editor and Publisher* (18 May 1940): 11.
63. "Scholarly," *Editor and Publisher*, 27.
64. "Inland Publishers Debate Public Criticism of Press," *Editor and Publisher* (19 October 1946): 11.
65. "Sulzberger Pleads for Responsible Press," *Editor and Publisher* (19 October 1946): 66. Also published as: "Responsible Journalism: A Cornerstone of Freedom," *Journalism Quarterly* 23 (December 1946): 353–359.

# CHAPTER 12

# Press Responsibility Confronted: 1942–1950

The steady criticism of the press and the mounting concern over threats to press freedom provided the context for Time Inc. publisher Henry R. Luce's proposal of a commission to study the problem.[1] Luce was not the first to suggest a national study, but he had the funds and the academic contacts. An effort by journalism scholars in 1924 to interest the Rockefeller Foundation in a major study had failed. The call of Dean Carl Ackerman of Columbia University's Graduate School of Journalism in 1936 for a journalism foundation and scientific study of the press in 1936–38 had not yet been heeded, nor had Harold Ickes' recommendation in 1939 for a congressional investigation.

Luce made the original suggestion for a study in 1942, when he asked University of Chicago Chancellor Robert M. Hutchins to head an inquiry into the freedom of the press issue. Hutchins, who had been an outspoken critic of the press, at first declined, but the next year he mentioned to Luce that "something probably could be accomplished by such an inquiry." Luce came up with the funding. Hutchins was free to appoint the thirteen-member Commission and to set the agenda.[2] Time Inc. was to keep hands off. In fact, Luce had to wait to be invited for a courtesy visit at the first Commission meeting.[3] As other scholars have pointed out, Hutchins appointed leading figures from the social sciences, law, and business, men who shared a circle of friends through connections with Yale University and the University of Chicago.[4]

It was a steller group: Zechariah Chafee, Jr., professor of law at Harvard University (vice-chairman of the Commission); John M. Clark, professor of economics at Columbia University; John Dickinson, professor of law at the University of Pennsylvania; William E. Hocking, professor emeritus of philosophy at Harvard University; Harold D. Lasswell, professor of law at

Yale University; Archibald MacLeish, poet and former assistant secretary of state; Charles E. Merriam, professor emeritus of political science at The University of Chicago; Reinhold Niebuhr, professor of ethics and philosophy of religion at Union Theological Seminary; Robert Redfield, professor of anthropology at the University of Chicago; Beardsley Ruml, chairman of the Federal Reserve Bank of New York; Arthur M. Schlesinger, professor of history at Harvard University; and George N. Schuster, president of Hunter College.[5]

The function of the Commission, as Hutchins saw it, was "to begin an inclusive inquiry into the nature, functions, duties and responsibilities of the press in America—using the word press in its broadest sense, to include not only everything that is printed, but also the radio, the newsreel and the documentary film." Hutchins intended to examine the limits placed on freedom of speech from government, readers, advertisers, and timid management.[6]

Luce, when interviewed about his reasons for sponsoring the study, explained that the matter was philosophical as well as practical. Luce was concerned about governmental censorship, the massive size of modern government, publicity bureaus, radio commentary, and news. He thought contemporary conditions were very different from those faced when the Constitution was adopted. The Commission should "inquire into the whole question once again, to reaffirm first principles, and possibly to arrive at new definitions and a new set of codes and practices to meet changed conditions."[7]

Luce told the commissioners at his first and only meeting with them that their aim should be to "make the public feel what the ideals of the press are, as well as tell an editor what he ought to do.... It is important to produce a broader understanding in the democratic society as to the agreed standards and the responsibilities of the press."[8] "You can't talk about freedom without postulating a theory of responsibility," he remarked. He refused to predict or set an agenda for the body and expressed delight with Hutchins' selection of commissioners—eminent leaders in their fields who would "ask the right questions."[9]

The Commission met about every other month for two and a half years, from February 1944 until December of 1946, before issuing a general statement and five individual studies covering the philosophy of the free press, international communication, government and communication, radio, and the movies.

## BEHIND CLOSED DOORS

*Editor and Publisher* first welcomed the Commission, so long as it was to be a fair and free examination, and agreed that newspapermen should not be members.[10] But the press and the Commission clashed as soon as it announced that its meetings would be held behind closed doors in order "to ensure frank discussion." Nine months after the first Commission meeting, *Editor and Publisher*'s reporter had pierced its secrecy to reveal that eight witnesses had testified. The magazine editorialized that the sessions ought to be "in a glass house, open for all to study."[11] But the doors stayed closed.

For two years there was silence, and then in March 1946 came the first report, *Peoples Speaking to Peoples*. It proposed an international agency on mass communication under the direction of the United Nations to oversee violations of peace treaties and to monitor media that were "fulminating discord."[12]

The reaction to this report was mild, but contained hints of what would come later. A major objection was to the proposed "czar" of information who would judge press wrongs and rights on an international scale. The danger, according to ASNE president John S. Knight, was that having an international supervisory body passing on whether reporters were stirring up feeling against a member of the UN or endangering world peace would bring a reporter "under the thumb of his competitors or the correspondents of other nations." Accrediting correspondents to the UN and a code of self-discipline would amount to a "polite form of *super-censorship*."[13]

The Commission wanted the press to publish "true information," and Knight asked, who would then decide what is true? He preferred to put his faith in good reporting. "The great strength and value of any good reporter, and his sole responsibility, is to serve his readers with factual, accurate news and not have his efforts approved or disapproved by any government or international copy desk."[14] It was clear to Knight that the commissioners hadn't the "slightest conception of the inner workings of the AP, the UP, or the INS," news agencies with "highly trained personnel . . . engaged in the production of a news report . . . not a nicely buttered-up fairy tale. . . ." Knight could support the recommendations for equality of access to news, transmission of information, and elimination of censorship. These were goals similar to those of ASNE's special mission for world press freedom begun in 1945.[15]

## GOVERNMENT NOT THE DANGER

The Commission's general report, *A Free and Responsible Press*, was released in March 1947, promoted by an ill-considered February press release that allowed opponents to attack the study on the basis of the release rather than after reading the full report. The press control issue was the center of objections. The editors saw the notion of a national citizens' panel to monitor the press and the implied threat that government might step in if the press did nothing to improve, as a direct invitation to government regulation. The battle lines were drawn.

The Commission said that the freedom of the press was in danger, not from government control, as the conservatives had been saying, but from commercialism. Publishers were not measuring up to their responsibilities to provide full facts and information and service to the people. The Commission warned that if the press did not heed these warnings, society might step in and right the balance.[16] The Commission affirmed its belief that the press must remain a private enterprise. Concerned as they were, the commissioners could not bring themselves to recommend licensing journalists, limiting the numbers of media units under any one ownership, or prohibiting cross-media ownerships, all ideas they had discussed.[17] Instead, like many press critics before them, they called for enlighted owners, more citizen involvement, and higher professional standards by the practitioners. They crystallized decades of debate in a social responsibility concept for the modern press.

The social responsibility theory was a safeguard against totalitarianism, according to professor Theodore Peterson. The writings of the Commission provided the "most unified discussion of the goals of social responsibility theory," as formulated by commissioner William Hocking, and suggested the direction in which criticism about the press was moving, explained Peterson. He noted that practitioners had contributed to shaping it, even if they didn't agree with its logical extension.[18]

The commissioners had discussed responsibility and accountability, but on the last draft of the title, the word accountability was replaced by responsibility.[19] The commissioners believed owners had to begin to show self-restraint and responsibility to the public, and that the public had to hold the press up to more high-minded standards. Accountability implied some mechanism to enforce standards; responsibility was self-imposed.

Archibald MacLeish preferred the term "accountability" and used it in his 1946 draft of the report, little of which remained in the final version. MacLeish argued that the American press had not developed a mechanism for enforcing its own standards of professionalism, either through codes of ethics, professional organizations, or journalism schools. Until it did this, he said, journalism "would not be a profession." Owners of newspapers, he believed, were the ones who needed to be accountable, not the working journalists. These owners were currently accountable to their associates in the business world, and reader demands would do little to change that, he thought. "Large circulation allows the press to ignore large parts of the public," he observed, but he believed that a diverse public and the democratic society needed a continuous forum for the discussion of public issues. The notion of citizens' councils to monitor press performance seemed to the commissioners to present a nonthreatening means of accountability that would, as MacLeish said, help the press "remain free."[20]

The Commission proposed that the American press fulfill five requirements:

1. A truthful, comprehensive, and intelligent account of the day's events in a context which gives them meaning.

**2.** A forum for the exchange of comment and criticism.
**3.** The projection of a representative picture of the constituent groups in the society.
**4.** The presentation and clarification of the goals and values of the society.
**5.** Full access to the day's intelligence.[21]

The new reality of the mass press meant "freedom *from* and freedom *for*," explained the report.[22] That meant that the press had to be free from the menace of external compulsions from all sources and free for the development of its own conception of service and achievement. That was social accountability.[23]

The Commission decided that the modern era did need a restatement of press freedom in terms of the realities of the urban, industrial mass society that had contributed to the rise of the mass press. The directors of the press had failed "to recognize the press needs of a modern nation and to estimate and accept the responsibilities which these needs impose on them."[24] Limited access to the press had become a danger to democratic society, but press freedom was not "being swept away overnight," nor were there simple, quick solutions. The Commission specifically said it was opposed to government ownership or control because that "might kill freedom in the process." The modern press, the public, and the government all had key roles in this three-part responsibility.[25]

Because the "modern agencies of communication" were of such enormous size, and had such tremendous audiences and speed of delivery, the Commission said they presented a "new phenomenon." They could "advance the progress of civilization or thwart it . . . debase and vulgarize mankind . . . endanger the peace of the world . . . play up or down the news and its significance, foster and feed emotions, create complacent fictions and blind spots, misuse the great words, and uphold empty slogans . . . and facilitate thought and discussion." They could do this by accident or by intent. Their scope and power were increasing every day, as new technology allowed them to spread lies faster and farther "than our forefathers dreamed when they enshrined the freedom of the press in the First Amendment to our Constitution."[26]

## A NEW ROLE FOR CITIZENS

In struggling to articulate a middle ground between libertarian and totalitarian forms of mass press, the Commission had proposed a tripartite sharing of responsibility among press, government, and people. Balancing these interests continues to provide the creative tension in the American press structure.

The proposal for an independent citizens' agency was the Commission's way of bringing the public into the accountability formula and is perhaps its most controversial suggestion. The Commission had discussed this idea in its first year of deliberations, and it had even considered how such an agency might be funded and organized. It is not clear whether Hutchins had this idea in mind when he agreed to set up this Commission, but it would not be surprising. Commissions were often used in the United States during this period to look into national problems. Press councils had been functioning in Sweden since 1916 and England since 1938 with good results. The subject came up in Commission documents as early as April 1944.[27]

By September 1945 the Commission had met or interviewed, among others, several editors and publishers, Newspaper Guild representatives, a journalism educator, a critic, and lawyer. Some members expressed their exasperation over the complacency of the press in thinking it was "doing a good job." It seemed, Hutchins remarked, that editors thought there was nothing wrong with the press if they could just "keep the government out and let them get behind the handouts and secrecy." Journalism clearly was not a profession, the Commission concluded, because it had "ambiguous standards of performance" and "the absence of any sanction on behavior."[28]

The proposal for a continuing citizens' agency to review press performance seemed an inviting alternative to the Commission. It was pointed out that it would be essential for this agency to be an independent citizens' group, neither a Hays office (the movie industry's self-censorship apparatus), a pressure group, nor a governmental body. It would be fact-finding and objective, and it would work to improve standards of practice and not just offer negative criticism, they said. To provide credibility and integrity for the agency, it was suggested that it be housed at a university and be funded by foundation grants. Members would be elected to three-to-five-year terms, and the first group might be proposed by the Hutchins Commission. They estimated a $5 million pricetag for the first ten years of such a commission's operation.[29]

The citizens' commission would be asked to monitor press performance and point out places where it was lacking; work for diversity in content and access; investigate charges of lying and misrepresentation by the press; encourage research and study of the press; and stimulate publicity and public discussion of press performance. The Hutchins Commission members were concerned that their proposal might appear to be an invitation to perpetuate the work of their own Commission. Nevertheless, they thought it wise to have plans ready for implementation, if the idea were accepted. None of this discussion was published at the time, and the proposal became too controversial to survive. The press responded that it would do its own policing and immediately cast the shadow of censorship over the proposal.

The Commission also recommended that the press serve as "common carriers of information and discussion . . . engage in vigorous, mutual self-criticism . . . increase the competence, independence, and effectiveness of its staff."[30] A designation as a common carrier signified to the press an abdication of editorial judgment and selection of content, another infringement on press freedom. Centers of advanced study, research, and publication in the field of communication and the broadest and most liberal training for students in schools of journalism were also suggested.[31] The press would remain legally free if it accepted its moral responsibility to be publicly accountable, the Commission warned.[32]

## A COOL RESPONSE

At a press conference introducing the report, Hutchins said that it was aimed at owners and managers, and was "not critical of reporters and staffs." The public deserved and wanted a better press, he said. The Commission fully supported the press as a private enterprise, Hutchins added, but believed that the press did a poor job in covering labor relations, race relations, national, and international affairs. The press needed more criticism, and that was the underlying purpose of the study, he said.[33]

It was unfortunate but predictable that editors and publishers responded with anger and resentment. Even Luce gave it a cool reception. The Commission had ignored their self-improvements, such as ethical codes and objective reporting. ASNE president and assistant editor of the New York *Herald Tribune* Wilbur Forrest charged that the report had "been influenced by a pattern of thought designed to undermine public confidence in the American press as an institution." He meant "left wing individuals and groups" who wanted eventual government regulation and control. To Forrest, who was engaged in promoting world press freedom, the report also threatened the very international credibility he and others thought they had succeeded in gaining for the American press.[34]

The Commission report was read, reviewed, discussed, and quickly buried. Although its specific recommendations had not been adopted, the report provided a "philosophical framework for reform," Professor Margaret Blanchard said in her study of the Commission.[35] It strengthened efforts by several editors and professional organizations that had been moving in this direction for the previous fifteen years.

## NEW STATEMENT OF THE IDEAL PRESS

The response to the Commission's additional reports was diluted, perhaps by lack of newspaper interest and the euphoria that came with peace. The Commission had said it was writing for about a decade hence. It would take that and more before many of its suggestions would be assimilated in to contemporary practice. But as Blanchard concluded: "Not only did the Commission make press criticism socially acceptable, it arrived on the scene at a most auspicious moment: it was an idea whose time had come."[36]

The Commission's deliberations were kept in closed archives until April 1962. After that it was possible to see that they struggled over various proposals of protective legislation, such as limits on corporate ownerships of media units, breaking up large groups, or prohibiting cross-media groups. This was a familiar line of argument promoted in the modern era by media critics from Upton Sinclair to Morris Ernst. Some of the commissioners were sympathetic, but they knew that such proposals would immediately associate their work with that of the "crackpots and socialists." Ernst's book was meeting stiff opposition during this time, and the Commission was aware of that.

In trying to find this middle way, Professor Jerilyn McIntyre points out, the commissioners were really trying to formulate policy and not philosophy.[37] Their policy was compatible with New Deal thinking, but that era was ending. A vitriolic analysis published by a *Chicago Tribune* writer did try to discredit the Commission as being tinged by communist thinking, and it illustrates early cold war rhetoric that would become familiar in the 1950s.[38]

Hutchins believed that the Commission's proposals were "not startling." He considered the suggestion for a citizens' agency as the most important item in the report and strongly urged its support.[39] After nine major revisions the commissioners had compromised, and the most strident parts were toned down to something all could support. Nevertheless, its liberal bias was obvious.

## NIEMAN FELLOWS' IDEAL NEWSPAPER

At about the same time as the Hutchins Commission report, the first postwar class of professional Nieman fellows in journalism at Harvard University developed a blueprint for the ideal newspaper. The fellowship had been established in 1937 in honor of Lucius W. Nieman, founder of the *Milwaukee Journal*, by his widow "to promote and elevate standards of journalism in the United States and educate people deemed especially qualified for journalism."[40]

"Newspapermen are incorrigible idealists or optimists . . . they are bitter or cynical because their idealism for the integrity of news has been frustrated . . . from venality or partisanship of publishers, from timidity or narrowness of editors, from prejudice and ignorance of community. . . ." said Louis M. Lyons, former *Boston Globe* star reporter and the first program director.[41] The fellows saw the central problem of the press in a democracy as having to serve the needs of the whole community, "the interests of the big and little fellow," while the control lay "wholly in the hands of the big fellow." The publisher, they believed, had to keep the paper open to the free flow of ideas, and to do this, had to have a "sense of trusteeship to the society."[42] This balancing of interests, they thought, was essential for the free press in a democratic society.

Their book, *Your Newspaper*, deplores the large gap between the press and the people and worries about the public's lack of trust in the press. Their three main criticisms were irresponsibility, arrogance, and monopoly ownership. The model they proposed would be devoted to a concern about the general welfare of the public. It would be better written, more interpretive, and more intelligent. They proposed fact and source checking for the newspaper as was done at the magazines. They wanted higher standards of education and professionalism for journalists that would give them more independence in standing up to owners, managers, and editors.

## MORE SELF-CRITICISM NEEDED

The press needed more self-criticism, they said. Newspapers should cover the press "as thoroughly and enterprisingly as any other important institution in American life," and it should become a regular department in the newspaper.[43] The press belonged in the group of opinion-influencing institutions, including "movies, theater, radio, books, religion, and schools." The press, they charged, was failing "to be a guardian of our liberties . . . when it fails to watch radio and itself."[44]

Their idea of press criticism was not "a flogging device" but "systematic coverage of the press as a proper news source, recording its achievements, problems, methods, stunts, wild goose chases, and impact on society." The press critic would need to be a "reporter who knows the history of the press and understands its peccadillos, who is aware of the interactions between the newspaper and its community, who possesses good judgment and a large bump of curiosity, and who can write with wit and fairness . . . [and] justly without scolding or fawning."[45]

The columns of *Editor and Publisher* bristled with reaction to the Commission report, but the Nieman fellows' book received minimal attention, although the ideas in it complemented the Commission's report. In fact, the Commission had solicited their ideas, but the two projects were carried on independently.

## JOURNALISM TEACHERS REACT

The journalism teachers were angered by the "imprudent and ill-considered" attack on the schools, which had not been examined or visited by any Commission members. As American Association of Schools and Departments of Journalism (AASDJ) president Robert W. Desmond pointed out, many of the standards and recommendations proposed by the Commission were already in place in the better schools.[46] The schools believed they were already providing constructive press criticism of press performance, as well as press institutes and short courses intended to raise the standard. The report was flawed by "serious shortcomings," Desmond said, and "may become merely a new stick with which to beat the press."[47]

The teachers invited Hutchins to their next meeting, where he lashed out at them, charging that "journalism training as now being conducted by 'most' schools is not a legitimate function of higher education."[48] Hutchins had long opposed professional education for undergraduates, favoring the liberal arts and great books approach that he introduced at the University of Chicago.

J. Edward Gerald of the University of Minnesota responded to Hutchins, saying he was "smearing the good name of education for journalism by using the hit-and-run tactics common to sensational journalists." Gerald explained that the "material from the liberal arts is made useful mainly by being discussed in the context of the modern world problems with which the journalist deals as reporter and editor."[49]

At the same meeting, Erwin D. Canham, editor of the *Christian Science Monitor*, said that publishers were working to improve the product. He regarded the distrust of the critics as a grave, long-range danger. Paul F. Lazarsfeld of the New York Bureau of Applied Research at Columbia University suggested that the new quantitative research might help take the emotional sting out of criticism. He proposed regional, lay fact-finding boards that would offer critical information on the mass media. Press criticism needed to be "as cool a topic as headline writing," he suggested, removed from the "present nervous and defensive atmosphere."[50]

## PRESS TAKES RESPONSIBILITY

Several activities were under way. The American Press Institute at Columbia, started in 1946, was offering regular seminars for editors and reporters on current topics of professional interest.[51] The University of Missouri in 1936 had established the Walter Williams Foundation for the specific study of the press, and the Lucius Nieman Foundation in 1938 at Harvard University began bringing professional journalists to campus for an intensive year of academic and professional study and debate. The first class finished in 1939. *Nieman Reports*, the first national academically based journalism review, begain in 1947.[52]

The AP managing editors in 1948 formed eleven continuing study committees for monitoring AP performance in key areas in an attempt to improve their news reports. Codes of ethics, similar to ASNE's canons, were being drafted in 1948 by the editorial writers and by Sigma Delta Chi, the professional journalism honorary society for men.[53]

When the editorial writers invited Hutchins to their meeting in 1948, he lit into them for misquoting and misunderstanding his report. The report had not come from "muckraking professional agitators," he said, but was the "serious study of sober men"; its charges were not to be shrugged off, as he suggested the press was doing. Of all people, the editorial writers should be taking a leading role in making the press responsible, he said. They should be a force for public enlightenment. The problem was how to make the owners of the press responsible and still maintain press freedom.[54]

The press should stop "exhibiting neurotic symptoms everytime anybody criticizes you. Such response suppresses criticism," said Hutchins. The editorial writers ought to "demand" the creation of an independent agency to criticize the press. "If you don't like the Commission's recommendations," Hutchins said, "think of something else that will give this result. Freedom requires responsibility."[55]

## JOINING PRESS AND CRITICS

That challenge was met by the press when *Editor and Publisher* proposed a meeting between the commissioners and members of the press. The magazine admitted that a continuing agency for appraising the press might be a good idea, but it ought to include newspapermen. The journal offered to cooperate in establishing such a board.[56] But nothing came of that. At a public session in March 1949, two of the former commissioners met with editors from several newspapers. The editors pointed out that they, too, were not satisfied with newspapers and wanted improvements. They were unhappy that the Commission had lumped the good with the bad newspapers. Specific studies were needed, all agreed, and there was a call for more research.[57]

No concrete steps were taken at this meeting because it was announced that ASNE was already forming a Committee on Responsibility to work on this subject of press criticism. ASNE agreed to "examine the desirability of sponsoring appraisals or studies of the press." The committee reported in 1950 with a mild statement favoring "informed criticism."[58] The journalism educators, newly united as the Association for Education in Journalism (AEJ), established a Committee on Professional Freedom and Responsibility in Press and Radio, to monitor the press on these critical matters.

B. M. McKelway, editor of the *Washington Star* and ASNE president in 1949, noted that the press commission idea had achieved modest success in some other countries but would not work in America. Who would pay for it and would a sponsor influence its work? "It is only a matter of time before evolutionary processes put the private policeman on the public payroll," he stated.[59] Codes of ethics, intelligent criticism and responsible behavior should come from within the institution of the press, he believed. In the end, the individual newspaperman, "his character and allegiance to responsibility—rather than the policing commission or enforced rules of conduct—are the best guarantors of continued self-improvement of the press." The press should "welcome criticism," he said. Many journalists agreed that news was "public property."[60]

The proposals found in the Hutchins Commission report were neither new nor original, but they attained the cachet of the eminent scholars on the

Commission. The direction of thinking since the turn of the century had been toward increasing professionalism and responsibility for the institution of the press and for its journalists and editors. The pressure added by the New Deal era, and its intensification and polarization of attitudes and political beliefs, raised the heat of the discussion, reminding all concerned of the ever-present threat of government intervention.

Hutchins predicted that it would take a decade for the impact and influence of the report to be felt. In fact, it took longer, but by the 1960s there were critical press reviews, newspaper ombudsmen, local press councils, academic research, professional seminars, and self-studies by the professional associations. Hundreds of journalism students absorbed the Commission's message of social responsibility through class discussions of the report, assigned reading of the report, and a classic study, *Four Theories of the Press*.[61] Press criticism and analysis remained sporadic in the popular magazines and news weeklies. Few newspapers ran regular press criticism, but there was some. Press ombudsman and editor's or publisher's viewpoint columns sometimes took up criticism and response in the 1970s and 1980s. The pioneering efforts at professional press criticism that began in the 1940s pointed the way toward what could become an emerging specialty.

## NOTES

1. James L. Baughman, *Henry R. Luce and the Rise of the American News Media* (Boston: Twayne, 1987), 174.
2. Philip Schuyler, "Government News Gag Press Freedom Problem," *Editor and Publisher* (8 April 1944): 7; and The Commission on Freedom of the Press Papers, Box 8, folder 9, item 119, "Summary of Discussion, Commission Meeting in Chicago," 15–17 September 1946 (Chicago: University of Chicago Library, Joseph Regenstein Library). Both the interview with Luce and Hutchins' comments agree on the origin of the idea. From Commission on Freedom of the Press papers, copyright © 1944–1947 by The University of Chicago, Reprinted by permission.
3. Commission papers, Box 1, folder 2, item 4a, "Conference on Freedom of the Press, with Henry Luce . . .".
4. Jerilyn S. McIntyre, "Repositioning a Landmark: The Hutchins Commission and Freedom of the Press," *Critical Studies in Mass Communication* 4 (October 1987): 6.
5. The Commission on Freedom of the Press, *A Free and Responsible Press* (Chicago: University of Chicago Press, 1947).
6. "New Commission to Study Press Freedom," *Editor and Publisher* (4 March 1944): 22.
7. "New Commission," 22.
8. Commission papers, Box 1, folder 2, item 4a.
9. Luce interview, *Editor and Publisher* 7.
10. "Editors Welcome *Time-Life* Inquiry into Press Freedom," *Editor and Publisher* (15 April 1944): 9.

11. "Two Civil Liberties Champions Clash on Press Freedom," *Editor and Publisher* (9 December 1944): 38.
12. Llewellyn White and Robert D. Leigh (Commission on Freedom of the Press), *Peoples Speaking to Peoples* (Chicago: The University of Chicago Press, 1946). See also: Editorial "Leigh-White Report," *Editor and Publisher* (30 March 1946): 42.
13. "Knight Assails Plan in Leigh-White Report," *Editor and Publisher* (20 April 1946): 120.
14. "Knight Assails," *Editor and Publisher*, 120.
15. "Knight Assails," *Editor and Publisher*, 120.
16. Commission, *Free and Responsible*, 131.
17. Commission papers, Regenstein Library. The papers document all the discussions and testimony heard by the group.
18. Theodore Peterson, "The Social Responsibility Theory of the Press," in Fred S. Siebert, Theodore Peterson and Wilbur Schramm, *Four Theories of the Press* (Urbana: University of Illinois Press, 1963), 82–85.
19. Commission papers, Box 9, folder 1: document 120, "Ninth Revision of the General Report," 15 October 1946.
20. Commission papers, Box 4, folder 8, "Draft of General Report," by Archibald MacLeish, 26 February 1946: 90–102.
21. Commission, *Free and Responsible*, 20–29.
22. Emphasis mine.
23. Commission, *Free and Responsible*, 18.
24. Commission, *Free and Responsible*, 2.
25. Commission, *Free and Responsible*, 2–3.
26. Commission, *Free and Responsible*, 3.
27. Commission papers, Box 4, folder 7, item 87, "Review of Material in Commission Documents," 29 January 1946. McIntyre says Merriam brought up the idea of citizen participation in 1944 (see: "Repositioning," 19, and n. 25.).
28. Commission papers, Box 3, folder 10, item 75, "Minutes of the Commission, Chicago," 17–19 September 1945: 25.
29. Commission papers, Box 4, folder 1, item 79, "Memorandum for the Commission on a Continuing Citizens' Agency in the Field of Mass Communication."
30. Commission, *Free and Responsible*, 92–95.
31. Commission, *Free and Responsible*, 99. The Gannett Center for Media Studies at Columbia University founded in 1984 is the first institute for advanced study.
32. Commission, *Free and Responsible*, 19.
33. "Report Aimed Directly at Owners—Hutchins," *Editor and Publisher* (29 March 1947): 8.
34. "Forrest Accuses Group of Damaging Prestige," *Editor and Publisher* (29 March 1947): 11.
35. Margaret Blanchard, "The Hutchins Commission: The Press and Responsibility Concept," *Journalism Monographs* 49 (May 1977): 51.
36. Blanchard, "Responsibility Concept," 52.
37. McIntyre, "Repositioning," 10. Not until 1973 did the U.S. establish a National Press Council, which lasted only a decade and died for lack of media support.
38. Frank Hughes, *Prejudice and the Press* (New York: Devin-Adair, 1950).
39. "Hutchins Chastises Editorial Writers," *Editor and Publisher* (27 November 1948): 6.

40. "The Nieman Foundation Celebrates Its 50th Birthday," *Nieman Reports* 63 (Spring 1989): 2.
41. Leon Svirsky, ed., *Your Newspaper: Blueprint for a Better Press* (New York: Macmillan, 1947), ix.
42. Svirsky, *Blueprint*, x.
43. Svirsky, *Blueprint*, 133.
44. Svirsky, *Blueprint*, 142.
45. Svirsky, *Blueprint*, 134.
46. Robert Desmond, president, American Association of Schools and Departments of Journalism, Editorial, *Journalism Quarterly* 24 (September 1947): 192.
47. Desmond, Editorial, 188.
48. "Journalism Teachers Parry With Hutchins," *Editor and Publisher* (3 January 1948): 10.
49. "Teachers," 10.
50. "Fact-Finding Boards on Press Advocated," *Editor and Publisher* (10 January 1948): 58.
51. "American Press Institute Seeks $850,000 Endowment," *Editor and Publisher* (28 June 1947): 10.
52. Some might argue that Seldes' *In Fact* should be called the first journalism review.
53. "Editorial Writers to Draft Code of Ethics, Standards," *Editor and Publisher* (27 November 1948): 5.
54. "Hutchins Chastises," 6.
55. "Hutchins Chastises," 50.
56. "An Offer to Hutchins," *Editor and Publisher* (27 November 1948): 38.
57. "E&P Panel Suggests Studies for Press Self-Improvement," *Editor and Publisher* (26 March 1949): 52.
58. Problems, 1947, 212.
59. "News, Public Property: Cornerstone of Free Press," *Editor and Publisher* (3 September 1949): 3.
60. "News, Property," 41.
61. Peterson, *Four Theories*.

# CHAPTER 13

# Toward a Professional Criticism: 1947 and Later

Two men in New York City—A. J. Liebling and Don Hollenbeck—in the 1940s laid the groundwork for what could become a professional genre of journalism criticism. Their efforts were primarily directed at their own city's newspapers, but New York sets the pace for journalistic innovation, so their work was noticed. What they chose to examine—content, form and style, motives, ethics, social worth, and responsibility—suggested a direction for future critics.

A. J. Liebling, a former *World-Telegram* feature writer, joined the staff of the *New Yorker* in 1935. After serving as a war correspondent in World War II for the magazine, he returned to revive "The Wayward Press" column. It had been started by humorist Robert Benchley in 1927 as an occasional item and had run for about a decade. Liebling continued it on a more regular basis until his death in 1963, producing about ninety columns, many later reproduced in book form. He gained a loyal and sophisticated following with his rapier wit, distinctive language, and forthright expression of likes and dislikes.

Don Hollenbeck, a former CBS war correspondent, was placed in charge of a new fifteen-minute weekly radio program on press criticism in 1947. He anchored "CBS Views the Press," which ran weekly on WCBS local radio for three years. Hollenbeck found soft spots in the news coverage and pointed out lapses of ethics and judgment in New York City journalism. Under Hollenbeck, the program was a hard-hitting critique of press coverage with occasional commendations when the press lived up to his belief that it should serve society's needs.[1]

Hollenbeck worked with reporters Joe Wershba and Edmund Scott to write the program. They solicited items from the CBS news staff and read nine daily New York City newspapers and other pertinent articles on the press.[2] The idea for the show emerged after hours of discussion and argument over radio and press coverage of political news, Hollenbeck recalled. It was CBS's way of helping newspaper readers "get their own perspective on what they see in print," he said. Criticism had been valuable in improving the performance of radio, but when "radio presumed to criticize the sacrosanct press, that was too much," said Hollenbeck.[3] Listeners predicted the quick demise of the show, but the program gained a reputation for accuracy. The news media needed public criticism, but an even better forum, Hollenbeck said, would be the local press and radio. The constant treatment of local performance begins to make listeners think more about what they are reading and hearing, and "when done locally, means more personally."[4]

Hollenbeck left the program in 1950 to moderate another CBS show, and he died in 1954.[5] He received the George Polk award in recognition of his outstanding achievement in press criticism, and the show earned five major awards. CBS retained no scripts of the program, but a long review in *Editor and Publisher* does give the flavor and moral tone of the first fifteen-minute Sunday afternoon show. Hollenbeck took to task the *World Telegram*, the *Journal-American* and the *Sun* for their "ostentatious coverage" of thirty-seven families (about 120 people) that the city had temporarily housed in hotel rooms.[6]

"The great ink-letting which resulted from the disclosure that a number of New York City families on relief had been housed in hotels has abated some, after having for about a week resembled a kind of newspaper lynching party," he remarked.[7] The uproar had resulted in getting families hustled out of the hotels into condemned tenements and city lodgings, according to Hollenbeck. He chided reporters for their implications that "these kinds of people" didn't rate maid service and radios in their rooms. Further, Hollenbeck revealed that the story had been brought to press attention by a disappointed office seeker out to discredit the mayor. The reporters had not checked and wound up victimizing the welfare families, and to make matters worse, he added, the local comedians were using the story in "distasteful" nightclub routines.[8]

The program reviewed all of New York City's newspapers, magazines, and wire services. Edward R. Murrow, then vice president and director of public affairs for CBS, had scheduled the program because he believed "freedom of the press and freedom of radio are inseparable," and "mutual criticism will benefit both."[9] Hollenbeck had worked as a newspaper reporter and editor for the *Omaha Bee*, *PM*, and the AP, and as a foreign correspondent for the OWI. He joined CBS radio after the war.[10]

Reactions to the show were mixed. The *New York News* charged that the press could "do a better job on radio any week," but the *New York Herald Tribune* praised CBS for its integrity and "honest and well informed" opinions.

*PM* and the *New York Post* thought mutual criticism between press and radio would benefit the press. The *New York Sun* sniped that "several newspapers follow the communist line, so why shouldn't a radio station?"[11]

In contrast to Hollenbeck, the press criticism of A. J. Liebling has been broadly available in reprinted collected editions. It was analyzed in a doctoral study by Edmund M. Midura, who says the critic's approach was to read widely in the New York press and occasionally the out-of-town papers, and then take up specific issues and cases. Liebling also attacked monopoly domination of the press, antilabor coverage, and conservative bias. He believed that publishers were "greedy, smug, clannish, reactionary, self-deluded, and contemptuous of the press." Columnists were also favorite targets of Liebling. Midura's analysis shows that Liebling promoted the best values in journalism and advocated better and more responsible reporting, interpretive backgrounding, honesty, accuracy, mutual self-criticism, and professionalism.[12]

Liebling regularly took on the day-to-day editing foibles of the press, such as exaggerated headline writing, labeling story victims or criminals with catchy names like "Lady in Mink," "Pig Woman," "Ripper," journalistic overwriting, or just bad reporting. Liebling's style left the reader with a clear impression of the issue being probed but hard pressed to excerpt a single line or paragraph that succinctly boiled down the point. Liebling was an engaging writer who set a literary standard for press criticism. His fans enjoyed following his wit, outrage, astonishment, wordplays, and literary allusions as he skewered his victims, revealing the warts and bumps of the press he loved.

One subject he returned to frequently, because it was so prevalent, was the death of a newspaper and the one-newspaper town:

> What you have in a one-paper town is a privately owned public utility that is constitutionally exempt from public regulation, which would be a violation of freedom of the press. As to the freedom of the individual journalist in such a town, it corresponds exactly with what the publisher will allow him. He can't go over to the opposition, because there isn't any. If he leaves, he ends his usefulness to the town, and probably to the state and region in which it is situated, because he takes with him the story that caused his difference with the management, and in a distant place it will have no value. Under the conditions, there is no point in being quixotic.[13]

Liebling decided that he had written so many newspaper obituaries that they could be done by formula:

> ... the gloom-fraught city room, the typewriters hopelessly tapping out stories for the last edition, the members of the staff cleaning out their desks and wondering where the hell they are going to go. The technique involves a certain amount of reference to earlier disasters of the same sort, as does a story about a hotel fire or the sinking of a submarine. One measure of such events is called in headlines the "Toll": the folding of the *World* put twenty-

eight hundred employees on the street, of the *Star* four hundred, of *the* Sun twelve hundred. Another is the age of the decedent.... [14]

In rereading his coverage of newspaper deaths over a period of twenty years, Liebling said: "I tried to isolate individual reasons for failures that would make a special case: in that of the *World* papers, a particularly pusillanimous ownership; in *PM*'s, a paper that never found its groove; in the *Sun*'s, a paper that couldn't get out of it. But the disturbing common factor was that nobody came to the rescue, and that nothing grew in the place of the dead trees."[15]

His concern about the future of the profession of journalism was also a continuing one. Perhaps nowhere else did he so succinctly capture the change taking place in journalism education as in his reaction to the $26 million bequest by publisher S. I. Newhouse to establish a School of Communications at Syracuse University after his death:

Communication means simply getting any idea across and has no intrinsic relation to the truth. It is neutral. It can be a peddler's tool, or the weapon of a political knave, or the medium of a new religion. "Journalism" has a reference to what happens, day by day, but "communication" can deal, just as well, with what has not happened, what the communicator wants to happen, or what he wants the dupe on the other end to think. Its general and increasing substitution, in the schoolmen's jargon, for harmless old journalism disturbs me, as the next little piece indicated:

Q. What do you do for a living?
A. I am a communicator.
Q. What do you communicate? Scarlet fever? Apprehension?[16]

Liebling often lectured at the Nieman fellows' sessions at Harvard University, where he enjoyed a vigorous give-and-take with professionals on a year's sabbatical from the daily grind. In the 1940s and 1950s Liebling personified the journalism critic, and perhaps he gave a bite and edge to that task that was revived in the turbulent 1960s when the press and most other institutions were under close scrutiny. *MORE*, a New York City journalism review of the period, sponsored annual meetings called the Liebling Counter Convention to underscore its anti-establishment challenge to the traditional publishers and editors who were meeting at the same time.

Midura says that Liebling was not a cynic. His associates said that Liebling "really believed he could do something about things." He often said that he didn't think that he had much impact on the press of his time, but that did not stop him from criticizing it. One of the "very few voices speaking out in his generation," Liebling helped shape the ideas of some journalists, Midura concludes, and his "consummate skill as a reporter and essayist should assure him a place in the annals of the profession."[17]

## CENTERS OF CRITICISM

Although earlier Liebling had expressed a negative view of journalism schools as a result of his own experience at Columbia, Midura says that later he saw those schools as potential centers for "carrying out qualitative criticism" and research on the press. The idea that the professional schools of journalism and the liberal arts colleges that housed journalism and media departments ought to be centers of criticism and ethical leadership was gaining some attention in the aftermath of the Hutchins Commission report.

One direct public challenge was made to establish a journal of press criticism by James S. Pope, the managing editor of the *Louisville Courier-Journal*, at a meeting of the Michigan press. He called on the University of Michigan "to set up a permanent committee to criticize the nation's newspapers." It should be a university-sponsored survey of newspapers along the line of drama, movie, and book criticism. "Someone will pioneer in the new art-science of measuring the accomplishments of the press," he said. "Why not the University of Michigan?"[18]

In following up on that speech, the then-chairman of the Department of Journalism, Wesley H. Maurer, said he "took the challenge very seriously" and consulted with the University's president and with his faculty colleagues, but he was thwarted by the state's publishers and editors, who were "definitely opposed" on the grounds of "freedom of the press." The issue was dropped in the face of "unresolvable problems and unwarranted criticism," and the department concentrated on teaching for the "profession of journalism" and demonstrating its criticism by example.[19]

Regular press criticism within journalistic circles was growing in the late 1940s in the *Nieman Reports*, books, studies, proceedings of national and state press groups' meetings, and seminars. Scholars' articles and books contributed analysis and some criticism. *PM*, *Time* and *Newsweek*, and the *Saturday Review of Literature* covered the press as news and included criticism. But it would not be until 1961 that the *Columbia Journalism Review* would make its appearance, and lead the way in regular monitoring and commentary on the performance of American journalism. It was joined later by *MORE* (1971–78) and the *Chicago Journalism Review* (1968–75), *Washington Journalism Review* (1977–), and several other local press reviews, including the *St. Louis Journalism Review* (1970–).[20]

## OVERVIEW OF PRESS CRITICISM

Throughout the seventy years covered by this study, lively and vibrant voices have identified problems and responsibilities of press-society relations. There have been responses and some changes. Issues arise and swell like a slowly approaching tide, and then recede to be replaced by new concerns.

In the 1880s and 1890s, there was concern about the raucous, popular mass journalism that threatened the stability of the Victorian way of life. Out of this clamor arose the notion of an ideal newspaper to serve the new urban inhabitants. Several alternatives were proposed, and in the end the popular newspapers toned down their sensationalism to more closely match the expectations of their audience. Reporters and editors began looking for ways to gain self-respect for their work by forming professional associations, and in the 1920s adopted national codes of ethics and behavior. Newly founded journalism schools and departments in the early twentieth century upheld these ideals and trained a new generation in socially responsible professional journalism.

The period spanning two world wars and a severe depression introduced a concern over the potential for good and evil in publicity and propaganda. The growth of modern social sciences and press research during the same time contributed to understanding of the role of the press in society.

Although the tabloids of the 1920s revived an old concern over sensationalism, the Depression and another war provided the context for serious partisan debate. Press criticism was embedded in pro- and anti-New Deal criticism in a struggle over who would wield power and shape public policy. New Dealers were likely to say the press had lost its political power since it could not influence the electorate away from the Democrats. The Republican-dominated newspaper owners contended that the power was there, and that they were serving the important function of keeping a popular administration under critical examination. Threats of government pressure and control and journalistic anguish over the fate of the free press flavored this era, but the wartime necessity of working together for the national interest kept some of the vitriol down.

The journalists' adoption of codes of ethics and performance standards without viable enforcement or licensing mechanisms for accountability created a double standard within the press and underscored the journalists' limited autonomy. Licensing had been considered but was dropped during the war fervor over the issue of government censorship.

Journalists and editors did not form one strong national union or professional association, preferring to cluster in specialized groups. The codes of ethics adopted by these groups of reporters and editors did have a certain uniformity of agreement, but there were no such codes for the owners of the press. What is considered unethical and damaging to press credibility, such as visible support for political or other special interest groups, is the natural prerogative of the corporate executive and owner. Their memberships in the city's most powerful social clubs, and service on boards of directors at banks and corporations and foundations, are obligatory management duties in corporate America.

In the matter of responsible treatment of sources, privacy, and sensitivity toward feelings, the codes were purely advisory and depended on enforcement by the editors and publishers. Nevertheless, the quality papers accepted the idealism expressed in these codes and edited that way. Others will continue to respond to the public's appetite for gossip, scandal, and violence. It is precisely the matter of business profits versus societal obligations that has given critics the most to chew on during the past century. This issue was in sharp focus in the New Deal era and again in the Vietnam War period. There are no laws to force the newspapers to operate in the public interest. An appeal to each individual's moral standard, the weight of journalistic tradition, and the focused voices of public criticism are the informal monitors on the press. Several New Deal critics attacked this casual system and proposed alternatives that would require accountability, or systems to limit the size of a single media ownership in the interest of keeping a plurality of voices.

The strong opposition to such efforts in the late 1940s and again in the 1980s illustrates the entrenched opposition to outside forms of monitoring journalistic content or performance beyond those required by law, such as libel, obscenity, slander, and treason. In the face of public pressure the journalistic profession has instituted codes of ethics and behavior and moderated its behavior to satisfy the most vociferous of public demands.

The 1930s provided the first strong test of factual, objective, unbiased reporting as the standard for the American daily newspapers. For about two decades, some editors and reporters pressed for a lessening of the rigid formula of objectivity that had become universal for the American press by the 1920s. The first pressure was to add interpretation and explanation in covering the causes and proposed remedies to the Depression, and later to explain Europe's fall into another world war. Objectivity was sharply tested in the 1950s by the skillful manipulative tactics of Senator Joseph McCarthy and his fight to rid America of communism. In that era, journalists eventually realized that giving a lie the same prominence as truth just because a public official had said it was as unfair and unethical as some of the practices that led to journalistic objectivity in the first place.

## RECENT PRESS CRITICISM

The themes of press criticism since the 1950s resonate with a certain familiarity against the background of press criticism offered by this study. The persistence of the social responsibility theme, first mentioned in 1900, suggests that it has become a key reinterpretation of the role of the free press in U.S. society, replacing the older libertarian view. But it brought with it the need to define the nature of the responsibility, and that changes depending on circumstances of the age. Press responsibility was sharply questioned during the Vietnam War and on issues of reporting on racism, sexism, crime, the environment, and presidential campaigns.

Objectivity was found equally incapable of describing the range and depth and emotional complexity of human rights issues in the 1960s. Another "new journalism" in the 1960s used the techniques of creative writing to heighten the drama and reporting about real people and events. This was suspected of parading opinion in the guise of fact. After a brief popularity in news reporting, "new journalism" was incorporated in newspaper feature writing. Its lesson was not lost. Fairness, accuracy, completeness became new terms to describe American reporting; objectivity became something to strive for and impossible to attain. The modern journalist could make use of interpretation, analysis, and creative techniques as required by the story and permitted by the editors, but most stories were reported straight in the old hard-news style.

Only a few critics have pointed out that objectivity as practiced not only encourages detachment, but also allows the journalist to avoid personal responsibility for his or her reports. Wire service reporting has been the epitome of objective reporting, and as former CBS news anchor and UPI reporter Walter Cronkite observed, it creates journalists who have to be "ideological eunuchs." Cronkite added that on television, too, he had to "hew absolutely to the middle of the road" with no prejudice or bias.[21]

The watchdog function of the press was temporarily given a new bite in the 1960s in the Watergate exposé of government corruption. The press was praised by many for exposing the Nixon administration's attempt to subvert the electoral process. But it was also subjected to a growing barrage of criticism from the right, charging that the press was unfair to business, unpatriotic, and untrustworthy in its political reporting. Pressure groups and special investigations of the media arose on all sides and the extent of the Nixon retaliation toward a press he considered personally unfriendly and hostile is documented in William E. Porter's *Assault on the Media*.[22] In the 1970s and 1980s, as in the FDR era, this time under popular Republican presidents Nixon and Reagan, press and political criticism melded. This time the press was charged with being too liberal and antibusiness.

A public that had expressed strong levels of confidence in the press during the postwar decade in 1983 applauded the Reagan administration's ban of reporters from its Grenada invasion. Juries that wanted to award millions of dollars in libel damages in this period were seen by the press as a sign of public hostility. The personal popularity of President Ronald Reagan and his skillfull management of the press and of his own popular image gave rise to some criticism that the press caved in to presidential pressure and was serving "on bended knee," as one critic put it.[23] Taking a page from FDR, Reagan also took his message directly to the public through television and regular weekly radio addresses. He was able to portray the press as a badgering nuisance to be avoided as much as possible.

The reality of declining readership in proportion to the population pushed newspaper managements of the 1980s into a frantic attempt to please readers and hold circulation and advertising rates. While some competing older papers gave up the battle and died, some established joint-operating agreements, which the government sanctioned with the 1972 Newspaper Preservation Act allowing shared production facilities as long as editorial units remained separate. *USA Today*, a new experimental paper introduced in 1982 for the mobile middle class attuned to television, jet travel, and uprooted families following the company, offered a fresh alternative national paper by providing ample color, graphics, and spritely, brief reports that covered most reader interests on a national scale. It gained a 1.7 million circulation in six years, while other papers were losing readers. The television news director's dogma that viewers had short attention spans was transferred to print, as more newspapers tried to compete by copying TV rather than offering a different and substantive product like the *New York Times*, *Los Angeles Times* or *Washington Post*. The ideal newspaper was beginning to sound like a marketing strategy.

In the current struggle for survival, the number two newspaper in the few remaining cities with newspaper competition is squeezed hardest, both by the loss of readers, and thus advertisers, and by transporation difficulties and costs in serving the expanding suburbs. The suburban press, on the other hand, seems healthy and expects good prospects in the future. It commands the local community news and attention and has its eye on dominating that advertising market. The daily newspaper in some cities still has a clear hold and solid base in audience and advertising. Elsewhere, the economic and delivery problems combined with the potential for a market-segmented product could begin to create a tiered class-market structure of newspapers on the European model.

## TELEVISION BECAME CRITICS' TARGET

While all these matters of concern to newspapers have been widely discussed in the turbulent 1970s and 1980s, the rapid prominence and dominance of television after World War II provided the real competition for the newspaper press. And it began, also, to draw off much of the political, social, and moral criticism. Television quickly became the main source of news for most people in the nation, and the criticism that followed was immediate and vigorous. Television, more than newspapers, let the public see the intrusive naked power and arrogance of journalists after their quarry, while it also taught interested activist individuals and groups that gaining the television spotlight was the fast lane into mainstream debate. Television, as the culmination of instantaneous journalism, was shaping much of the nation's vision of reality. Information was power. Access to information meant control of what got discussed and how it got discussed. Misuse of this information power and the unfair allocation of that power to white males became a hot topic for criticism in the 1960s.

Unlike print journalism, the criticism of television entertainment and television news fell easily into a pattern of regular newspaper coverage by the movie and arts reviewers. Scholarly work, too, starting in the 1960s emphasized the role, power, and effects of mass media. A recent analyst pointed out that, while television news adopted the norm of journalistic objectivity, the objective report is not neutral—it tends to reflect the perspectives of official sources and dominant values. This analysis has been made of print journalism, but the stakes seem higher with television. As this study warns: "TV has become a mature and powerful force in American politics. In commanding attention and shaping opinion, television is now an authority virtually without peer."[24] Objectivity also has again become the subject of scholarly and popular criticism, with one analyst offering alternative approaches to break the objective-subjective stalemate in these discussions and to focus on the ideological and cultural nature of the context of editing and audience response.[25]

A sizable body of scholarly and popular television criticism has already emerged, perhaps because most of television falls into the entertainment sphere. Television study has attracted the attention of literary, film, and culture critics as well as social scientists. They are bringing to television analysis a maturity and depth of insight that is still lacking for print.[26] Print press criticism stumbles along, offering useful insights but turning over much old ground. Further, it tends to be read by "insiders" who are already knowledgeable, while it gets little support or attention from the "industry," press foundations, and academe.

The television network news organizations, the wire services, and the big city newspapers may be today's dinosaurs, but they have served a useful function in providing some of the social glue that connects an enormous multiethnic and economically diverse nation. Each new mass medium has swept in and rearranged the structure of the industry, generally by ascribing somewhat narrower functions to each participant. We have yet to see the impact of the latest technologies on the structure and function of the existing mass media, but the indications are that a resplintering of the mass into audience-defined interests and targeted markets will characterize more and more of the media. This could open up greater diversity and a wider range of cultural and intellectual choices of content if each of the smaller markets is strong enough to support the enterprise. Newspapers could go the way of radio and magazines and find themselves part of large information conglomerates. Some already are.

## THINKING IN MASS

Concern about vulgarization, the degradation of high artistic and cultural achievements by ever-greater emphasis on mass and lowest-common-denominator appeals, lies behind much contemporary criticism of journalism, mass media, and the arts. English professor and literary critic John Aldridge makes this clear: "Rampant mediocrity has become a major characterizing feature of our time, reducing differences and compromising standards." When this is applied to journalism, it takes on the added dimension of a threat to informed self-government.[27]

"The real threat of mass production of ideas, of vulgarization," said *New York Times* editor Simeon Strunsky decades earlier, "is when a middle class begins to think in the mass." It becomes a danger to the vigor of the society and its intellectual leadership and imagination, if the few millions of the best educated people lose individuality and in their mental life tend to become a herd." He was talking about tabloid newspapers and radio, but the point is apt today.[28]

In the absence of any forms of mandatory accountability or enforceable professional standards for print journalism, the role of criticism assumes greater weight. The public can clearly benefit from informed criticism and participation in debate over press performance. Owners and managers in time may come to see that responsible and responsive criticism is helpful in building public respect and credibility and maintaining a dialogue between press and community.

The old newspaper editors who were personalities in their communities have disappeared from the urban scene. The newspaper has become more important as an entity than have any of the individuals who own or create it. Sometimes, the mass daily newspaper seems a faceless and soulless thing, unreachable, untouchable by ordinary people. Readers bring more than pennies and buying power to the newspaper; they bring expectations about the role of the press and the conduct of professional journalists in reporting and writing the news. They expect information and explanation along with the entertainment and emotion. If the public stops caring and assumes the press is unapproachable and removed, it may stop attending to the message and finally stop the subscriptions. That ultimate critical act is one that worries not only the publishers but social critics as well. Press, people, and government all have a stake in keeping an open society informed and dynamic. Criticism plays an important part by furnishing an informal means of "quality control" in this newspaper industry that is much more than just another business.[29]

## THE MATTER OF AUTONOMY

Journalistic professionalism as a means of raising the quality of journalistic performance in the United States was fraught with troublesome logic. The American press is an institution that is part business and part public service, and its freedom rests on the primacy of free speech and absence of prior restraint to that speech, such as licensing and censorship. A profession, on the other hand, perpetuates and protects its mystique and power by limiting access through licensing and educational requirements and policing its own group members' infractions through license suspension or disbarment, for example. Most modern daily journalism is a big business bureaucracy, not a personal, client/professional relationship. No matter how high minded, ethical, and independent a journalist or editor may be, it is still the publisher-owner who pays the bills and ultimately sets the tone.

This means that most journalists have limited autonomy—some more than others and some very little. But autonomy is a key element in professionalism. journalists are hired employees or paid freelancers. Their professionalism demands accuracy, objectivity, and ethical behavior, but because it lacks a means for social accountability, it is a flawed professionalism. On the one hand, objectivity asks that journalists treat subjects and people with detachment and fairness, yet empathy and creativeness often make a better story. Objectivity commands, stay out of the story; reality presents a wider range of choices. Professionalism requires ethical behavior, but the ethical reasoning used in journalism is most often utilitarian—the greater good at balance against an individual's discomfort.

From time to time a case stirs broad concern, and the reaction readjusts institutional behavior. For example, when the Pulitzer Board took the Mirage Tavern story award away from the *Chicago Sun-Times* to express disapproval of the covert investigation that had been the basis for the story, it sent a message to journalists nationwide. That kind of behavior was not going to be rewarded with prizes. And when a fictional story is passed off as a fact, discovery of the fraud may result in firing of the offender. Recreation of events treated as news offends journalists and the public, as ABC network news discovered in 1989, when it staged footage of an alleged spy passing documents to a contact and let it appear to be action news. In dozens of similar instances, journalistic practice has determined ethical boundaries.

Competition, too, has provided an informal accountability. There was some assurance when newspapers had direct competition in their home markets that a story was not going to be missed or mishandled for long. There was always an alternative. But that no longer exists, and competition is not always a good substitute for editors and journalists having to think through and weigh the moral arguments *before* publication. Lacking other forms of accountability, when standards are breached, the law may finally decide.

In the 1980s, for example, ostensibly because of the large dollar amounts awarded in many libel cases, news organizations were being advised *not* to put codes of ethics and practices in writing, in order to avoid their use as standards in lawsuits. If the law and commerce are to make these most fundamental decisions in journalism, where does that leave the ideal of professional accountability? Impaired, to say the least.

The institution of journalism needs to come up with an appropriate mechanism for accountability, one that suits the unique character of this quasi-profession, and one that does not give up professional idealism, press freedom, or commercial success. Countless books, articles, and studies of modern journalism, including this one, arrive at the same end—moral responsibility ultimately lies with each individual journalist *and* with a public opinion that either tolerates the journalism it gets or demands change. There is no reason for journalists to shun criticism; in fact, criticism provides a court of public opinion and is the surest means of involving public participation. Criticism, in fact, offers cultural and political leverage for ethical journalists against the power and influence of corporate mass media. Regular criticism may offer a way out of the dilemma of the First Amendment versus professionalism.

## NOTES

1. Saul Carson, "On the Air: The Reformed Gadfly," *New Republic* 128 (20 April 1953): 10–12.
2. Don Hollenbeck, "Who Is Right?" *Atlantic Monthly* (September 1948): 49.
3. Hollenbeck, "Right," 50.
4. Hollenbeck, "Right," 51.
5. Obituary, *New York Times* (23 June 1954): 16. His death was a suicide.
6. "CBS Station in New York Starts Criticism of Press," *Editor and Publisher* (7 June 1947): 11.
7. "CBS Station," *Editor and Publisher*, 11.
8. "CBS Station," *Editor and Publisher*, 11.
9. "CBS Station," *Editor and Publisher*, 11.
10. Don Hollenbeck, *Current Biography* (February 1951): 29.
11. Erik Barnow, *The Image Empire* (New York: Oxford University Press, 1970), 55: and obituary, *Time* (5 July 1954).
12. Edmund M. Midura, "An Evaluation of A. J. Liebling's Performance as a Critic of the Press," Ph.D. dissertation (University of Iowa, 1969), 32, 215.
13. A. J. Liebling, "Do You Belong in Journalism?" in *The Press* (New York: Ballantine Books, 1975 rev. ed.), originally published May 14, 1960.
14. Liebling, *Press*, 60, originally "Dismally," 28 January 1950.
15. Liebling, *Press*, 63.
16. Liebling, *Press*, 36.
17. Midura, "Evaluation," 33–35.
18. "Editor Proposes Criticism Project," *Editor and Publisher* (7 February 1948): 32.
19. Letter from Wesley H. Maurer, Sr., to the author, 29 November 1988.
20. Richard A. Schwarzlose, *Newspapers: A Reference Guide* (New York: Greenwood Press, 1987), 309.
21. Jeremy Gerard, "Walter Cronkite: Speaking His Mind," *New York Times* (8 January 1989): H 29–30.
22. William E. Porter, *Assault on the Media: The Nixon Years* (Ann Arbor: University of Michigan Press, 1976).
23. Mark Hertsgaard, *On Bended Knee: the Press and the Reagan Presidency* (New York: Farrar, Straus & Giroux, 1988).

24. Shanto Iyengar and Donald R. Kinder, *News That Matters* (Chicago: University of Chicago Press, 1987), 133.

25. Robert A. Hackett, "Decline of a Paradigm? Bias and Objectivity in News Media Sources," *Critical Studies in Mass Communication* 3 (1984): 229–59.

26. See for example: Richard Campbell and Jimmie L. Reeves, "Covering the Homeless: The Joyce Brown Story," *Critical Studies in Mass Communication* 6 (1989): 21–42; and James Carey, ed., *Media, Myth and Narrative* (Beverly Hills: Sage, 1988).

27. John W. Aldridge, *The American Novel and the Way We Live Now* (New York: Oxford University Press, 1985), 156.

28. Simeon Strunsky, *The Living Tradition* (New York: Doubleday, Doran, 1939), 271.

29. Professor Jonathan Friendly suggested the expression "quality control" as applied here.

# CHAPTER 14

# The Nature of Criticism

The American press has received ample criticism, and yet it lacks a theory of press criticism and pays scant attention to what might be called a critical tradition. The profession of press critic, which might be applied to a few writers from the 1930s through the 1950s, still describes but a handful of specialists who critique the press. Press criticism has grown like Topsy, emanating from whatever individual or group has a gripe about a favored topic and its press coverage. Hurt feelings, anger, pride, moral outrage, political or social goals are more likely to fuel this spontaneous criticism than an analytical or intellectual appraisal.

It is not clear why no genre of press criticism has developed as a mature specialty. The few journals of criticism that have emerged in recent years provide an opportunity for sustained, professional press criticism, but still few people do this work for a living. Press criticism might logically have arisen from among the literary essayists and magazinists in American press history. Perhaps it is simply that Americans believe the newspapers are practical information and a part of daily civic life, but not works of artistic merit nor of lasting social or cultural worth.

The names that newspaper owners give their publications suggest that they hold a more elevated view than that of their paper's functions: beacon, light, sun, world, star, messenger, courier, herald, item, ledger, news, and journal are all popular titles. The journalistic historic tradition places a high value on the importance of the press as a popular educator and upholder of citizens' interest in public affairs. An institution with such fundamental centrality in American life and one provided special constitutional protection in the First Amendment would seem ripe for some form of public scrutiny. But the freedom of speech protection has also restrained any form of governmental interference with content as censorship. Editors will say that the public votes daily on the performance of its local newspaper by continuing or stopping their subscriptions.

Perhaps this answer sufficed in an era with directly competing newspapers in most communities beyond the village size, where public scrutiny by neighbors, business associates, and the competition was immediate and direct. Frontier journalists, for example, had to contend with irate readers brandishing sticks and revolvers. Partisan editors took great joy in berating each other in their editorial columns. When the urban daily shed its partisan and community character and became a smorgasbord for the masses, it shifted direct contact to such forms as letters to the editor, phone calls, or libel suits. The urban press became a powerful social and cultural institution whose importance in the daily life of the nation has become better understood in the post–World War II period of mass media research. But this knowledge has still not led to a movement to create a genre of specialty press criticism by the institution itself nor to much regular, vigorous critical analysis from the schools of journalism, which should have this as a key responsibility. In contrast, movies, radio, and television fell quickly into place as subjects suitable for critical evaluation by the press.

The ephemeral nature of the mass media, the range of the content from quality to trash, and a broad intellectual range within the audience characterizes print as well as broadcast and film. The medium itself doesn't dictate audience or cultural level. The elite and popular differentiation as a reason for the presence or absence of regular criticism of one medium over another doesn't hold, but function may be the key. The newspaper has been a part of the political world since its inception. In America the newspaper has been associated with mainstream popular democracy at least since the Jacksonian era. It is informer, popular educator, gossip, town crier, messenger, whistle blower, and cheerleader. It is criticized as a quasi-institution, more akin to the schools and the government than to the arts.

The modern newspapers envisioned by Joseph Pulitzer was to "speak to a nation" and not to a select committee. Catering to an entire population meant content, style, and appeal had to be broadened in order to capture the masses. The high value placed on an open, democratic society also meant that the popular press had to stay in touch with current interests and mores. An artful balance is required to serve both the marketplace of ideas and that of commerce. It is the perceived success or failure of this balancing act that generates the most press criticism, especially from the guardians of the high culture who keep a sharp eye out for overweighting the commercial side. So the criticial battleground for the press has been over matters not so much of form and style, but of content and behavior, intent and impact on individuals and society.

## NEWS AS A LITERARY FORM

Only occasionally has the issue of literary form or creativity been raised about journalistic work, although contemporary researchers are starting to address this. The poet Archibald MacLeish described the commonality of poetry and journalism in a dramatic call to bridge the artificial gulf he saw between seeing and feeling in the late 1950s.[1] Helen M. Hughes and Michael Schudson, sociologists a generation or more apart, have called attention to the story form of news reporting as contrasted to the information form.[2]

Much more has been learned about journalism's role in putting the "pictures in our heads," as Walter Lippmann described it in 1922. Later scholars have explained the media role in the creation of social reality, role modeling, cultural myths, and texts.[3] Journalism's role as an agent of change, an agenda setter and messenger of good and bad news is studied by contemporary mass media researchers. There is general agreement that daily journalism plays a vital role in modern society.

MacLeish put it compellingly when he warned that the "crisis of modern civilization" was the "crisis of the life of the imagination." There was an artificial gulf between the objective detachment of journalistic reporting of events and poetry's emphasis on feeling. Both journalism and poetry "recreate the world we have," but "feeling without knowing does not make a work of art." Objective "detachment at the cost of its emotional significance" is harmful to society. MacLeish was concerned that his contemporaries seemed unfeelingly to face the prospect of "nuclear extermination," and he thought education might be the starting point for relearning the lesson. "The life of imagination" had to be restored to modern society, he said, because without it people were unfree, heedlessly following the decisions of others.[4]

The new culture-based research is trying to fill this gap. Similarly, a new "new journalism" in the late 1960s used fictional techniques to probe deeper in a time of social turbulence and shifting values. That journalism tried to get inside other people's heads and ways of living in order to supplement the routine, "objective" reporting of events. It is a difficult artistic style to master, and the dichotomy between fact and opinion in the modern American news tradition is very deep. The "new journalism" inexpertly done can turn into propaganda and preaching, or into reenactments and ficionalized treatments of real events.

As the modern press matured from sensationalism and yellow journalism through tabloid journalism into the omnibus, general-interest newspaper for the mass urban society, a set of values and standards about press performance also evolved. The essence of American journalism is to be a public informant, providing the forum for debate and discussion, popular education, edification, and amusement. Wars and domestic strife raised new issues for the press and new challenges to journalistic reporting and analysis. The press brings the good and the bad, the tawdry and the sublime, the dreams and the fears into the public arena for view and review.

## DEFINING PRESS CRITICISM

In 1974, James W. Carey, head of the School of Communication at the University of Illinois, issued a call for "sustained, systematic, and intellectually sound criticism." The press, he said, as one of our most important institutions is not subject to this analysis—not in public, and rarely within the universities or the press itself.[5] He offered three "modes" of criticism that should contribute to the criticial community: (1) "criticism by standards of public or social responsibility," (2) "scientistic criticism" by the social scientists, and (3) "cultural criticism" or the "ongoing process of exchange of debate between press and its audience" over the role and performance of the press in a democratic society.[6] Carey emphasized cultural criticism. To Carey, all press criticism is "essentially the criticism of language," and is analogous to literary or arts criticism. It requires, he says, "close public attention to the methods, procedures, and techniques of journalistic investigation and the language of journalistic reporting. This is the basic critical act in journalism...." But Carey noted that it was also the least available to the general public because it was mostly in journals.[7]

But how shall journalism criticism be done, and who shall do it? The professional journalists and scholars who study the press and educate the future journalists have the primary responsibility. Indeed, they know the institution, its aspirations and its limitations. They know something of its traditions, history, laws, and ethics. They understand the art/science of reporting and telling stories in words and pictures. As Dean Theodore B. Peterson at the University of Oregon put it in 1959: "If journalism schools are to achieve the professional status we all speak so glibly of, criticism is one of their inescapable functions."[8]

The themes still echo today. The lack of a regular press criticism is one of the most dangerous shortcomings of the press, said Jody Powell, former press secretary for President Jimmy Carter, because it "inhibits attempts to correct or at least alleviate all other problems."[9] Norman E. Isaacs, former president of the American Society of Newspapers Editors and of the Associated Press Managing Editors and chairman of the National News Council from 1977 to 1982, challenged print and broadcast journalists to live up to the highest standards intended by the founding fathers. The media "don't take themselves and their role seriously enough," he said, quoting Douglass Cater of the Aspen Institute. "They refuse to admit that those who are involved in the communications of a democracy play a major role in its governance."[10]

Isaacs recalled Alexander Hamilton's warning of two centuries ago that the security of a free press, "whatever fine declarations may be inserted in any Constitution respecting it, must altogether depend on public opinion and on the general spirit of the people and of the government."[11]

## DISENCHANTED AUDIENCE

Today, public opinion polls show a public disenchanted with big government and big media. The press should not be just a "money machine" or an exciting game, said Isaacs. "What it all boils down to is values," he asserted. The only way "democracy can work successfully is through a value system that puts honorable public service in the reporting of events as accurately as possible, interpreting them honestly, and analyzing them fairly. That kind of journalism can win back the confidence of the citizenry." The news organizations need a lot of "painful reappraisal and reorganization," said Isaacs, including better budgets, more reasonable news space, a sense of mission, greater accountability, ethics, and compassion.[12]

Time magazine in a 1983 cover story charged the press with arrogance, insensitivity, sensationalism, and indifference toward the public except to gain them as readers. The journalist is no longer seen as a popular crusader for justice but as an ethical compromiser, according to Time. The daily newspaper seems as remote as other big corporations; journalists appear to be insensitive and prying scribes who badger suffering victims. Time reminded its readers of the importance of the press to society and urged press accountability by means of ombudsmen, news councils, correction boxes, courts of review, and press critics, who would provide a needed "moral compass" for readers.[13]

While the press fretted over its loss of credibility, opinion polls in the early 1980s showed the public also distrusted television, the federal government, and Congress.[14] Surprisingly, a survey by the Los Angeles Times-Mirror/Gallup organization in 1986 clouded the issue by saying there was "no credibility" crisis for the media if researchers used the term "believability." People wondered if both findings could be right. A study by Professor D. Charles Whitney of the University of Illinois Institute for Communication Research further pointed out that the public has generally held a favorable and supportive view of the importance of the press over the past fifty years, but that significant and vocal minorities, often the people who are the most heavy viewers and users of the media, do show high degrees of concern.[15]

## ASSURING A HIGH STANDARD

In a widely publicized libel action in 1985 contesting CBS' portrayal of General William Westmoreland during the Vietnam War, the General characterized the process as "unsatisfactory." Ironically, he wished for a better way than libel action to handle a public airing of journalistic procedure and to assure a high standard of ethics in journalism—something like the recently expired National News Council.[16] After only a decade, the council had died under-supported and little publicized. Once again, there was no way to insist that the press publish the council's findings, which some of the daily press objected to as undue outside pressure.

Lacking a national council, the use of press ombudsmen to look into the public's complaints about specific news media has been helpful. But there are only thirty-three such reader representatives, mostly at the larger newspapers.[17] Most of them write regular columns appraising and taking stands on the performance of their newspapers in response to their own and to readers' observations. In 1980 they formed a professional association, the Organization of Newspaper Ombudsmen, which includes members from the United States, Canada, and other countries. Because of its local nature, the ombudsman concept of direct community response and impartial monitoring, while still not widely used by the 1,645 dailies in the United States, may have a better chance for survival than the national council.

"Why aren't there more ombudsmen?" Isaacs, former editor of the *Louisville Courier-Journal*, which employed the first ombudsman in the United States, was asked. "It takes a smart, tough editor to decide a paper needs an ombudsman. And a wise, strong publisher to back up that editor," he replied. Too many editors and publishers are fearful of offending top management and being unpopular with their staffs, he explained. Too much of journalism is caught up in a "tribal culture" whose anthem is: "We stand by our story."[18]

And yet, Isaacs sees the ombudsman concept as the one bright hope for responsible, contemporary American journalism. It "offers the citizen-readers direct access to an executive officer to whom they can tender their protests, complaints, or views about the paper's effectiveness." It puts the newspaper back in direct contact with the readers, and it monitors journalistic values and ethics. "The free press has an immense role to play—that of being the nation's intellectual life line." Isaacs sees the ombudsman role as serving in that spirit and helping the newspaper live up to its public accountability.[19]

One study of editor/publisher attitudes toward press accountability found they voiced strong opposition to any form of uniform control, because they believe it would quickly lead to censorship.[20] This is not to suggest that the leaders of the press are unwilling to improve their image and restore public respect. The nation's newspapers grew up with strong community involvement and individual rights. Local authority is also deeply embedded in U.S. law, in the schools, and governmental services. Individual efforts by newspapers to live up to a voluntary standard of values and behavior have so far been the most successful method for raising the standards of the press. The voices of the citizen-critics also figure in the process.

"A real threat to free expression is coming soon," John Siegenthaler, publisher of *The Tennessean* and president of ASNE, predicted in 1989. He urged newspaper people to get behind support of free speech for television as well as for print, or they may find themselves facing not only the restoration of the Fairness Doctrine for TV but also one introduced for print. One such bill to make the Fairness Doctrine a law is already before Congress, he said, and Siegenthaler thinks Congress and the public would support the legislation because of their exasperation with the press and its arrogance. "How can there be free, open, lusty debate in a free, open society if broadcasters are intimidated, harassed, or chilled?" he asked.[21]

"Newspapers must be more critical of each other in print," he said. "Many papers have TV critics, but few have writers who point the finger of criticism at themselves." He said the press needed to "find ways to explain our positions on journalistic ethics, conflicts of interest, confidential sources —or why we do what we do the way we do it . . . we need to open up to the sunshine as much of our process of news decision-making and editorial opinion-making as soon as possible."[22]

## MODELS FOR PRESS CRITICISM

To look to literature and the arts as models for press criticism is only partially rewarding. There are correspondences in the area of broad objectives, but criticism of the high arts tends to look at the artistic merit first and context second, if at all. Press criticism would have at its center the analysis of the message in its social context and then the influence of language, style, and form. Some assistance may come from research techniques for studying material culture, which focus on the ways a culture is revealed in material objects, but here the emphasis is also from form to context.[23] Cultural analysis and institutional analysis along with social and intellectual history may offer useful insights.[24]

But there is no apt, single model of criticism that fits the press exactly. Press criticism as a genre will have to emerge from the nature of the press, from its rich history and tradition, its professional values, its legal and ethical constraints, and the interplay of style, form, and technology. Some influences will certainly include the evolution of objectivity and separation of fact from opinion as core values, as well as the underlying ideal of press freedom as a bulwark for other individual freedoms. The emphasis on mass rather than class and the limited autonomy of the journalist are other important factors shaping modern journalism.

The press does try to mirror life, but it also shapes and fashions reality by packaging it in story and visual forms, which are intended for information, sometimes for explanation and persuasion and example. But what the audience does with these stories and the information, what it brings to the experience, is largely unknown, and audience studies are only now attracting increased attention from media analysts.[25] This research will certainly help the critics' understanding of audience perceptions and reactions to media content.

Some literary critics look for models of reality in literature; others emphasize that literature is a product of the imagination with only "some" relation to reality.[26] At least most literary schools believe that the role of the critic is socially valuable in serving as "tastemaker" for society, helping to "educate the imagination" of readers, in encouraging the best work and highest standards, and providing a context or ranking of a contemporary work as compared to the classics and tradition. The importance of criticism is to teach the individual that he is not unique and has much in common with other individuals, says W. H. Auden, and to spread that knowledge to the audience.[27]

In the same way, press criticism as a subgenre of literary criticism, would be socially valuable. The press critic would also work on the same three levels set forth by literary critics: the individual, personal response; the interpretive or explanatory response for the audience; and the evaluative response that judges quality.[28]

The press critic would serve society and profession by continually bringing up for debate and analysis these issues, values, and standards, encouraging wider public debate on a less personalized and more analytical and intellectual plane. Too much press criticism in the past has attacked the writer or publisher for evil intentions or character defects rather than examining the institutional performance or social utility of the reportage.

The modern corporation with its mix of product and service and its national and expanding international reach can no longer afford to rely on a trickle-down method for establishing standards of journalistic performance and quality control. There is no assurance that the next chief executive officer will have any training, interest in or understanding of journalism's role in the American culture, however expert that officer may be in finance and marketing. The modern corporation and business world in the last two decades has taken a greater interest in business ethics and quality control in order to assure better and longer-lasting product satisfaction. If the media executives begin to see professional press criticism as a form of quality control that not only improves the product but also fosters public credibility, reader loyalty, and profits, the speciality will grow.

## FUTURE INDICATORS

There are a handful of positive indicators of what journalism criticism can be if it includes all forms of media and is open to research approaches from the humanities and social sciences. First, there is the growing evidence of support for the improvement of journalistic ethics within journalism in the form of college classes, professional seminars and workshops, and newsroom training sessions. Case studies of ethical choices made by journalists and editors are widely published and adopted in university classes, suggesting receptivity toward moral as well as social responsibility in this field. It could translate into a rising ethical consciousness for the journalistic profession; the critic would help sustain this dialogue and aid the public's understanding. This 1980s development has produced centers of study for media ethics, texts, courses, and a scholarly quarterly, *The Journal of Mass Media Ethics*.

Second, there is the modest growth of a form of monitoring that involves the public in the process. News councils and ombudsmen arrived in the 1970s. The ombudsmen represent thirty-three daily newspapers of varying size, while the only really successful news council is the one in Minnesota, formed in 1971 for the entire state. Some newspapers have created less formal means of discussing ethics and news play with their readers through reader response and letter columns, better display of corrections, and publisher's or editor's weekly columns.

Third, the growth of journalistic ethics classes fosters critical analysis and study of press performance as students have to review and ultimately question the thinking and standards that were operating in the case studies they read.

Fourth, there are regular sources of press criticism in national specialized professional journals (*Columbia Journalism Review*, *Nieman Reports*, *St. Louis Journalism Review* and *Washington Journalism Review*), and in a few television programs and scholarly associations. A new journal, *The Journal of Critical Studies*, includes journalism in its coverage.

Finally, there are a few professional press critics working full time or part time on press criticism and media reporting at a few top daily newspapers and news magazines and broadcast outlets. Scholars in journalism and communication, political science, sociology, anthropology, and American Culture have taken new interest in the subject and enriched the field by their research. CBS offered press criticism by Charles Collingwood in the 1960s on WCBS-TV, and ABC's "Viewpoint" and PBS' "Inside Story" frequently take up media issues today.

Jeff Greenfield, now a political analyst for ABC News, has held the job of media critic for both CBS and ABC News, and he covers print and broadcast media in his critical pieces for television and in magazines. Greenfield said it was difficult to do media criticism on network television because the affiliate stations do not like to run programs that might turn audiences away from their programming. He pointed out that in a world of busy, dual-career families, however, the critic might be useful in drawing audience attention to better or more popular programs as people become more selective with their viewing time.[29]

There have been media reporters and critics at various times in the recent decade at the top urban newspapers: the *New York Times*, *Washington Post*, *Los Angeles Times, Newsday* and *Wall Street Journal*. And the *Village Voice*, the *New Yorker*, *Time*, and *Newsweek* have also had press or media critics. In all cases the assignments varied and usually included reporting as well as criticism and analysis.

Perhaps best known of the professional contemporary media critics who criticize the press are: David Shaw, Ben Bagdikian, Ed Diamond, and Alexander Cockburn. Shaw, who since 1974 has had a special arrangement with the editor and publisher of the *Los Angeles Times* to do long, in-depth studies of the American press, including his own newspaper, writes about four or five pieces per year. He travels and consults widely while researching topics that have included press treatment of politics, polling, medicine, celebrities, sports, travel, and food and wine. His work has been collected and published in book form. His experience as a critic taught him that colleagues might be a bit cool or even hostile after being featured in one of his columns, but he has learned to have "the guts to say what I believe."[30]

Ben Bagdikian, reporter, magazine editor, ombudsman, and professor of journalism earned a 1978 citation of merit as "journalism's most perceptive critic" from the American Society of Journalism School Administrators.[31] His books include *The Information Machines* and *The Media Monopoly*. He served as project director for a Markel Foundation study of newspaper survival and has been a supporter of press councils. His writing has often rankled the industry and has stirred up debate. "Critics, like journalists, are not placed on this earth in order to be loved," he remarked, recalling earlier put-down labels like "a so-called critic" or an "alleged critic." But, he pointed out that there was no other way to become a press critic than to start writing and freelancing.[32]

He charged in his acceptance speech that the newspaper business was dominated by a "Manhattanitis" that assumes what happens in New York City is true of the nation. This, Bagdikian asserted, promotes a false myth of newspaper poverty. Because five dailies failed in New York City in the 1960s, people seem to ignore the fact that nationwide the newspapers make a "20 percent return on sales and on equity of 15 percent."[33]

Bagdikian predicted the conflict in the future of journalism as one between the steady growth of professional journalists and "the conversion of the news media organizations to huge corporate structures."[34] The professionals are not satisfied with old reporting formulas, and they know how to use investigative and social science research techniques to make comprehensive and understandable reports, he said. The journalists will push for greater freedom on how and what to report, while corporate management will press for "controllable, mass-produced goods." Although the press was in a transition era when he spoke, the multinational corporation was coming to dominate business, and that would include the mass media, he believed.[35]

In his challenging study published in 1983 he documented that *The Media Monopoly* consisted of fifty top interconnected ownerships and that these structures engaged in favoritism and news bias and fostered homogenization and blandness of content, to the detriment of the ideal of an informed citizenry. He charged that mass advertising had pushed the press from 40 to 60 percent advertisements, and encouraged "fluff" and noncontroversial news. The objectivity standard, "which sounded splendid," also led to politically neutral reporting and "lack of intelligent examination by the journalists," as the McCarthy era aptly demonstrated.[36]

These modern developments, Bagdikian warned, have encouraged reader apathy toward media and little loyalty to specific papers. His solution would be to distribute media power and limit the number of media outlets under one ownership in an attempt to bring back the vital diversity of ideas and the engagement of readers and reporters in the community and its activities. His lamentations went unanswered; instead, the corporate conditions he outlined continued as marketplace conditions were allowed to determine the future of journalism in the United States. But another trend that he noted, the increased use of market research to carve out more specific markets and the new technological possibilities with cable, video, and satellites, may create a more diverse set of choices even though the ownerships continue to congeal.

Ed Diamond, currently affiliated with New York University where he heads a media study group on political news coverage, was a former senior editor at *Newsweek*. He left the magazine to start a study group at MIT, and has taught and presented media criticism on Boston area television. He has published several books of media criticism, including the *Tin Kazoo* and *Good News, Bad News*. His work relies heavily on careful analysis of media content and trends in the coverage and is well regarded in academic media research circles.

Alexander Cockburn, media critic for the *Village Voice* for a decade before going to the *Nation* and the *Wall Street Journal*, raises ideological issues and social questions in the tradition of Seldes, Bent, and Liebling. Beyond these, there are few individuals who do regular press criticism on local or alternative newspapers, and there still is no recognized press criticism speciality at most daily newspapers. Most of the news of the media industry, therefore, is handled by nonspecialists, and most criticism continues to be hit and miss, following contemporary enthusiasms and notable ethical lapses in press performance.[37]

## CRITICIZING TELEVISION AND PRINT

A long-standing enmity born of competition and jealousy—and perhaps to some extent a preference for and belief in the primacy of the word on paper—exists between print and nonprint journalists. The differing legal basis for print and broadcasting in the United States has added to that split, as have the media owners' battles over turf as each technological development dislodged the earlier forms.[38]

Should print and television journalists ever reach an understanding of their common traditions, roles, goals, and self-interests vis-à-vis speech and press freedom, social responsibility, public enlightenment, and civic leadership, the role of journalism critic could become even more vital. Such a media/press critic, as in the arts, would foster high standards of journalism, raising issues for public debate and providing context and background to aid public understanding in matters of news judgment and the importance of language and imagery in public opinion. The critic could explain the potential for creativity and technological expertise as well as the limits and pitfalls, and could educate the public to be more journalistically literate.

The indicators of a serious interest in journalistic criticism are strong enough to suggest that it is time to take a look at the criteria that might be applied to this new professional genre. Contemporary press critics range from those with ideological attitudes to promote to those who refrain from subjectivity and offer more objective or contextual analysis. The genre should—as in arts criticism—accommodate a variety of approaches and voices and styles to give the widest potential debate and context for the critical discussion.

## THE PRESS CRITICS' CHALLENGE

The Information Age of computer-cable-video-laser-satellite technology is merging the forms of news and entertaiment media. This development should be covered as a political, social, and economic issue. Without serious public discussion, market and technological demands are restructuring the industry and its news products, making the issue of balancing financial success with the responsibility of providing quality news coverage more vital than ever as newspapers and network news cut budgets, target affluent markets, and emphasize soft and service features over hard news and analysis. The old challenge has resurfaced.

The "new reshaping of the news content of the press is happening without plan or public criticism," says journalism professor and media critic Felix Gutierrez. He feels that "the profitable side will have to subsidize the general news," but the question will be how much news and what kind? The press must show "stewardship of its responsibility to the people," he says, or he expects that the public will see less hard news and more "soft and salable" news in their daily newspapers.[39]

Regular daily coverage of such issues by professional critics of journalism would provide a forum for informed public discussion. This criticism would teach the public about the realities of daily journalism while also serving as a monitor against the deliberate disregard of those ethics. Thoughtful criticism would reward the responsible journalists and expose the irresponsible to the glare of public scrutiny, a searchlight the press willingly shines on all others.

The professional critic is a transmitter of the traditions and values in literary and artistic works, an interpreter of the contemporary shape of that genre and a goad that helps push out the boundaries of established art forms. The critic holds up the new to past standards, judges the results, and introduces new developments and insights.

Studies and polls of contemporary audiences of print and broadcast journalism indicate that the public has little understanding of what goes on in the newspaper or television newsroom. In fact, popular entertainment such as movies and television shows featuring journalists add to the public's exaggerated ideas of the best and worst traits of working journalists. So do the interviews and profiles of celebrity-status journalists with their spectacular salaries and presumed personal power. These glamour images are just as inaccurate as the earlier Bohemian image, and the press itself has a large challenge to counter that image with something approaching reality. In this arena, as in others, the press critic can help provide an alternative under-standing by focusing on the art and ethics of reporting and the hard work and sometimes staggering impact a reporter's story may have on a person or issue as well as the frustration over seeming public indifference to serious news reporting.

The press in a democratic society is a conservator of mainstream values as well as an introducer of new and challenging values. It occupies a place be-tween the individual and many well-defined and well-funded special interests, businesses, institutions, and industries. Because the press has a specially pro-tected freedom, society has learned to expect it to be responsible. One major responsibility has been to rise above the battle and observe and comment and cry alarm on behalf of the larger society instead of special interests. This means, of course, that someone is always upset over a particular news item. Criticism of this sort, no matter how valid, is also often emotional and thoughtless. Publishers say the press is tested daily in the market of public opinion, but that kind of testing is the superficial, personal reaction or indifference of the hurried reader. The act of subscribing or tuning in is not necessarily a critical act. Professional criticism is.

Insider criticism of contemporary journalism is readily available and con-sumed by journalists, scholars, and other media enthusiasts. But this dis-cussion, significant and useful as it is, does not often get aired in the public press. Professional press criticism needs to be part of the public forum, and it would have to gain credibility based on performance. The public would quickly spot a critic who engaged in special pleading or propaganda for the institution producing the critic's paycheck. It may be asking a lot of a commercial, quasi-public institution to provide and pay for its own public critical apparatus and also maintain a "hands off" policy, but that is where *all* the theoretical argu-ments over press accountability end. Lacking any form of government control, seeking something more reliable than hit-and-miss criticism, the analyst is forced to think of ways the press can do a better job of policing itself.

## CHALLENGES FOR THE 1990s

Journalism must reappraise and readjust to maintain its centrality to the eternal need for information in a democratic society. Technology, redistribution of the audience, and marketing support for the mass media are at the heart of the current problem. Most daily newspapers are run as part of large corporations and conglomerates, often with publicly traded stock and "bottom line" profit mentalities. Journalists move from city to city in the quest of better jobs, and may have slight interest in their place of residence. Marketing strategies and surveys are used to determine reader interests instead of the old method of letting the publisher/editor figure out what the community wants and needs. The daily newspaper's close connection with the fabric of its city and citizens has lessened in most places, leaving that function to a thriving suburban press.

The gulfs between thinking and feeling, between social responsibility and profits, between people and faceless institutions seem wider than ever. The stepped-up competition among all mass media for power and profits once again is submerging the concern for ideals and values. In such times the commercial drive lurches toward greed, sensation, and trivia, while social conscience starves. The reverse potential also exists; newspapers can regain the trusted role as guardian of the public's liberties through tough-minded independence, social responsibility, and a willingness to demonstrate some credible method of public accountability.

The press in the United States has been local or at most regional, with only a few national newspapers serving small, specialized audiences. The general-interest newspaper that serves everyone has been the model of choice in cities and towns of all sizes. No other medium could match the local, daily newspaper for local news coverage or local advertising. If that special condition changes and a tiered system of national newspapers emerges (now at least technically feasible with satellite printing plants and skillful computerized target marketing), the daily newspaper may be forced to make a hard choice between mass and class, and the determining factor is going to be economics.

So far the industry response has been to keep lowering the intellectual quality, cutting the story length, and offering more entertaining and service features in the quest of a fickle audience. A far different response might be to let newspapers find their appropriate and interested audience, a still large slice of the total mass that wants more printed information, more analysis, more news in context in a daily printed form. Television already has captured the mass quick-fix news audience. Magazines and radio faced the same dilemma after World War II as television swept over the nation.

If newspapers begin to adopt the market segmentation approach of the magazine and radio industry, the traditions and values that were so central in the formation of omnibus newspapers will be raised again. What impact would a new press industry structure have on the democratic forum? The *forum* is essential, but does the *form* matter? Change is not the threat, but loss of public interest and lack of public participation in the debate over the future and responsibility of this important institution is. It is the frequency of reports of growing disenchantment and disillusion by a large part of the public that most concerns this author. This study has reaffirmed the continuing need for robust public debate on journalistic performance by the critics, the public, press, and government in order to keep the press alive and in turn to keep democracy healthy.

## NOTES

1. Archibald MacLeish, "The Poet and the Press," *Atlantic Monthly* 203 (March 1959): 40–46.
2. Michael Schudson, *Discovering the News: A Social History of American Newspapers* (New York: Basic Books, 1978), Chap. 5; and Helen MacGill Hughes, *News and the Human Interest Story* (Chicago: University of Chicago Press, 1940).
3. Gaye Tuchman, *Making News: A Study in the Construction of Reality* (New York: Free Press, 1978); and James W. Carey, *Communication as Culture: Essays on Media and Society* (Boston: Unwin Hyman, 1989).
4. MacLeish, "Poet," 46.
5. James W. Carey, "Journalism and Criticism: The Case of an Undeveloped Profession," *The Review of Politics* 36 (April 1974): 227.
6. Carey, "Case," 242–44.
7. Carey, "Case," 244.
8. Jay W. Jensen, "A Method and a Perspective for Criticism of the Mass Media," *Journalism Quarterly* 37 (Spring 1960): 251.
9. Jody Powell, *The Other Side of the Story* (New York: William Morrow, 1984), 292.
10. Norman E. Isaacs, *Untended Gates—The Mismanaged Press* (New York: Columbia University Press, 1986), 218.
11. Isaacs, "Gates," 223, quoted from Alexander Hamilton in *The Federalist* 94 (28 May 1788).
12. Isaacs, "Gates," 224.
13. William A. Henry III, "Journalism Under Fire," *Time* (12 December 1983): 91.
14. Henry, "Fire," 79.
15. D. Charles Whitney, *The Media and the People: Americans' Experience with the News Media: A Fifty-Year Review* (New York: Gannett Center for Media Studies at Columbia University, 1985), 24.
16. "Westmoreland Reflects," *Editor and Publisher* (23 March 1985): 7.
17. *Editors for the Public*, pamphlet (Sacramento: Organization of Newspaper Ombudsmen, 1989).
18. Norman Isaacs, speech to Organization of Newspaper Ombudsmen, Boston, 18 April 1988.
19. Isaacs, speech, Boston.
20. Barbara Hartung, "Attitudes toward the Current Applicability of the 1947 Hutchins Report on Social Responsibility of the Press," unpublished Ph.D. dissertation (San Diego: U.S. International University, 1979).
21. "Come to the Aid of Broadcasters," *Editor and Publisher* (18 February 1989): 14, 43.
22. "Come to the Aid," 14.
23. Thomas J. Schlereth (ed.) *Material Culture Studies in America* (Nashville: The

American Association for State and Local History, 1982); and Schlereth (ed.), *Material Culture: A Research Guide* (Lawrence, Kans.: University Press of Kansas, 1985).

24. Carey, *Communication*, and Dave Nord, "A Plea for Journalism History," *Journalism History* 15: 1 (Spring 1988): 8–15.
25. Andrea Press, *Women Watching Television* (Philadelphia: University of Pennsylvania Press, due 1990).
26. V. F. Calverton, *The Newer Spirit: A Sociological Criticism of Literature* (New York: Boni and Liveright, 1925); and Carl Grabo, *The Creative Critic* (Chicago: University of Chicago Press, 1948).
27. W. H. Auden, "Criticism in a Mass Society," from *The Intent of the Critic* by Edmund Wilson et al. (Gloucester, Mass.: Peter Smith, 1941/1963), 120.
28. Northrop Frye, *The Critical Path: An Essay on the Social Context of Literary Criticism* (Bloomington: Indiana University Press, 1971); and Frye, *The Educated Imagination* (Bloomington: Indiana University Press, 1964).
29. Jeff Greenfield, lecture at University of Michigan Department of Communication, 6 April 1987. His suggestion has obvious parallels with the way that people use book, movie, and theater reviews.
30. David Shaw lecture, University of Michigan Department of Communication, 10 September 1987.
31. "ASJSA Honors Ben Bagdikian as Journalism's 'Most Perceptive Critic,'" *Journalism Educator* 33 (October 1978): 6–12.
32. "Perceptive," 7.
33. "Perceptive," 7.
34. "Perceptive," 10.
35. "Perceptive," 12.
36. Bagdikian, *Monopoly*, 132.
37. The first book to discuss press criticism was: Lee Brown, *The Reluctant Reformation: On Criticizing the Press in America* (New York: David McKay, 1974).
38. Czitrom, *American Mind*.
39. Felix Gutierrez, associate dean and professor of journalism, University of Southern California, speech, University of Michigan Department of Communication, January 1988.

# Epilogue

What should we expect of this professional critic of journalism?

Traditionally, the critic evaluates, offers insights, provides context, and expresses opinions. The critic offers a sustained critical dialogue between artist and society. The media critic would measure the actual performance of the journalistic medium against a set of standards that included the social philosophy, and professional codes, traditions, ethics, and aesthetics.

The media critic would also provide news of developments within journalism, relating current practices and standards to the historical traditions and values of journalism in America. And the critic would be expected to offer educated and penetrating opinions that were supported by evidence and by clear, unprejudiced thinking. The profession of media criticism could be as stimulating and challenging, especially in the Information Age, as that of art, music, theater, film, or literary criticism.

In making a plea for press criticism, Jay Jensen said in 1960 that such criticism in order to be valid should be "made with adequate understanding of the nature of the object," should be conducted in an objective manner (without bias and treating journalism as an object of study), and should be grounded in the historical development of the media and with due regard for the contextual relationships of the media and their environment.[1]

Although the media critic would probably not be loved by the journalistic profession at first, in time that profession might recognize the value of airing its problems and conflicting points of view. It is just possible that more understanding of the journalist and journalism could result. It is certainly hoped that the press critic of the future would not be charged, as Will Irwin was in 1911, with "fouling his own nest" for his muckraking criticism.

The ombudsmen, who serve as local critics of their newspapers, respond in public to reader inquiries and criticism and take up those issues with editors and staff. They have found guarded acceptance from their colleagues. It is much easier for reporters and editors to disregard criticism from outsiders as crank calls than it is to ignore the professional staffer who has worked among them in the newsroom.

In time even the thinnest-skinned practitioner in journalism may realize that professional criticism is preferable to government regulation that would be permitted by a public that believed an arrogant press must be checked. Declining public confidence in the mass media may be a part of a general decline in confidence in the institutions of contemporary society, but taking that line of defense offers little help in restoring public confidence in the press. If it is true that there are signs that society is wearying of the pursuit of selfish pleasure and profit and welcoming a restoration of public-spirited community values, it would be an appropriate time to firmly establish the profession of media critic.

## THE CRITIC'S PREPARATION

The media critic would need to have thorough knowledge of the history of American journalism with its special protection under the Constitution. Knowledge of Enlightenment thinking and the Libertarian and Progressive strands in U.S. history that influence attitudes about and within the press would be critical. Understanding of Socialist and Marxist thought and conservative ideology would be useful in analyzing the various critical stands taken on mass media.

Working knowledge of the journalist's daily routine in newspapers, news magazines, radio, and television news operations would be essential. In order to criticize the performance of print and broadcast journalists, the critic would need a thorough understanding and familiarity with the codes and practices and news values that guide daily journalistic work. The realities of deadlines, the limits of technology, the formulas for storytelling, and the pressures of competition must be part of the critic's experience and understanding. The critic must also know the ideals and the drive for improvement expressed by the best practitioners in the field, as well as the history of press criticism.

The critic must know the laws that limit journalistic performance, such as libel, privacy, and copyright, and the laws pertaining to national security and broadcast regulation. The working of and the reason for the Freedom of Information Act and the Open Meeting Acts, Shield Laws, and press and bar standards for reporting trials should be a part of the critic's intimate understanding in order to judge how well the press performs under these restrictions.

Beyond that, the critic would have to have an appreciation for the shadowy lines between what is normal practice for reporters covering a story and what may be tolerated and why, whether legally or ethically. A critic must have worked through the many kinds of ethical problems that face the journalist and editor daily and needs a standard for evaluating the choices made and the alternatives. The critic will also need to understand and be able to use information-gathering strategies and tactics that best serve the writer and reporter in a world rich in information. The critic will constantly raise the question of whose interest is being served—public, publisher, reporter, source—and which should predominate or does predominate in specific cases and in principle. It will take a facile writer to articulate these ethical choices in terms the public will appreciate and digest.

Accuracy, fairness, timeliness, clarity, and good taste are still the accepted contemporary standards for reporting. Concern for freedom of the press and for the rights of individuals as well as concern for the general social good are fundamental values in most ethics codes for journalists. These codes and standards form the basis against which a critic may judge performance. But the critic will always have to evaluate these in the light of new conditions and circumstances.

Language and image as shaping, enhancing and distorting the messages should also be considered by the media critic. The artistic and psychological power of words and images is too often neglected in press criticism, and here the critic will learn from a large body of work in literature, art, and music and new research in culture/critical studies of the media.

The media critic must have thought deeply and considered carefully the role of journalism in American society, its potential and its weaknesses. The critic must have a clearly articulated set of standards for the profession against which to judge, but these must be capable of growth and change as in the other arts. The fragile balance between individual and institution, responsibility and profit provides a basic framework for the critical evaluation of the media. It would be wise for the critic to have a good understanding of media systems elsewhere in the world in order to provide a fresh perspective and to be current with international media developments that impact on the United States.

Finally, the critic will have to be an independent individual with the self-confidence and courage to speak out with conviction. It will require the unyielding support and understanding of employers. The press critic, then, would serve as watchdog of the watchdog, evaluating standards and helping to maintain them, analyzing and interpreting journalistic actions and their cultural impact, teaching the public about journalism and journalists and their special role and responsibility in the democratic marketplace of free expression. In the end, the critic would be a truly civilizing force on the press.

## NOTE

1. Jay W. Jensen, "A Method and Perspective for Criticism of the Mass Media," *Journalism Quarterly* 37 (Spring 1960): 261.

# Bibliography

## BOOKS OF CRITICISM AND JOURNALISTIC ETHICS: 1880–1950

Bent, Silas. *Ballyhoo*. New York: Boni & Liveright, 1927.

———. *Newspaper Crusaders*. New York: McGraw Hill, 1939.

Brucker, Herbert. *Freedom of Information*. New York: Macmillan, 1949.

Crawford, Nelson A. *The Ethics of Journalism*. New York: Knopf, 1926.

Ernst, Morris. *First Freedom*. New York: MacMillan, 1946.

Flint, Leon Nelson. *The Conscience of the Newspaper: A Case Book in the Principles and Problems of Journalism*. New York: Appleton-Century, 1925.

Gibbons, William Futhey. *Newspaper Ethics*. Ann Arbor: Edwards Brothers, 1926.

Holt, Hamilton. *Commercialism and Journalism*. Boston: Houghton Mifflin, 1909.

Hughes, Frank. *Prejudice and the Press*. New York: Devin-Adair, 1950.

Ickes, Harold L. *America's House of Lords*. New York: Harcourt, Brace, 1939; Vanguard, 1941.

———, ed. *Freedom of the Press Today: A Critical Examination by Twenty-eight Specialists*. New York: Vanguard, 1941.

Irwin, Will. *The American Newspaper*. Ames, Iowa: Iowa State University Press, 1969.

Kinsley, Philip. *Liberty and the Press*. Chicago: Chicago Tribune, 1944.

Lahey, Thomas A. *The Morals of Newspaper Making*. Notre Dame: University of Notre Dame Press, 1924.

Liebling, A. J. *The Press*. New York: Ballantine Books, 1975. Originally published May 14, 1960.

Lippmann, Walter, *Liberty and the News*. New York: Harcourt, Brace & Howe, 1920.

———. *The Phantom Public*. New York: Macmillan, 1930.

———. *Public Opinion*. New York: Macmillan, 1922.

Lundberg, Ferdinand. *America's 60 Families*. New York: Vanguard, 1937.

Nash, Vernon. *What Is Taught in Schools of Journalism. Bulletin 29, #54.* Columbia, Mo.: University of Missouri, 1928.

Nevins, Allan. *The Evening Post: A Century of Journalism.* New York: Boni & Liveright, 1922.

Reid, Whitelaw. *American and English Studies II.* London: Smith, Elder, 1914.

Rogers, James Edward. *The American Newspaper.* Chicago: University of Chicago Press, 1909.

Salmon, Lucy Maynard. *The Newspaper and Authority.* New York: Oxford University Press, 1923.

——. *The Newspaper and the Historian.* New York: Oxford University Press, 1923.

Seitz, Don. *Training for the Newspaper Trade.* Philadelphia, Pa.: J. B. Lippincott, 1916.

Seldes, George. *Freedom of the Press.* New York: Garden City, 1937.

——. *Lords of the Press.* New York: Julian Messner, 1938.

——. *1,000 Americans.* New York: Boni & Gaer, 1947.

——. *The People Don't Know.* New York: Gaer & Associates, 1949.

——. *Tell the Truth and Run.* New York: Greenberg, 1953.

Sinclair, Upton. *The Brass Check: A Study of American Journalism.* Pasadena, Calif.: printed by the author, 1920.

Svirsky, Leon, ed. *Your Newspaper: Blueprint for a Better Press.* New York: Macmillan, 1947.

Thorpe, Merle. *The Coming Newspaper.* New York: Henry Holt, 1915.

Villard, Oswald Garrison. *The Disappearing Daily.* New York: Knopf, 1944.

——. *Some Newspapers and Some Newspaper-men.* New York: Knopf, 1923.

Warner, Charles Dudley. *The American Newspaper.* Boston: I. R. Osgood, 1881.

White, Llewellyn and Robert D. Leigh, (Commission on Freedom of the Press). *Peoples Speaking to Peoples.* Chicago: University of Chicago Press, 1946.

Williams, Talcott. *The Newspaper Man.* New York: Scribners 1922.

Yost, Casper S. *The Principles of Journalism.* New York: Appleton, 1924.

## SPECIAL REPORTS, SUPPLEMENTS, PROCEEDINGS

American Academy of Political and Social Science. "Ethics of the Professions and of Business." *Annals of the American Academy of Political and Social Sciences* 7: 169–87. Supplement. Philadelphia: 1922.

——. "Freedom of Inquiry and Expression." *Annals* 200 (November 1938). Supplement.

——. "The Place of the Press in Modern Life." *Annals* 219 (1942). Supplement.

American Society of Newspaper Editors. *Problems of Journalism: Proceedings of the ASNE.* Washington, D.C.: 1923+. Published annually.

The Commission on the Freedom of the Press. *A Free and Responsible Press.* Chicago: University of Chicago Press, 1947.

Organization of Newspaper Ombudsmen. *Editors for the Public.* Sacramento: 1988.

University of Kansas, Department of Journalism. "Proceedings of the First National Journalism Conference Held During Kansas Newspaper Week, University of Kansas, Department of Journalism, May 10–14." Lawrence, Kans.: 1914. (*University of Kansas News Bulletin*).

## CRITICAL ARTICLES AND EDITORIALS AND PUBLISHED LECTURES BY NAMED AUTHORS DURING PERIOD STUDIED: 1880–1950

Abbott, Lawrence. "An Apology." *Outlook* 143 (13 January 1926): 283–84.

Agar, Herbert. "Rights are Responsibilities." In *Freedom of the Press Today: A Clinical Examination by 28 Specialists*, ed. by Harold L. Ickes. New York: The Vanguard Press, 1941: 19–25.

Alger, George W. "Sensational Journalism and the Law." *Atlantic Monthly* 91 (February 1903): 145–51.

Allen, Eric W. "Review of *Brass Check*." *Editor and Publisher* (8 January 1921): 1.

———. "Newspapers Need Criticism." *Editor and Publisher* (8 September 1923): 1.

Allen, Frederick L. "Newspapers and the Truth." *Atlantic Monthly* 129 (January 1922): 44–54.

Allport, Gordon W. and Janet M. Faden. "The Psychology of Newspapers: Five Tentative Laws." *Public Opinion Quarterly* 4 (December 1940): 687–703.

Atwood, M. V. "Proposed Plan for Certifying to Capability of Persons in Journalism." *Journalism Quarterly* 8 (March 1931): 24–29.

Banks, Elizabeth. "American 'Yellow Journalism.'" *Nineteenth Century* 44 (August 1898): 328–340.

Bent, Silas. "Lindbergh and the Press." *Outlook* 160 (April 1932): 214–40.

Berger, Meyer. "Surrender of Privacy." *Scribner's* 105 (April 1939): 16–21, 105.

Bleyer, Willard Grosvenor. "Journalism in the U.S.: 1933." *Journalism Quarterly* 10 (1933): 296–301.

———. "Bleyer Says Journalism Is Only Unorganized Profession." *Editor and Publisher* (18 October 1924): 8.

Bliven, Bruce. "Balance Sheet for American Journalism." In Ickes, *Specialists*: 29–39.

———. "Our Changing Journalism." *Atlantic Monthly* 132 (December 1923): 743–50.

Brice, Paul M. "Newspaper Ethics." *Editor and Publisher* (29 July 1905): 7.

Brisbane, Arthur. "The American Newspaper: Yellow Journalism." Part 4. *Bookman* 24 (June 1909): 400–404.

Brown, Robert U. "ASNE to Strive for Free Press Principle Internationally." *Editor and Publisher* (29 April 1944): 17.

Brown, Roscoe C. E. "The Menace to Journalism." *North American Review* 214 (November 1921): 610–18.

Browne, Junius Henri. "'Newspaperism' Reviewed." *Lippincott's Monthly Magazine* 38 (November 1886): 721–28.

Brucker, Herbert. "The Glut of Occurrences." *Atlantic Monthly* 156 (August 1935): 204.

Camp, Eugene M. "Journalists: Born or Made?" Paper for Alumni Association of Wharton School, First Annual Reunion, University of Pennsylvania, March, 27, 1888. Philadelphia: Philadelphia Social Science Association, 1888. Fifteen-page pamphlet.

Carson, Saul. "On the Air: The Reformed Gadfly." *New Republic* 128 (20 April 1953): 10–12.

Casey, Ralph D. "The Press, Propaganda and Pressure Groups." In *Annals* 219 (1942): 66–75.

————. "Reform From Within, Trend of U.S. Press." *Editor and Publisher* (8 September 1923): 1.

Chambers, Julius. "The Press and the Public Official." *Forum* 44 (July 1910): 14–25.

Chandler, Harry. "Our Day of Responsibility." *Editor and Publisher* (April 1932): 7.

Clapper, Raymond. "A Free Press Needs Discriminating Public Criticism." In Ickes, *Specialists*: 83–93.

Clark, Carroll D. "Yellow Journalism as a Mode of Urban Behavior." *The Southwestern Social Science Quarterly* 14 (1933): 238–245.

Cobb, Frank I. "Frank I. Cobb Urges the Restoration of the Free Play of Opinion." *Editor and Publisher* (8 January 1920): 6.

Commander, Lydia Kingsmill. "The Significance of Yellow Journalism." *Arena* 34 (August 1905): 150–55.

Connolly, Charles B. "The Ethics of Modern Journalism" *Catholic World* 75 (July 1902): 453–62.

Crawford, Nelson Antrim. "The American Newspaper and the People: A Psychological Examination." *Nation* 113 (13 September 1921): 249–52.

Creelman, James. "Joseph Pulitzer—Master Journalist." *Pearson's* 21 (March 1909): 246.

Dana, Charles Anderson. "The Modern American Newspaper." In *The Art of Newspaper Making*. New York: Appleton, 1895: 1–19.

Dawson, Mitchell. "Paul Pry and Privacy." 150 *Atlantic Monthly* (October 1932): 385–94.

Desmond, Robert. Editorial. *Journalism Quarterly* 24 (September 1947): 188–192.

Ellis, William T. "Rockefeller Money Backs Scientific Probe of News Methods and Sources." *Editor and Publisher* (6 September 1924): 3.

Fenton, Frances. "The Influence of Newspaper Presentation Upon the Growth of Crime and Other Anti-Social Activity." Part 2. *The Journal of Sociology* 16 (January 1911): 538–564.

Gannett, Frank E. "Sensational Newspapers Near End of Vogue Here and Abroad." *Editor and Publisher* (18 April 1931): 30.

Garnsey, John Henderson. "The Demand for Sensational Journals." *Arena* 18 (November 1987): 681–86.

Gilder, Richard Watson. "The Newspaper, the Magazine and the Public." *Outlook* 61 (4 February 1899): 317–21.

Godkin, E. L. Editorial. *Nation* 68 (27 April 1899): 295.

————. Editorial. *Nation* 66 (5 May, 1898): 336.

————. "Newspapers Here and Abroad." *North American Review* 150 (February 1890): 197–204.

Hadley, Arthur Twining. "Is Honest Journalism Possible?" *Current Literature* (June 1909): 47–48.

Hapgood, Norman. *Everyday Ethics: Page Lecture Series*. New Haven, Conn.: Yale University Press, 1910.

Harmsworth, Alfred. "The Simultaneous Newspapers of the 20th Century." *North American Review* 172 (January 1901): 72–90.

Harvey, George. *Journalism, Politics and the University*. Bromley Lecture at Yale University, March 12, 16, 1908. New Haven, Conn.: Yale University Press, 1908.

Haste, Richard A. "The Evolution of the Fourth Estate." *Arena* 41 (March 1909): 348–52.

Herrick, Robert. "The Paper War." *Dial* 66 (8 February 1919): 113–14.

Hitchcock, Curtice N. "Review of the *Brass Check*." *Journal of Political Economy* 29 (April 1921): 366–48.

Hollenbeck, Don. "Who Is Right?" *Atlantic Monthly* 182 (September 1984): 49–51.

Holt, Hamilton. "A Plan for an Endowed Journal." *Independent* 73 (8 August 1912): 299–301.

Hoopes, Roy. "When Ralph Ingersoll Papered Manhattan: The Saga of *PM*, A Revolutionary Newspaper." *The Washington Journalism Review* 6 (December 1984): 25.

Ingersoll, Ralph. "A free Press—for What?" In Ickes, *Specialists*: 137–142.

Irwin, Will. "If You See It in the Paper, It's—?" *Colliers* 72 (18 August 1923): 11–14, 26–28.

———. "The Press Agent, His Rise and Decline." *Colliers* (8 December 1911): 24–25, 39.

Johnson, Gerald W. "Freedom of the Newspaper Press." *Annals* 200 (1938): 60–75.

Keating, Isabelle. "Reporters Become of Age." *Harper's Monthly* 170 (April 1935): 601–12.

Keller, J. W. "Journalism as a Career." *Forum* 15 (August 1893): 691–704.

Kiplinger, W. M. "Interpret the News." *Journalism Quarterly* 13 (September 1936): 289–294.

Krock, Arthur. "The Press and Government." *Annals* 180 (July 1935): 162–67.

Lee, James Melvin. "Review of Some *Newspapers and Some Newspaper-men*." *Editor and Publisher* (17 November 1923): 12.

Leupp, Francis. "The Waning Power of the Press." *Atlantic Monthly* 105 (February 1910): 145–156.

Lilly, W. S. "Ethics of Journalism." *Forum* 7 (July 1889): 503–07.

Lippmann, Walter. "Two Revolutions in the American Press." *Yale Review* 20 (March 1931): 433–441.

——— and Charles, Merz. "A Test of the News." *New Republic* 23 supplement (August 1920): 1–42.

Lloyd, Alfred H. "Newspaper Conscience—A Study in Half Truths." *American Journal of Sociology* 27 (September 1921): 197–210.

Lord, Chester S. "'Boss' Lord Praises Journalism Schools." *Editor and Publisher* (13 May 1916): 1563.

McCormick, Robert R. "Bureaucracy is Greatest Threat to Press Freedom—McCormick." *Editor and Publisher* (28 September 1940): xiv.

MacLeish, Archibald. "The Duty of Freedom." In Ickes, *Specialists*: 187–191.

McAnney, B. O. "Preparing Students for Strenuous Newspaper Life." *Editor and Publisher* (13 June 1914): 1082.

May, Ronald. "Is the Press Unfair to McCarthy?" *New Republic* 128 (20 April 1953): 10–12.

Mencken, H. L. Editorial. *American Mercury* 2 (October 1924): 155–59.

Mott, Frank Luther. "Development of News Concepts in American Journalism." *Editor and Publisher* (28 February 1942): 36.

Murray, W. H. H. "An Endowed Press." *Arena* 2 (October 1890): 553–59.

Nizer, Louis. "The Right of Privacy: A Half Century's Development." *Michigan Law Review* 39 (February 1941): 526–560.

Olson, Kenneth E. "The Newspaper in Times of Social Change." *Journalism Quarterly* 12 (March 1935): 9–19.

Pallen, Conde Benoist. "Newspaperism." *Lippincott's Monthly Magazine* 38 (November 1886): 470–77.

Park, Robert E. "The Natural History of the Newspaper." In *The City* by Park, Robert and Ernest W. Burgess. Chicago: University of Chicago Press, 1925/1968: 80–98.

———. "News and the Power of the Press." *American Journal of Sociology* 47 (July 1941): 1–11.

———. The Yellow Press." *Sociology and Social Research* 12 (1924): 3–11.

Peck, Harry Thurston. "A Great National Newspaper." *Cosmopolitan* 24 (December 1897): 209–20.

Perry, John W. "Scope of U.S. Journalism Widening." *Editor and Publisher* (April 1932): 7.

Peterson, Frederick. "The Newspaper Peril, a Diagnosis of A Malady of the Modern Mind." *Editor and Publisher* (1 September 1906): 7.

Pulitzer, Joseph. "The College of Journalism." *North American Review* 178 (May 1904): 641–80.

Pulitzer, Ralph. *The Profession of Journalism: Accuracy in the News—An Address.* New York: Columbia University School of Journalism, 1912.

Reid, Arnot. "The English and the American Press." *Nineteenth Century* 22 (August 1887): 529–36, 691.

Reid, Whitelaw. "The Future of the Newspaper." *Nation* 95 (26 June 1897): 432–33.

———. "Journalism as a Career." In *American and English Studies II*. London: Smith, Elder, 1914: 193–230.

———. "Journalistic Duties and Opportunities." In *American*: 313–344.

———. "The Practical Issues in a Newspaper Office." In *American*: 231–280.

Robb, Arthur. "Shop Talk at 30." *Editor and Publisher* (21 September 1940): 44.

Roche, John F. "False Rumors and Demands for Press Silence Complicate Lindbergh Kindnapping Story." *Editor and Publisher* (12 March 1932): 1.

Ross, Edward Alsworth. "The Suppression of Important News." *Atlantic Monthly* 105 (March 1910): 303–311.

Rosten, Leo. "The Social Composition of Washington Correspondents." *Journalism Quarterly* 14 (June 1937): 125–132.

———. "The Professional Composition of the Washington Press Corps." *Journalism Quarterly* 14 (September 1937): 221–225.

Schlesinger, Arthur Hays. "Responsible Journalism: A Cornerstone of Freedom." *Journalism Quarterly* 23 (December 1946): 353–359.

Schuyler, Philip. "Government News Gag Press Freedom Problem." *Editor and Publisher* (8 April 1944): 7.

———. "Willis Abbott Visions a Press Devoted to 'Good News of the World.'" *Editor and Publisher* (12 July 1924): 3.

Scott, Frank W. "College Training for Journalism." *Independent* 69 (13 October 1910): 814–17.

Seitz, Don C. "The American Press." (Six-part series). *Outlook* 143, Part 1 (6 January 1926): 20–22; Part 2 (13 January): 66–68; Part 3 (20 January) 110–112; Part 4 (27 January): 136–38; Part 5 (3 February): 176–177; Part 6 (10 February): 209–210.

Speed, J. J. Gilmer. "Do Newspapers Now Give the News?" *Forum* 15 (August 1893): 705–11.

Steffens, Lincoln. "The New School of Journalism." *Bookman* 18 (September 1903): 173–177.

Thomas, W. I. "The Psychology of Yellow Journalism," *American Magazine* 65 (March 1908): 492.

Villard, Oswald Garrison and Martin Weyrauch. "Are Tabloids a Menace?" *Forum* 77 (April 1927): 485–501.

Ward, Julius. "The Future of Sunday Journalism." *Lippincott's Monthly Magazine* 37 (June 1886): 389–398.

Warner, Charles Dudley. "Better Newspapers." *Journalist* (1 May 1897): 14. (Excerpted from *Harper's Monthly*: April 1897).

———. "Newspapers and the Public." *Forum* 9 (April 1890): 198–207.

Warren, Samuel D. and Louis D. Brandeis. "The Right to Privacy." *Harvard Law Review* 4 (15 December 1890): 193–220.

Watterson, Henry. "English and American Journalism." *Munsey's* 34 (January 1906): 423–428.

White, Horace. "The School of Journalism." *Journalist* (16 January 1904): 220.

Willey, Malcolm M. "The Function of the Newspaper." *Annals* 200 (1942): 18–24.

Wilcox, Delos F. "The American Newspaper: A Study in Social Psychology." *Annals* 16 (July 1900): 56–92.

## CRITICAL ARTICLES AND EDITORIALS WITHOUT NAMED AUTHORS (ARRANGED CHRONOLOGICALLY)

"American Newspaper Press." *Fortnightly Review* 44 (1 December 1885): 827–37.

Editorial. *Dial*. 14 (16 January 1893): 35–37.

Editorial. *Dial*. 15 (16 August 1893): 79–81.

Editorial. "The Decay of American Journalism." *Dial* 19 (16 April 1897): 238.

Editorial. *Journalist* (1 May 1897): 12.

"Yellow Journalism." *Inland Printer* (October 1901): 89.

Letter to Editor. "Newspaper Responsibility for Lawlessness." *Nation* 77 (20 August 1903): 151.

"That School of Journalism." *Journalist* (29 August 1903): 292.

Editorial. *Journalist* (10 October 1903): 388.

Editorial. *Journalist* (9 July 1904): 190.

A Newspaper Reader. "Lessons in Crime Fifty Cents per Month." *Outlook* 84 (2 February 1907): 276.

Editorial. "Newspapers' Sensations and Suggestions." *Independent* 62 (21 February 1907): 450–51.

"A New College of Journalism in the West." *Harper's Weekly* (27 June 1908): 22.

A New York Editor. "Is an Honest Newspaper Possible?" *Atlantic Monthly* 102 (October 1908): 441–47.

An Independent Journalist. "Is an Honest and Sane Newspaper Press Possible?" *American Journal of Sociology* 1t (November 1909): 321–34.

Editorial. "What the Public Wants." *Dial* 32 (16 December 1909): 500.

"First National Newspaper Conference, August 1912, Madison." *Outlook* (17 August 1912): 847–48.

"Licenses of Journalists." *Literary Digest* 54 (7 April 1917): 1021.

"Has the Press Hampered the Search for the Lindbergh Baby?" *Literary Digest* (30 April 1932): 3–35.

Editorial. "Public Opinion and the Press." *Commonweal* 25 (20 November 1936): 85–86.
"Faith in Power of Editors Shaken." *Literary Digest* 122 (19 December 1936): 42.
"The Press and the Public." *New Republic* 91 (17 March 1937): 78–91.
"The Nieman Foundation Celebrates its 50th Birthday." *Nieman Reports* 63 (Spring 1989): 1–47.

## CRITICAL ARTICLES AND EDITORIALS IN *EDITOR AND PUBLISHER* (ARRANGED CHRONOLOGICALLY)

"School of Journalism." (22 August 1903): 274–75.
"The Pulitzer School." (22 August 1903): 1–2.
"Reports on School." (10 October 1903): 1.
"General Taylor's Review." (21 November 1903): 4.
Editorial. "The College of Journalism." (7 May 1904): 4.
Review of W. D. Scott's *Psychology of Advertising*. (26 September 1908).
"Press as Civilizer." (19 June 1909): 4.
"Equipment for Journalism." (20 August 1910): 4.
Editorial. "Licensing for Newspaper Men." (4 May 1912): 8.
"Teachers' Conference." (7 December 1912): 1.
Editorial. "Should Reporters Be Licensed?" (16 October 1915): 476.
"American Journalists' Forum." (5 June 1920): 19.
"Rockefeller Money Backs Scientific Probe of News Methods and Sources." (6 September 1924): 3.
"Rockefellers Disclaim Press Probe—Lee." (20 September 1924): 10.
"Licensing Idea for Journalists Given Trial." (25 July 1925): 9.
Editorial. "Do It!" (2 January 1926): 24.
Editorial. "Professional Status." (13 March 1926): 32.
"State Certificates for Newspaper Men Advocated by Illinois Press." (13 March 1926): 32.
"Shadow of Censorship Menaces Press: Many Editors Revolt at Browning Smut." (5 February 1927): 1.
Editorial. "Censorship or—?" (5 February 1927): 34.
"Vice Society Hales *N.Y. Graphic* to Court." (12 February 1927): 5.
"Planning to 'Professionalize' Press Agentry." (2 April 1927): 9.
"NY State Committee Hits Crime News." (9 April 1927): 35.
Editorial. "A Strange Report." (9 April 1927): 48.
"Institute of Journalists Called U.S. Need." (6 October 1928): 5.
"Five Years of Newspaper Experience Suggested for Journalism Teachers." (5 January 1929): 16.
"Lippmann Sees Passing of Popular Press." (17 January 1931): 41.
"Editors Differ on Kidnap Broadcast." (19 March 1932): 9, 62.
"F. G. Bonfils, Denver Publisher Dies." (4 February 1933): 7.
"Bullen Tells How Institute Works." (30 December 1933): 7, 33.
"Win Public Confidence, Press Told." (22 December 1934): 9.
Editorial. "Welcome Criticism." (21 September 1935): 26.

"Regulation of Trial Coverage Urged in Bar Association Report." (18 September 1937): 5.

"Gannett Defends Press as Fair." (21 January 1939): 29.

"Ickes Charges News Distortion by Press in Debate," (21 January 1939): 4.

Editorial. "Mr. Ickes Again." (28 January 1939): 32.

"Ickes Broadens Attack on Press in New Speech." (18 February 1939): 14.

"More Scholarly Newspapermen Needed, Felix Morley Says." (18 May 1940): 11.

"Election Proved Freedom of Press Tripp Says in Letter to Ickes." (16 November 1940): 3.

"Shop Talk at 30." (21 September 1940): 44.

"Higher Journalistic Standards Reported by Pulitzer Judges." (24 May 1941): 9.

"New Commission to Study Press Freedom." (4 March 1944): 22.

"*Editor and Publisher* Marks Its Sixtieth Anniversary." (25 March 1944): 7.

"Editors Welcome *Time-Life* Inquiry into Press Freedom." (15 April 1944): 9.

"Canham Cites Enterprise." (29 April 1944): 19, 62.

"Knight Discusses U.S. Censorship in London." (29 April 1944): 123.

"Knight Asserts Press Will Not Give Up Freedom." (9 December 1944): 1.

"Two Civil Liberties Champions Clash on Press Freedom." (9 December 1944): 38.

"Shop Talk at 30." (21 March 1945): 68.

"Seltzer Sees Youth Needed to Revitalize Newspapers." (8 December 1945): 8.

"Canham Visions Trend to Daily News Magazine." (19 January 1946): 9.

"Books in Review." (30 March 1946): 58.

Editorial. "Leigh-White Report." (30 March 1946): 42.

"Knight Assails Plan in Leigh-White Report." (20 April 1946): 120.

"Sulzberger Pleads for Responsible Press." (19 October 1946): 66.

"Inland Publishers Debate Public Criticism of Press." (19 October 1946): 11.

"Forrest Accuses Group of Damaging Prestige." (29 March 1947): 11.

"Report Aimed Directly at Owners—Hutchins." (29 March 1947): 8.

"CBS Station in New York Starts Criticism of Press." (7 June 1947): 11.

"American Press Institute Seeks $850,000 Endowment." (28 June 1947): 10.

"Journalism Teachers Parry With Hutchins." (3 January 1948): 10.

"Fact-Finding Boards on Press Advocated." (10 January 1948): 58.

"Editor Proposes Criticism Project." (7 February 1948): 32.

"Lester Markel Thinks Press Neglects Interpretive Role." (3 April 1948): 61.

"An Offer to Hutchins." (27 November 1948): 38.

"Hutchins Chastises Editorial Writers." (27 November 1948): 6.

"Editorial Writers to Draft Code of Ethics, Standards." (27 November 1948): 5.

"*E & P* Panel Suggests Studies for Press Self-Improvement." (26 March 1949): 52.

"News, Public Property: Cornerstone of Free Press." (3 September 1949): 3.

"Hearst-Pulitzer Feud Cost Millions. Ended in Draw." (27 June 1957): 182–84.

"How Newspapers Can Win Battle to Retain Subscribers." (3 September 1988): 52.

## ARCHIVES

Chicago, Illinois: The University of Chicago Library, The Joseph Regenstein Library: The Commission on Freedom of the Press papers.

New York, N.Y.: Columbia University, The Butler Library: The *World* (N.Y.) archives;
Bureau of Accuracy and Fair Play.


## UNPUBLISHED DISSERTATIONS, CORRESPONDENCE

Daley, Patrick Jay. *Radical Currents in Twentieth Century American Press Criticism: Notes for the Future.* Unpublished doctoral dissertation, University of Iowa, 1983.
Hartung, Barbara. *Attitudes Toward the Current Applicability of the 1947 Hutchins Report on Social Responsibility of the Press.* Unpublished doctoral dissertation, U.S. International University (San Diego), 1979.
Midura, Edmund M. *An Evaluation of A. J. Liebling's Performance as a Critic of the Press.* Unpublished doctoral dissertation, University of Iowa, 1969.
Petersen, Barbara K. "Thinking the Unthinkable: Licensing of Journalists in America —An Historical Perspective." Unpublished doctoral student paper, University of Michigan Department of Communication, March 1988.
Phillips, George Howard. *An Analysis of 835 Articles in the Leading American Periodicals for the Period 1890–1914 to Determine What Was Said about American Daily Newspapers.* Unpublished doctoral dissertation, University of Iowa, 1962.
Reynolds, William Robinson. *Joseph Pulitzer.* Unpublished doctoral dissertation, Columbia University, 1950.
Shilen, Ronald. *The Concept of Objectivity in Journalism in the U.S.* Unpublished doctoral dissertation, New York University, 1955.
Winfield, Betty H. "FDR's Publicity Foundation for a Modern Presidency." Unpublished paper, AEJMC History Division Convention, 1981.
Personal letter from Wesley H. Maurer, Sr. 29 November 1988.
Personal letter from Richard A. Schwarzlose. 25 May 1989.
Personal letter from Lee Stinnet. 13 July 1989.


## LECTURES

Greenfield, Jeff, Lecture on media criticism at University of Michigan Department of Communication, 6 April 1987.
Gutierrez, Felix. Lecture on media and minorities at University of Michigan Department of Communication, January 1988.
Isaacs, Norman. Speech to Organization of Newspaper Ombudsmen, Boston, 18 April 1988.
Shaw, David. Lecture on media criticism at University of Michigan Department of Communication, 10 September 1987.


## BOOKS AND ARTICLES: HISTORY, BACKGROUND, AND LATER CRITICISM

Aldridge, John W. *The American Novel and the Way We Live Now.* New York: Oxford University Press, 1985.
Armstrong, William M. *E. L. Godkin: A Biography.* Albany: State University of

N.Y.U. Press, 1978.

Ashmore, Harry S. *Unseasonable Truths: The Life of Robert Maynard Hutchins*. Boston: Little, Brown, 1989.

"ASJSA Honors Ben Bagdikian as Journalism's 'Most Perceptive Critic.'" *Journalism Educator* 33 (October 1978): 6–12.

Auden, W. H. "Criticism in a Mass Society." In *The Intent of the Critic*, by Edmund Wilson et al. Gloucester, Mass.: Peter Smith, 1941/1963.

Bagdikian, Ben H. *The Media Monopoly*. Boston: Beacon Press, 1983.

Barnouw, Erik. *A History of Broadcasting in the U.S.* Vol. 1, *A Tower in Babel*. New York: Oxford University Press, 1966.

———. *The Image Empire*. New York: Oxford University Press, 1970.

Baughman, James L. *Henry R. Luce and the Rise of the American News Media*. Boston: Twayne, 1987.

Beasley, Maurine. "Women in Journalism Education: The Formative Period 1908–1930." AEJMC Convention paper, Memphis State University, August 1985.

Bernays, Edward L. *Biography of an Idea: Memoirs of Public Relations Counsel Edward L. Bernays*. New York: Simon & Schuster, 1965.

———. *Crystallizing Public Opinion*. New York: Horace Liveright, 1923.

———. *Propaganda*. New York: Horace Liveright, 1928.

Bessie, Simon M. *Jazz Journalism: The Story of the Tabloid Newspaper*. New York: Dutton, 1938.

Blanchard, Margaret. *Exporting the First Amendment*. New York: Longman, 1986.

———. "The Hutchins Commission: The Press and Responsibility Concept." *Journalism Monographs* 49 (May 1977).

Bledstein, Burton J. *The Culture of Professionalism*. New York: Norton, 1978.

Brendon, Piers. *The Life and Death of the Press Barons*. London: Secker & Warburg, 1982.

Brown, Lee. *The Reluctant Reformation: On Criticizing the Press in America*. New York: McKay, 1974.

Burns, James MacGregor. *The Workshop of Democracy*. New York: Knopf, 1985.

Calverton, V. F. *The Newer Spirit: A Sociological Criticism of Literature*. New York: Boni & Liveright, 1925.

Campbell, Richard and Jimmie L. Reeves. "Covering the Homeless: The Joyce Brown Story." *Critical Studies in Mass Communication* 6 (1989): 21–42.

Cahham, Erwin D. *Commitment to Freedom*. Boston: Houghton Mifflin, 1958.

Carey, James W. *Communication as Culture: Essays on Media and Society*. Boston: Unwin Hyman, 1989.

———. "Journalism and Criticism: The Case of an Undeveloped Profession." *The Review of Politics* 36 (April 1974): 227–49.

———, ed. *Media, Myth and Narrative*. Beverly Hills: Sage, 1988.

Cashman, Dennis. *America in the Gilded Age*. New York: New York University Press, 1984/1988.

Christians, Clifford G. "Fifty Years of Scholarship in Media Ethics." *Journal of Communication* 27 (Autumn 1977): 19–29.

Cooley, Charles Horton. *Social Organization: A Study of the Larger Mind*. New York: Scribner's, 1909/1925.

"Come to the Aid of Broadcasters." *Editor and Publisher* (18 February 1989): 14, 43.

Cooper, Kent. *The Right to Know: An Exposition of the Evils of News Suppression and Propaganda*. New York: Farrar, Straus & Cudahy. 1956.

Cox, Betty W. "Spoon-Feeding the Baby Bomers." *APME News* (15 June 1989): 3.

Czitrom, Daniel J. *Media and the American Mind: From Morse to McLuhan*. Chapel Hill, N.C.: University of North Carolina Press, 1982.

Davis, Elmer. *But We Were Born Free*. New York: Bobbs-Merrill, 1952.

Dennis, Everette E. and Claude-Jean Bertrand. "Seldes at 90: They Don't Give Pulitzers for That Kind of Criticism." *Journalism History* 7 (Autumn/Winter 1980–81): 81–86, 120.

de Tocqueville, Alexis. *Democracy in America*. New York: Modern Library, 1981. (Original 1835).

Dornfeld, A. A. *Hello Sweetheart, Get Me Rewrite!* Chicago: Academy Chicago Publications, 1988. (Originally *Behind the Front Page*, 1983.)

Emery, Edwin, *The History of the American Newspaper Publishers Association*. Minneapolis: The University of Minnesota Press, 1950.

—— and Michael Emery. *The Press and America*. 5th ed. New Jersey: Prentice-Hall, 1984.

—— and Joseph P. McKerns, eds. *AEJMC: 75 Years in the Making*. Journalism Monographs 104 (November 1987).

Frye, Northrop. *The Critical Path: An Essay on the Social Context of Literary Criticism*. Bloomington: Indiana University Press, 1971.

——. *The Educated Imagination*. Bloomington: Indiana University Press, 1964.

Gamst, Glenn, Tim Alldridge, and Steve Bush. "Effects of Targeted Sales Messages on Subscription Sales and Retention." *Journalism Quarterly* 64 (Summer 1987): 463–472, 554.

Gerard, Jeremy. "Walter Cronkite: Speaking His Mind." *New York Times* (8 January 1989): H 29–30.

Glasser, Theodore L. "Objectivity Precludes Responsibility." *Quill* (February 1984): 102–07.

Good, Howard. *Acquainted with the Night: The Image of Journalists in American Fiction, 1890–1930*. New Jersey, Metuchen: Scarecrow, 1986.

Grabo, Carl. *The Creative Critic*. Chicago: University of Chicago Press, 1948.

Hackett, Robert A. "Decline of a Paradigm? Bias and Objectivity in News Media Sources." *Critical Studies in Mass Communication* 3 (1984): 229–259.

Harris, Leon. *Upton Sinclair: An American Rebel*. New York: Thomas Y. Crowell, 1975.

Henry, William A. III. "Journalism Under Fire," *Time* (12 December 1983): 76–93.

Hertsgaard, Mark. *On Bended Knee: The Press and the Reagan Presidency*. New York: Farrar, Straus & Giroux, 1988.

Hollenbeck, Don. *Current Biography*. (February 1951): 29.

Hoopes, Roy. *Ralph Ingersoll: A Biography*. New York: Atheneum, 1985.

Hudson, Robert V. *The Writing Game: A Biography of Will Irwin*. Ames: Iowa State University Press, 1982.

Hughes, Helen MacGill. *News and the Human Interest Story*. Chicago: University of Chicago Press, 1940.

Ingersoll, Ralph McAllister. *Point of Departure: An Adventure in Autobiography*. New York: Harcourt, Brace & World, 1961.

——. "Postscript to *PM*." *Nieman Reports*. (September 1963): 11.

Irwin, Will. *The Making of a Reporter*. New York: Putnam, 1942.

Isaacs, Norman E. *Untended Gates: The Mismanaged Press*. New York: Columbia University Press, 1986.

Iyengar, Shanto and Donald R. Kinder. *News That Matters*. Chicago: University of Chicago Press, 1987.

Jackson, Holbrook. *The Eighteen Nineties*. New York: Knopf, 1922.

Jensen, Jay W. "A Method and a Perspective for Criticism of the Mass Media," *Journalism Quarterly* 37 (Spring 1960): 261–66.

Judis, John B. "The Hart Affair." *Columbia Journalism Review* 26 (July/August 1987): 21–25.

Juergens, George. *News from the White House: The Presidential-Press Relationship in the Progressive Era*. Chicago: University of Chicago Press, 1981.

Kingsbury, Susan Myra. *Newspapers and the News*. New York: Putnam, 1937.

Lee, James M. *A History of American Journalism*. Garden City, N.Y.: Garden City 1917/1923.

Lieberman, Jethro K. *The Tyranny of the Experts*. New York: Walker, 1970.

MacDougall, Curtis D. *Newsroom Problems and Policies*. New York: Dover, 1963.

———. *Interpretative Reporting*. New York: Macmillan, 1938.

McIntyre, Jerilyn S. "Repositioning a Landmark: The Hutchins Commission and Freedom of the Press." *Critical Studies in Mass Communication* 4 (October 1987): 4–28.

MacLeish, Archibald. "The Poet and the Press." *Atlantic Monthly* 203 (March 1959): 40–46.

McKerns, Joseph P., Carole L. McNall, and Elisabeth M. Johnson. "Mass Media Criticism: An Annotated Bibliography." *Mass Communication Review* 3 (Winter 1975/76): 9–18.

MacNeil, Neil. *How to be a Newspaperman*. New York: Harper & Row, 1942.

Marzolf, Marion T. "The American 'New Journalism' Takes Root in Europe." *Journalism Quarterly* 61 (Autumn 1984): 529–36, 691.

———. *Up from the Footnote: A History of Women Journalists*. New York: Hastings House, 1977.

May, Henry F. *The End of American Innocence*. New York: Knopf, 1959.

May, Ronald and Jack Anderson. *McCarthy the Man, the Senator and the Ism*. Boston: Beacon Press, 1952.

Mott, Frank Luther. *American Journalism*. New York: Macmillan, 1962.

———. *A History of American Magazines*. Vol. IV, 1885–1905. Cambridge: Harvard University Press, 1957.

Niebuhr, Reinhold. "The Role of the Newspapers in America's Function as the Greatest World Power." In *The Press in Perspective*, Ralph D. Casey, ed. Baton Rouge, La.: Louisiana State University Press, 1963: 38–49.

Nord, Dave. "A Plea for Journalism History." *Journalism History* 15 (Spring 1988): 8–15.

Peterson, Theodore. "The Social Responsibility Theory of the Press." In *Four Theories of the Press* by Fred S. Siebert, Theodore Peterson, and Wilbur Schramm. Urbana: University of Illinois Press, 1963: 73–103.

Porter, William E. *Assault on the Media: The Nixon Years*. Ann Arbor: University of Michigan Press, 1976.

Powell, Jody. *The Other Side of the Story*. New York: William Morrow, 1984.

Press, Andrea. *Women Watching Television*. Philadelphia: University of Pennsylvania Press, due 1990.

Rivers, William. *The Opinionmakers: The Washington Press Corps*. Boston: Beacon Press, 1965/67.

Rosten, Leo C. *The Washington Correspondents*. New York: Harcourt Brace, 1937.

Salisbury, William. *The Career of a Journalist*. New York: Dodge, 1908.

Schlereth, Thomas J., ed. *Material Culture Studies in America*. Nashville: The American Association for State and Local History, 1982.

————, ed. *Material Culture: A Research Guide*. Kansas: University Press of Kansas, 1985.

Schlesinger, Arthur M. *The Rise of the City, 1878–1898*. Vol. 10, *A History of American Life*. New York: Macmillan, 1933.

Schudson, Michael. *Discovering the News: A Social History of American Newspapers*. New York: Basic Books, 1978.

Schwarzlose, Richard A. *The Nation's Newsbrokers*, Vol. 1. Evanston: Northwestern University Press, 1989.

————. *Newspapers: A Reference Guide*. New York: Greenwood, 1987.

Shaw, Donald L. "News Bias and the Telegraph: A Study in Historical Change." *Journalism Quarterly* 44 (Spring 1967): 3–12, 31.

Steele, Richard W. *Propaganda in an Open Society: The Roosevelt Administration and the Media 1933–1941*. Westport, Conn.: Greenwood Press, 1985.

Stensas, Harlan S. "Development of the Objectivity Ethic in U.S. Daily Newspapers." *Journal of Mass Media Ethics* 2 (Fall/Winter 1986–87): 50–60.

Stevens, John D. "Journalism Instruction at the University of Michigan, 1929–1979." Ann Arbor: Department of Journalism, 1979.

————. "Social Utility of Sensational News: Murder and Divorce in the 1920's." *Journalism Quarterly* 61 (Spring 1985): 53–58.

Still, Bayrd. *Mirror for Gotham*. Washington Square: New York University Press, 1956.

Strunsky, Simeon. *The Living Tradition*. New York: Doubleday, Doran & Co., Inc., 1939.

Sutton, Albert Alton. *Education for Journalism in the United States from its Beginning to 1940*. Evanston, Ill.: Northwestern University, 1945.

Sutherland, Frank. "Journalist Groups Arguing Over Need for Strong Ethics Codes." *ASNE Bulletin* (1987): 4–5.

Tomsich, John. *A Genteel Endeavor: American Culture and Politics in the Gilded Age*. Stanford, Calif.: Stanford University Press, 1971.

Tuchman, Gaye. *Making News: A Study in the Construction of Reality*. New York: Free Press, 1978.

Weinberg, Julius. *Edward Alsworth Ross and the Sociology of Progressivism*. Madison: State Historical Society of Wisconsin, 1972.

Weinfeld, William. "The Growth of Daily Newspaper Chains in the U.S.: 1923, 1926–35." *Journalism Quarterly* 13 (December 1936): 357–380.

"Westmoreland Reflects." *Editor and Publisher* (23 March 1985): 7.

White, Graham J. *FDR and the Press*. Chicago: University of Chicago Press, 1979.

Whitney, D. Charles. *The Media and the People: Americans' Experience with the News Media: A Fifty-Year Review*. New York: Gannett Center for Media Studies at Columbia University, 1985.

Wiebe, Robert H. *The Search for Order: 1877–1920*. New York: Hill & Wang, 1967.

Winfield, Betty H. "FDR Wins (and Loses) Journalist Friends in the Rising Age of News Interpretation." *Journalism Quarterly* 64 (Winter 1987): 698–706.

# Index

White, William Allen, 139, 143, 145
Whitney, D. Charles, 195
Wilcox, Delos F., 28–29, 47. *See also*
  Social responsibility
Willey, Malcolm M., 157
Williams, R. Gray, 40
Williams, Talcott, 66, 99
Williams, Walter, 55–56
Winfield, Betty, 138, 147 n.27
Wright, H. J. 91
Women, status of in journalism, 60 n. 27,
  29

Yale University, 54
*Yellow Book*, 23

"Yellow Kid" ("Hogan's Alley"), 23
Yellow journalism: and class conflict, 30;
  crime emphasis, 36–40; criticized,
  25–29, 36, 42; crystallization of
  sentiment against, 27, 29; defended,
  24, 26, 35–36; defined, 23, 34–35, 38;
  morbid appeal, 37–38, 64; softening
  the brain, 36; Spanish-American War,
  26–27; trial by newspaper, 29–30;
  truce of Pulitzer and Hearst, 30–31;
  women reporters exploited, 24. *See
  also* Circulation
Yellow press. *See* Yellow journalism
Yost, Casper S., 91, 98
*Your Newspaper*, 170